A UNIVERSITY OF TRADITION

A UNIVERSITY OF TRADITION

THE SPIRIT OF PURDUE

Second Edition

COMPILED BY THE
PURDUE REAMER CLUB

PURDUE UNIVERSITY PRESS
WEST LAFAYETTE, INDIANA

"Standing Tall" chapter opening image courtesy of NASA; "The Spirit of Purdue" chapter opening image courtesy of Janet Stephens, THGphotography.

Special appreciation to Purdue University photographers Mark Simons and Andrew Hancock.

Dust jacket and book designed by Heidi Branham.

Library of Congress Cataloging-in-Publication Data

A university of tradition : the spirit of Purdue / compiled by The Purdue Reamer Club. -- 2nd ed.
        p. cm.
    ISBN 978-1-55753-630-3 (pbk. : alk. paper) -- ISBN 978-1-61249-249-0 (epdf) -- ISBN 978-1-61249-250-6 (epub) 1. Purdue University--History. I. Purdue Reamer Club.
    LD4673.A2 2013
    378.77295--dc23
                                        2012021005

Dedicated to ALL Boilermakers—Past, Present, and Future.

HAIL PURDUE!

CONTENTS

HERE'S TO THE BLACK AND GOLD

MENTIONING THE HONORABLE

THE SPIRIT OF PURDUE

APPENDICES

PREFACE

ANY COMPREHENSIVE HISTORY OF PURDUE IS
increasingly difficult to produce. If you work and study at
one of the world's leading universities, change just becomes a
way of life. New buildings are erected, new discoveries made,
people come and go. Only one thing is constant—the spirit
of Purdue lives on.

As members of the Purdue Reamer Club, the student authors
of this book, we are committed to fostering school traditions,
to supporting major and Olympic sports, and to aiding in
the development of proper school spirit. This second edition,
substantially expanded and in full color, accounts for much of
the history of our alma mater. We've tried our best to present
an accurate account, but sometimes the records are silent
or contradictory, and other times we may just have made a
mistake. We do believe, however, that readers will find plenty
of interesting information, some surprises, and a healthy dose
of entertainment in the pages that follow.

Many people were involved in the production of this book,
including past and present Reamer Club members too
numerous to name. You know who you are, and we thank
you. Thank you to the team at Purdue University Press who

assisted in developing the book and also to all the patient staff at the Purdue University Libraries Archives and Special Collections Division, Purdue Office of Marketing and Media, and Purdue Athletics Department.

One hundred and fifty years since the Morrill Land-Grant College Act laid the foundations for institutions like ours, and a century since the authors of "Hail Purdue" gave the University its rally cry, we dedicate this book to our community of knowledge on the banks of the Wabash. We look forward to cataloging new traditions, celebrating new triumphs, and boosting school spirit for many years to come.

Boiler Up, Hammer Down, Hail Purdue!

FIAFW,

—The Students of the Purdue Reamer Club

THE
LAND GRANT
COLLEGE
· 1862 ·

THE LAND GRANT
COLLEGE ACT

FROM THE GROUND UP

PURDUE UNIVERSITY, like other land-grant colleges, was from its beginnings a uniquely American institution, founded upon ideas of equality and practical education. This philosophy remains the cornerstone of Purdue's mission. Another essential foundation for Purdue's birth and growth was giving—donors who gave generously of their time, wealth, and land. A task as monumental as launching a university doesn't happen overnight, and Purdue's founders were faced with countless decisions before the first day of classes in 1874. These pioneers, and the generations of visionary men and women who succeeded them, have given rise to a wealth of traditions, making Purdue the diverse institution it is today.

John Purdue.

JOHN PURDUE

John Purdue was born October 31, 1802 near Shirleysburg, Pennsylvania, on the eastern slopes of the Alleghenies. The only son in a family of nine children, he obtained what schooling was available near his home. In 1823, he moved with his parents and siblings to Ross County, Ohio. Their home was in Adelphi, a tiny community in south-central Ohio. He taught school there and became friends with one of his pupils, Moses Fowler. They later became business partners.

After teaching in Pickaway County, Ohio, Purdue, not yet thirty years old, bought 160 acres in Marion County, Ohio. He farmed for a year before starting his career in business.

By taking hogs to the market and selling them on consignment for his neighbors, he made a considerable profit for himself. In 1833, he and Fowler opened a general mercantile store in Adelphi. They moved their business to Lafayette in 1839.

Purdue had visited the Lafayette area in 1837 and immediately had been enraptured by it. The dry goods store he and Fowler started was soon a success. In little time, Purdue became one of the leaders of his community in both charitable and governmental concerns. At various times, he was a member of the city council and the school board, and was well-known for his interest in education.

Over the next few years, Purdue expanded his business interests, including the purchase of the *Lafayette Journal,* which he later tried to use during an unsuccessful campaign for Congress.

He continued his philanthropic interests—preferring to give to causes that would put his name on them. His longtime interest in matters of education led to his support when the state looked to establish a land-grant college.

On March 3, 1869, State Senator John A. Stein read a letter to the Senate from John Purdue offering $100,000 to establish the new state agricultural college at Battle Ground in Tippecanoe County, provided that it "by law have his surname identified with the name of the college." On April 2, six days before a special legislative session to decide on the land-grant college,

Purdue raised his original proposal by $50,000. This, coupled with offers of $50,000 from Tippecanoe County and 100 acres of land from local residents, swayed the legislature. After much debate, Purdue's offer was accepted, making him the only person for whom a Big Ten school is named.

John Purdue began to battle illness in the summer of 1876, although he remained active in the community and with the University. September 12 was the first day of classes for the third academic year of his namesake University. Purdue visited the campus, chatting with faculty and students, and inspecting the construction of a new building that would become University Hall, before returning home. He died later that day and was laid to rest on the grounds of Purdue University as he requested.

The long life of the deceased was filled with beneficent activity; and his business enterprise will be long felt in Lafayette, but one act that crowned his life and makes the name of John Purdue immortal, was his magnificent donation to this University.
—President White, Purdue's funeral oration

THE MORRILL ACTS

The Morrill Act, also called the Land-Grant College Act, was first introduced by Senator Justin Smith Morrill of Vermont and then signed into law by President Abraham Lincoln on July 2, 1862. The act stated that each state would receive 30,000 acres of federal land for each congressional representative from that state to be sold to provide an endowment for ". . . at least one college where the leading object shall be, without excluding other scientific and classical studies and including military tactics, to teach such branches of learning as are related to agriculture and the mechanic arts."

The land donated to the states was to be sold and the money invested in U.S. Bonds or other safe securities. The interest from these securities would form a continuous supply of money to the states for the purpose of funding the land-grant institutions. A second Morrill Act, passed August 30, 1890, concerned further endowment of the land-grant colleges.

FOUNDING OF THE UNIVERSITY

In 1865, the Indiana General Assembly voted to participate in the Morrill Act. On May 6, 1869, the General Assembly decided to locate the institution near Lafayette and accepted John Purdue's offer to pay $150,000, Tippecanoe County's offer to pay $50,000, and the 100 acres of land offered by local residents.

Many lawmakers and local citizens participated in establishing the University, but four stand out as those who forged the institution in its early days:

- JOHN PURDUE, a Lafayette businessman, who pledged money and his name to the University.
- JOHN COFFROTH, an early trustee and ally of John Purdue.
- MARTIN PEIRCE, an early treasurer of the Board of Trustees and a friend of John Purdue.
- JOHN STEIN, an early secretary of the Board of Trustees who, with Peirce, administered the day-to-day affairs of the University before any staff hires were made.

In December 1869, the Board of Trustees officially named the college Purdue University. At the same time, John Purdue was granted broad powers to build a university and was named a member of the board. He purchased 100 acres of land southwest from the corner of State and Marsteller streets (now part of south campus). Coffroth, Peirce, and Stein joined the board in 1870.

Through 1870 and early 1871, board meetings centered on the location of various campus buildings. Much disagreement ensued; so much that Purdue vacated his chairmanship of the board, leading to the election of Peirce as the new president of the board.

In January 1872, the board asked Purdue to buy another tract of land. Purdue turned over a deed for 84 acres north of the 100-acre tract in April of that year. After that meeting, Peirce and John Hougham, who later would become the first faculty member of the University, made a trip to the northeast to research buildings at several existing colleges. At the August 1872 board meeting, their report recommended that construction start immediately on a "dormitory," "boarding house," and "laboratory" on the 84-acre tract. When classes started two years later, those were the main buildings on campus. Also in August 1872, the University hired Richard Owen as its first president,

BOILER BYTE

HOG WILD

Purdue's short-lived first president, Richard Owen, was obsessively detail-oriented. In drawing up plans for the fledgling University, he painstakingly included guidelines for students' diet, "avoiding the free use of pork, meats fried in grease, rich pastry and the like, a being highly injurious to those having much more work of the brain than the muscles." However, Owen's very job was due to the "free use of pork"; John Purdue had made his fortune from selling the meat, and he was even chief supplier of pork and pork products to the Union armies during the Civil War.

but he resigned in March 1874 before classes ever started.

In August 1873, the board directed Hougham to begin classes by October 1. However, the buildings were not completed in time. In January 1874, the board agreed that Hougham should start classes March 1. Some preliminary classes—higher arithmetic, algebra, physical geography, natural philosophy (natural sciences), physiology, and chemistry—were taught in a short session through June 12.

. . . at least one college where the leading object shall be, without excluding other scientific and classical studies and including military tactics, to teach such branches of learning as are related to agriculture and the mechanic arts.

—Land-Grant College Act

Abraham Shortridge, superintendent of Indianapolis Public Schools, was hired as president in June of 1874, and by July he had drawn up a rough plan of study. The first official semester began on September 16, 1874 with thirty-nine students and six faculty members. At that moment, the University was no longer a work in progress, but the land-grant college envisioned five years earlier when John Purdue and others from Tippecanoe County had come forward with pledges of money and land.

OLD GOLD AND BLACK

In the fall of 1887, it was decided that official school colors were necessary for the football team to achieve distinction in collegiate athletics. At the time, Princeton was the most successful football team in the country and was acclaimed by the press as the Eastern Champions. J. B. Burris (class of 1888), captain of the first Purdue team, proposed that Princeton's colors be adopted to give Purdue quick distinction. Princeton's colors, actually orange and black, were said by some to be "yellow and black." Since Purdue team members hardly felt "yellow," they decided to change that color to a distinguished Old Gold and to accept the Black. The motion to accept these as University colors carried.

BOILERMAKERS

Legend has it that in 1889 the two newly hired Purdue football coaches were quite discouraged by the scrawny volunteers that turned out for the team. Not to be outdone by anyone, the coaches recruited several husky boilermakers from the Monon Railroad Shops and a few burly policemen as well. After enrolling these men in one University course, they set out to play football. This resulted in victory after victory. When the team beat Wabash College, the Crawfordsville newspapers became incensed and wrote a few uncomplimentary articles, labeling the team members from Purdue everything from "railsplitters" to "haymakers." But, as with many legends, this tale is part fact and part fiction.

Slaughter of Innocence: Wabash Snowed Completely Under by Boiler Makers from Purdue.

—Daily Argus News

In truth, the year was 1891. No members were actually recruited from the Monon Shops, which did not come to Lafayette until 1895. Purdue, however, did trounce Wabash College in a memorable game; however, no Crawfordsville newspaper used the term "Boilermaker" when telling the game story.

On October 26, 1891, Purdue beat Wabash 44–0. The local Crawfordsville papers mourned the loss, with the greatest laments coming from the *Daily Argus News*. Beneath the main headline, "Slaughter of Innocence," was a key secondary head: "Wabash Snowed Completely Under by Boiler Makers from Purdue." The Lafayette papers quickly picked up on the unique moniker. By October 1892, the writers at *The Purdue Exponent* were using the name regularly. Purdue students fancied the name "Boilermakers" and have been proud to be known as such ever since.

OFFICIAL UNIVERSITY SEAL

In the United States, colleges and universities have had seals since early colonial days. Purdue's first seal—the first of nine—was introduced in 1890. Undergraduate Bruce Rogers, who became a noted book designer, created the first seal and modified it in 1894. The University never officially adopted either version. Abby Phelps Lytle, head of the art department, was asked by the administration to design a new version in 1895. She introduced the slanted shield, the Uncial typeface, and the symbol of the griffin, a traditional symbol of strength. Each version since has incorporated these three elements.

The Lytle version was reworked in 1905 as part of a student project. In 1909, Charles H. Benjamin, the engineering dean, reworked the seal yet again. This version was first used in the 1909–10 *Purdue University Catalogue* and would continue to be used for the next sixty years.

Three other variations were proposed—one used occasionally—through the years. However, the University continued to use Benjamin's seal.

The current seal, the official emblem of Purdue, was formally inaugurated during the University's centennial in 1969. Al Gowan, at that time an assistant professor of creative arts, designed this version. Gowan's design refined the seal's concept while maintaining the symbols developed in 1895. His design continued the use of the griffin, although in a stylized, simplified version. He also retained the symbol of the shield, with the three parts of the shield representing the three stated aims of Purdue University: service, research, and education. These replaced the curriculum-based aims of the previous version: science, technology, and agriculture. The five feathers on the back of the griffin's head represent the five campuses of Purdue, spread throughout the state of Indiana. Gowan also retained Lytle's use of the Uncial typeface in the text of the "Purdue University" surrounding the griffin.

The Board of Trustees approved Gowan's design in 1969, replacing one that had been used historically but never officially adopted.

Rogers, 1890.

Rogers, 1894.

Lytle, 1895.

Gowan, 1969.

Benjamin, 1909.

BOILER BYTE

ANCIENT ORDER OF THE DORMITORY DEVILS

The Ancient Order of the Dormitory Devils was an "organization" of upperclassmen who lived in Purdue Hall. Members used to "welcome" new residents by dousing them with water in the middle of the night, and then forcing them to make a speech. To bother those who were studious, one of the Devils' favorite pranks was "blowing the gas." The burner jet would be removed from a lamp fixture and the gas blown through the piping back into the gas tank, the result being complete darkness since the lamps could not be lit. The Devils also tore up beds, caused trouble, and generally raised hell.

To evade a few classes, students would stack snowballs around the outside door. They would freeze there, and that way they could not get out and the janitor could not get in. The AODD even dunked President James H. Smart under the Old Pump. He was reportedly a good sport.

It is believed the group was last active in the fall of 1963.

Top: Purdue campus, 1876.

Middle: Purdue campus, 1896.

Bottom: Purdue campus, 1924.

Top: Purdue campus, 1938.

Middle: Purdue campus, 1952.

Bottom: Purdue campus, 2006.

HITTING THE BOOKS

IT BEGAN AS A CHOICE: school of agriculture or school of engineering? When Purdue opened its doors in 1874, only two options were offered to its all-male student body. Today, there are hundreds of majors to choose from within Purdue's curriculum. By adapting to the needs of the students, as well as to the changing times and social structures, Purdue's expansive range has grown to include eleven schools and colleges, spanning the full scope of human endeavor.

A Purdue food sciences student doing research with an oven that fries food without an oil bath, developed by Kevin Keener, associate professor in the Department of Food Science (left).

COLLEGE OF AGRICULTURE

Authorized by the Indiana General Assembly in 1869, under the Land-Grant College (Morrill) Act of 1862, the Division of Agriculture was established when the University opened in 1874.

The College of Agriculture officially became a school at Purdue University in 1907 and now offers more than fifty majors, ranging from agricultural communication to wildlife management. Departments of the College include Agriculture and Biological Engineering, Agricultural Economics, Agronomy, Animal Sciences, Biochemistry, Botany and Plant Pathology, Entomology, Food Science, Forestry and Natural Resources, Youth Development and Agricultural Education, and Horticulture and Landscape Architecture.

Research was an early focus of the school and continues to be an essential aspect of its operation. The Hatch Act of 1887 led to the creation of the Agricultural Experiment Station, and the Smith-Lever Act of 1914 created the Cooperative Extension Service, completing the teaching, research, and service triad integral to land-grant institutions.

COLLEGE OF EDUCATION

Purdue's preparation of teachers began in 1908. The earliest courses included general and educational psychology, history and principles of education, principles and methods of teaching, school organization and management, and secondary and industrial education. These courses have adjusted with the times and remain an integral part of the preparation process for new teachers that graduate from the University.

Until 1989, education faculty members at the University were divided into several departments, including the School of Humanities, Social Science, and Education. At one time, the school was known as the Division of Education and Applied Psychology and offered the first University course in sociology. In 1989, the independent School of Education was officially created to take on all of these formerly separate divisions of the education program, removing the school from the larger College of Liberal Arts. In 2005, Purdue renamed the school to the College of Education.

Today, students major in Elementary Education, Social Studies Education, and Special Education. Additionally, large numbers of education students are enrolled as secondary education majors in various other schools and colleges of the University. The school also offers master's and doctoral programs to students. Students enrolled in the College of Education, now housed in Beering Hall, are granted opportunities to explore education as a career through various courses and graduate with qualifications necessary to obtain licensure to teach in many states across the country.

COLLEGE OF ENGINEERING

One of the most significant and well-known educational trademarks of Purdue is its College of Engineering. The University's reputation as an excellent source of engineering education has earned it worldwide recognition. Engineering instruction has been offered at Purdue University since the institution first opened its doors to students. In the fall of 1876, only one student had registered in civil engineering; June 1878 saw the first degree awarded in engineering.

The School of Mechanics, established in 1879, led to the founding of the School of Mechanical Engineering in

A student in chemical engineering performs an experiment growing algae in a "bioreactor" at Purdue as part of a federally funded effort aimed at creating genetically engineered algae for biodiesel production.

Civil Engineering students standing in front of the Civil Engineering Building (now Grissom) ready to survey the world, 1915.

September 1882. Although Civil Engineering was the first technical subject to be taught at the University, a department was not established until 1887. Electrical Engineering—now referred to as Electrical and Computer Engineering—was organized as a separate school in 1888.

Today the College of Engineering is composed of the School of Aeronautics and Astronautics, the Department of Agricultural and Biological Engineering, the Weldon School of Biomedical Engineering, the School of Chemical Engineering, the School of Civil Engineering, the Division of Construction Engineering and Management, the School of Electrical and Computer Engineering, the School of Engineering Education, the School of Industrial Engineering, the School of Materials Engineering, the School of Mechanical Engineering, and the School of Nuclear Engineering.

COLLEGE OF HEALTH AND HUMAN SCIENCES

The study of "home economics" at Purdue dates back to 1887, when Professor Emma P. Ewing set up a three-year course of study called "Domestic Economy" within the science curriculum. Although the classes Ewing developed were offered only through 1889, her initial efforts were emulated by others who recognized the need for education focusing on home and families.

In 1905, President Winthrop E. Stone announced the creation of the Department of Household Economics within the science curriculum. He noted that "Purdue should offer to women opportunities comparable in scientific and technical value with those enjoyed by men." By 1919, the curriculum included a master's program in home economics. Laboratory education was vital to the curriculum early on, with facilities including labs for teaching foods, clothing, dietetics, food chemistry, and textile chemistry.

In 1926, the School of Home Economics was created, separating it from the School of Science. Over the years,

Two students from the College of Health and Human Services reading books to children at the Ben and Maxine Miller Child Development Laboratory School.

the program has broadened, with disciplines added in child development, institutional management, and marriage and family therapy. The name was changed to the School of Consumer and Family Sciences in 1976.

In February 2010, a decision was made by Purdue's Board of Trustees to realign the colleges in order to create opportunities that enhanced health and human sciences programs without disturbing the number of colleges on the West Lafayette campus. The College of Health and Human Sciences was launched on July 1, 2010, encompassing the departments of Health and Kinesiology; Psychological Sciences; Speech, Language, and Hearing Sciences; Human Development and Family Studies; Nutrition Science; Consumer Sciences and Retailing; Hospitality and Tourism Management; Nursing; and Health Sciences.

Previously, these nine different departments were spread across three separate colleges. Combining them allows for an

Purdue nursing students participate in a patient care scenario using one of the high-fidelity simulators in Nursing's simulation lab.

easier means of creating and improving programs that enhance student learning for success in a changing world, and promotes cross-disciplinary research and scholarship.

KRANNERT SCHOOL OF MANAGEMENT

In 1956, Purdue established the Department of Industrial Management and Transportation within the Schools of Engineering. Emanuel T. Weiler headed this newly founded department, in addition to the Department of Economics, which was, at the time, part of the School of Science. The two departments merged in 1958 to create the School of Industrial Management, later renamed the School of Management.

In 1962, thanks to a $2.73 million endowment from Herman C. and Ellnora Decker Krannert, the Krannert Graduate School of Industrial Administration became Purdue's first named school. The Krannerts' relationship with Purdue began in 1960, when Herman approved Purdue faculty to teach a management development program for the executives of his Indianapolis-based firm, Inland Container Corp. In addition to the endowment, the Krannerts provided additional funds for the construction of a new management building. In 1965, the first classes were held in the newly completed Krannert building.

Today, the school includes undergraduate programs in Accounting, Management, Industrial Management, and Economics. The school also provides executive education programs and administers several research centers. Krannert offers four master's degrees: the Master of Business Administration, the Master of Science in Finance, the Master of Science in Human Resource Management, and the Master of Science in Industrial Administration. PhD programs include qualifications in Economics, Management, and Organizational Behavior and Human Resource Management.

These buildings shall crumble to dust, the very ground on which we stand may be a wilderness and the owls hoot in the branches above this place, but every truth and good impulse given here will never die, but live forever in the hearts of the students here instructed.... We may engrave upon brass and rear temples, but they will crumble into dust; but he who writes upon the tablet of the human soul does that which no time can efface—which will grow brighter throughout the age of eternity.

—President Emerson White

COLLEGE OF LIBERAL ARTS

In the earliest years of the University, all liberal arts courses were offered solely through the School of Science. It was not until 1953 that the liberal arts mission was officially recognized with the formation of a separate school, the School of Science, Education, and Humanities.

Purdue trustees approved the Bachelor of Arts degree in 1959, recognizing that humanities and liberal arts had "come of age" at the University, something that had not been expected at the founding of the land-grant college. In 1963, the name of the school was changed to the School of Humanities, Social Science, and Education. At this time, the School of Science was pulled away to become a separate school and administrative unit. The School of Education split away from the School of Humanities, Social Science, and Education in 1989, leaving only the School of Liberal Arts.

Today, the school is known as the College of Liberal Arts and represents the second largest college at the University. Departments of this college include Anthropology; the Brian Lamb School of Communication; English; the School of Languages and Cultures; History; Philosophy; Political Science; Sociology; and the Patty and Rusty Rueff School of Visual and Performing Arts. To better accommodate the educational needs of students, as of July 1, 2010, the departments of Health and Kinesiology, Psychological Sciences, and Speech, Language, and Hearing have been relocated to the College of Health and Human Sciences. In addition to the College of Liberal Arts' wide range of opportunities for disciplinary inquiry, the school offers seventeen interdisciplinary programs.

COLLEGE OF PHARMACY

The School of Pharmacy at Purdue was established as a two-year school in 1884 in response to a demand for theoretical education and practical training in pharmacy and related subject areas. The name was changed to the School of Pharmacy and Pharmaceutical Sciences in 1963.

Now the school offers a six-year program leading to the doctor of Pharmacy degree as well as bachelor's and graduate degrees in pharmaceutical sciences. Departments include Industrial and Physical Pharmacy, Medicinal Chemistry and Molecular Pharmacology, and Pharmacy Practice.

A Purdue Pharmacy student working on a lab project.

On July 1, 2010, the College of Pharmacy, Nursing, and Health Sciences was revamped, leading to the departure of Nursing and Health Sciences. Today, these two schools are included in the College of Health and Human Sciences, leaving the College of Pharmacy to stand alone.

COLLEGE OF SCIENCE

Science courses were already a basic foundation when the University first opened its doors in September 1874. In 1876, President Emerson E. White developed a preparatory curriculum and created a College of General Science to prepare students for entry into the Schools of Science and Technology. It was not until 1907 that the School of Science was officially formed, with Stanley Coulter as the founding dean. In 1953, liberal arts and education were formally added into the school and the name was changed to the School of Science, Education, and Humanities. Those curricula were separated in 1963 and the name reverted to the School of Science.

The school is now made up of seven departments: Biological Sciences; Chemistry; Computer Science; Earth, Atmospheric, and Planetary Sciences; Mathematics; Physics; and Statistics. One of the largest of its kind in the nation, the Purdue Department of Chemistry provides introductory chemistry instruction to nearly 4,500 students every semester. The Department of Computer Science was formed in 1962, the first of its kind in the United States.

The Department of Earth, Atmospheric, and Planetary Sciences, along with other areas of study like physics and zoology, had its beginning with the founding of the University. The geology program started at Purdue when the doors opened in 1874 and was a required field of study for students in engineering, agriculture, and technology programs. Purdue became involved with the atmospheric sciences when the Indiana State Weather Service was transferred to the University in 1883.

The second person appointed to the Purdue University faculty was a professor of mathematics—William B. Morgan of Indianapolis. The program was almost exclusively concerned with undergraduate instruction, as a formal graduate school was not established until 1929. The Department of Statistics was developed in 1963 as a part of the Division of Mathematical Sciences. In 1968, the department became a separate entity within the School of Science.

COLLEGE OF TECHNOLOGY

Charles H. Lawshe, dean of University Extension, noted after several meetings of the American Society of Engineering Education that there were two paths emerging in engineering education: engineering science and engineering technology. In September 1960, he proposed that the Schools of Engineering reorganize into two divisions: the Division of Engineering Sciences and the Division of Engineering Technology. This plan, however, lacked faculty support and was dropped before being formally presented.

Lawshe, however, did not dismiss the basic idea of his original plan. As dean, he was in charge of the Purdue Technical Institute, a technology extension program that offered classes in Fort Wayne, Hammond, Indianapolis, and Michigan City. He believed it would be an ideal foundation on which to build a stand-alone technology curriculum.

In July 1963, Lawshe presented a plan for the creation of a new undergraduate school. A committee of faculty and administrators studied the proposal, and on February 15, 1964, the Board of Trustees acted affirmatively on the proposal, thus creating the School of Technology on July 1, 1964. Lawshe was named dean of the new school.

Purdue Aviation Technology student pilots Chantel Steele, right, and Amanda Keck preparing to fly a nearly 3,000-mile course from Arizona to Ohio during the 2012 Air Race Classic.

This newly created school was charged with providing educational programs for students whose technological interests and aptitudes were not being served adequately in existing curricula. Practical, hands-on training was a focus. The school began with seven academic departments: Technical and Applied Arts; Industrial Education; Nursing; Applied Technology; Aviation Technology; Architectural and Civil Engineering Technology; and Electrical Engineering Technology. Current departments are Aviation Technology; Building Construction Management; Computer Graphics Technology; Computer Information Technology; Electrical and Computer Engineering Technology; Mechanical Engineering Technology; and Technology Leadership and Innovation.

COLLEGE OF VETERINARY MEDICINE

The origin of veterinary medicine at Purdue can be traced back to 1877, when a Department of Veterinary Science was established in the School of Agriculture. The separate School of Veterinary Science and Medicine was not established until 1957, when the Indiana General Assembly passed an act that allowed for its creation. The first class of the Department of Veterinary Science began in the fall of 1959, and the cohort, composed of forty-three male students, graduated in 1963. Female students did not enter the school until 1960.

In March of 1974, the school was renamed the School of Veterinary Medicine, which became fully accredited before its first class had graduated. This accomplishment is something that is unsurpassed in veterinary education in the United States. Today, Veterinary Medicine, renamed a College in 2012, consists of three academic departments: Veterinary Clinical Sciences; Basic Medical Sciences; and Comparative Pathology. A year after the school's change of name in 1975, the Veterinary Technology Program was introduced. Now, the program offers both associate's and bachelor's degrees. This Veterinary Technology Program is unique in the fact that it is offered through the College of Veterinary Medicine rather than through a technology school or a separate community college.

Purdue's College of Veterinary Medicine is the only one in the state of Indiana and is one of twenty-eight veterinary medical schools in the United States. The change from "School" to "College" of Veterinary Medicine reflects the variety and depth of programs offered.

Purdue veterinary clinician Steve Thompson examines the wing feathers of a Moluccan cockatoo held by Mary Rakowski, a senior in veterinary medicine and assisted by second-year veterinary technician student Rebecca Cripe.

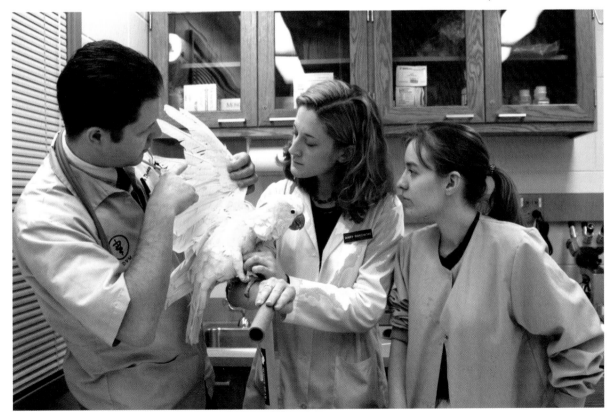

THE GRADUATE SCHOOL

On April 10, 1929, the University Board of Trustees authorized the establishment of a separate graduate school at Purdue. Graduate study was initiated in 1922, when President Edward C. Elliott appointed a committee of faculty to outline steps for the organization, establishment, and maintenance of a graduate school. The faculty, acting on the committee's recommendations, authorized the initiation of graduate study leading to both master's and PhD degrees on January 5, 1925. Although a few advanced degrees, including the PhD, were awarded prior to 1922, the first doctorate following the appointment of a supervising faculty committee for graduate study was awarded in June 1928.

The dean of The Graduate School is the principal administrative officer of The Graduate School. Administrative offices are located on the first floor of Young Graduate House. Many faculty members involve graduate students in their research projects. Other graduate students serve as teaching assistants in schools throughout the University.

The existence of The Graduate School unites the other schools around campus, creating a standard program for awarding higher degrees. In many of the buildings around

Purdue graduate students working on a test rocket that might be used in a vehicle to land on the Moon. The work is part of the NASA-funded Project Morpheus, which includes research to develop new technologies for future trips to the Moon, Mars, or asteroids.

campus, there are individual graduate offices that handle specific application and admissions processes before reporting their students and files to The Graduate School.

THE PURDUE MACE

Historically, the mace has been a symbol of authority. In the Middle Ages, maces were weapons—giant clubs with spiked iron heads capable of breaking armor—used by knights in battle. They also were borne by a royal bodyguard to protect the king in processions.

Over time, maces assumed more ceremonial functions, losing their warlike appearance as they began to be decorated with jewels and precious metals.

At Purdue University, the Mace is carried before the president and other dignitaries in the platform party during commencement processions and other special events. As a reflection of the modern vision of the University, the design of the Purdue Mace embraces sweeping thrusts and counterthrusts to create a vital energy within an otherwise clean, linear aesthetic. The Purdue seal is located in the center of the head of the mace; bounding the seal are two sweeping silver wings.

The Purdue Mace was designed and crafted in the 1980s by David Peterson, then a professor of art and design who taught jewelry and metalsmithing.

Purdue Mace.

THE PRESIDENTIAL MEDALLION

Closely allied with maces and seals as symbols of stature or authority are the collars of office worn by many officials, including chancellors and presidents of universities. Collars usually include a medallion inscribed with the seal of the institution and are worn over the academic gown on public occasions, particularly at commencements.

Located in the center of Purdue's Presidential Medallion is the griffin symbol used on the University seal. The Medallion, as well as the Mace, was handcrafted from sterling silver, ebony, and gold using centuries-old techniques.

Presidential Medallion.

With a Purdue diploma in hand, the world awaits.

Top: Commencement, 1902.

Bottom: Commencement parade on Hello Walk, June 1924.

COMMENCEMENT

In May 1875, Purdue held its very first commencement, awarding the Bachelor of Science degree to a class of one, John Harper, a transfer student from Northwestern Christian University (now Butler University in Indianapolis). In 1903, commencement ceremonies, which had been held either in Military Hall or outdoors on the Oval, were moved to the newly completed Eliza Fowler Hall. The steady growth of the size of the graduating class necessitated moving the events to ever larger and larger facilities, including Memorial Gymnasium, the Armory, and the Fieldhouse. In 1940, commencement ceremonies were moved to the Hall of Music, now referred to as the Elliott Hall of Music, where they continue to take place today.

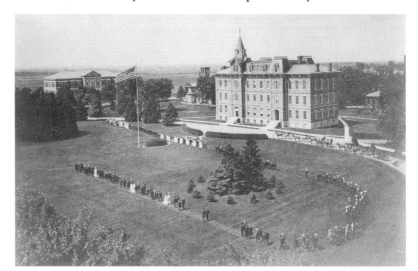

Top: Commencement, June 1926. Left to right: Frank Baldwin Jewett, speaker; Honorable Chase Osborn, awarded B.S. for class of 1880; Dean Stanley C. Coulter; John T. McCutcheon, awarded honorary degree Doctor of Human Letters; C.H. Robertson, awarded honorary Doctor of Science; George Ade, awarded honorary Doctor of Humane Letters; and President Edward C. Elliott.

Middle: Commencement, 1964.

Bottom: Commencement, 2010.

BOILER BYTE

AN EGO AS WIDE AS THE WABASH

John Purdue had a rather high opinion of himself. After he gave $1,000 toward the construction of the Second Presbyterian Church in Lafayette, he was invited to the dedication service. Entering the church just as the congregation rose to sing the first hymn, he mistook their action as a gesture in his honor. Ever "humble," his voice rang out: "Keep your seats ladies and gentlemen; don't mind me."

LEADING THE WAY

THEY HAVE LAID CORNERSTONES, fostered ideas, and encouraged advancement. They have been educators, researchers, school superintendents, scholars, armed forces veterans, and public servants. Their educations have come from several countries and many disciplines. They have led us in times of progress, depression, tragedy, and triumph. They have built upon the dreams of those who aided in establishing this institution, all the while quietly leaving their own legacies. Their numbers are small, yet their accomplishments are huge. They are the presidents of Purdue University.

Richard C. Owen.

RICHARD C. OWEN
(PRESIDENT, 1872–74)

Born January 6, 1810, in New Lanark, Scotland, Richard C. Owen was the youngest son of Robert Owen. He received his education in Switzerland and Glasgow and, at the age of eighteen, moved with his family to the United States. The Owen family settled in Indiana, where Robert founded the utopian community of New Harmony in 1825.

Owen's father was a great educator and Richard followed in his father's footsteps. His stints of teaching were interrupted, however, with military service in the Mexican and Civil Wars. During the Civil War, Owen was director of Camp Morton, a prison camp in Indianapolis. He improved conditions at the camp and treated the prisoners so well that, after the war, Confederate veterans presented a bust of Owen to the State of Indiana.

Upon leaving active duty, Owen was named a geology professor at Indiana University. This role was fitting considering he had briefly served as an Indiana State Geologist prior to the Civil War. In addition to geology, he taught such diverse subjects as natural philosophy, German, French, and chemistry.

With the passage of the Morrill Act in 1862, Owen became intrigued with its provision for an agricultural college. Owen studied the virtues of the idea and potential problems that creating an educational institution such as this would pose. Both his interest in this concept and his reputation as an educator led to his appointment to the presidency in 1872. He accepted a salary of $3,500 a year, which included bringing his considerable fossil and mineral collection, acquired through his interest in geology, to the University.

His first desire was to be virtuous, his second to be wise.
—Epitaph of Richard C. Owen

In May 1873, the newly established Purdue Board of Trustees asked Owen to draft a plan on how he would organize the University. He proceeded to develop a long memorandum of recommendations on dormitories, military and moral training, fire protection, and physical facilities. Although an experienced educator, Owen devoted more attention to the physical details of the new campus than was necessary, largely ignoring plans for classes, curriculum, and administrative organization.

When the report became public, there was an uproar. Journalists quickly condemned the paper as "impractical and inadequate." Amid this storm of criticism, Owen resigned as

Purdue's first president on March 1, 1874, the day before a special seminar was taught to meet a legislative deadline for the first class to begin.

Richard Owen returned to Indiana University to teach and engage in research. After his retirement in 1879, his continuing geological research took him across Europe and the Middle East. He eventually returned to New Harmony, where he died on March 25, 1890, at the age of eighty, from accidentally drinking embalming fluid. He is buried in an old cemetery in New Harmony, Indiana, where his epitaph reads: "His first desire was to be virtuous, his second to be wise." Owen Residence Hall, located on the north side of campus and home to over 700 students, was named in his honor.

ABRAHAM C. SHORTRIDGE
(PRESIDENT, 1874–75)

Abraham C. Shortridge was born in Henry County, Indiana, on October 22, 1833. Educated in Richmond, Indiana, he taught at Milton and Dublin College for three years before becoming a professor of mathematics at Whitewater College.

At age thirty, Shortridge was named the first superintendent of schools in Indianapolis, a position he held until Purdue hired him in 1874. A power in Indiana public education, he had helped organize the Indiana State Teachers Association in 1854.

With his experience as an educational administrator and a champion of the land-grant philosophy, Shortridge was named Purdue's second president in 1874. He is credited with opening the University's doors as classes began September 16, 1874. He also encouraged the trustees to add industrial education so that "young men who desire to fit themselves technically" need not go elsewhere for their instruction. The University responded by announcing four-year courses for physics, civil, and mechanical engineering.

Although he did manage to get the University open, Shortridge was not happy in his position at Purdue. He found John Purdue difficult to get along with and the faculty grew dissatisfied. Shortridge presented the first degree from

Abraham C. Shortridge.

Young men who desire to fit themselves technically to become leaders in these industrial pursuits should no longer be compelled to go elsewhere for their educations.
—President Abraham C. Shortridge

the new University in June 1875 and retired in December of that year, after only eighteen months in office.

In 1897, Shortridge was honored by the city of Indianapolis, with the renaming of Indianapolis High School as Shortridge High School in recognition of his work establishing the public school system of the city. Shortridge died on October 8, 1919.

JOHN S. HOUGHAM
(ACTING PRESIDENT, 1876)

John S. Hougham.

Born in 1821 near Connersville, Indiana, John S. Hougham graduated from Wabash College in 1846 and continued his studies at Brown University. He became a professor of mathematics and natural philosophy at Franklin College and later became the acting president of the same institution until a permanent replacement could be found. From there, he accepted a professorship at Kansas State Agricultural College in 1868, teaching science and agriculture.

Hougham moved to Purdue in May 1872, where he became the first faculty member of the new University. In addition to teaching science and agriculture, he was instrumental in helping guide the building program of the fledgling institution.

Beginning January 1, 1876, Hougham was asked to fill the vacancy left by the resignation of President Shortridge until a permanent president could be found. The search ended in May of that year with the appointment of Emerson E. White, after which Hougham returned to Manhattan, Kansas, where he devoted himself to manufacturing physical and chemical laboratory equipment. He passed away on March 31, 1894.

EMERSON E. WHITE
(PRESIDENT, 1876–83)

Emerson E. White was born January 10, 1829, in Mantua, Ohio. Until 1856, White worked as an educator and an administrator in the Cleveland school system. Following that, he relocated to Portsmouth, Ohio, and began work there as the superintendent of public schools. He remained at this post until he was chosen as Ohio's superintendent of schools in 1860. Later that same year, he purchased *Ohio Educational Monthly* and made it one of the leading educational publications in the country.

White steadily gained an excellent reputation in the educational community, and on February 17, 1876, he was appointed president of Purdue University. He took office on May 1 of that year, and on July 16, he gave his inaugural address stating his educational goals for Purdue: that Purdue should concentrate on applied sciences and supplement that course of study with a "liberal" education that concentrated on mathematics and science. With that address, he set a clear direction for the University, emphasizing its land-grant roots.

"It [the University] must be content to begin with cultivation of a narrow field," he said, "and to do the works so well that it may confidently look to the future to widen its domain and fill the import of its university title." Although White did not encourage the study of literature at Purdue, he was the only president to carry the title of Professor of English Literature.

Emerson E. White.

White's tenure came to an end when he met with one of the most divisive issues in Purdue history: the issue of students' right to belong to fraternities and other "secret societies" around campus. He wanted nothing to do with any "so-called Greek or other society" on campus. At the time, University regulations stated that if a student were to join such an organization, he would not be promoted at the end of the school year and would be dishonorably dismissed from the University.

Court actions ensued in reaction to the University's harsh regulations. Ultimate action on the matter came from the Indiana legislature. The 1883 General Assembly attached a rider to the appropriations bill that forced faculties of state-supported institutions to repeal all anti-fraternity regulations before funds would be released by the state. In the summer of 1883, when Purdue was faced with the prospect of losing state funds due to White's policies, he resigned from the presidency. He then moved to Cincinnati and served briefly as the superintendent of public schools before returning to writing and editing educational journals. He died in Columbus, Ohio, on October 21, 1902.

It [the University] must be content to begin with cultivation of a narrow field and to do the works so well that it may confidently look to the future to widen its domain and fill the import of its university title.

—President Emerson E. White

James H. Smart.

JAMES H. SMART
(PRESIDENT, 1883–1900)

Born on June 30, 1841, James H. Smart was the son of a physician and received his early education at home in Center Harbor, New Hampshire. High school began for him at the impressive age of eleven, but he dropped out only one year later in order to seek his fortune elsewhere.

Later in his life, Smart finally returned to high school and eventually became a teacher himself. He progressed into school administration, serving as principal of a school in Laconia, New Hampshire. Smart then moved to a principal position at a school in Toledo, Ohio. By 1865, Smart had managed to work himself up to the position of Superintendent of Public Schools in Fort Wayne, Indiana.

From there, Smart moved to Superintendent of Public Instruction for the State of Indiana in 1874, a position to which he would be reelected twice. He was the first person to ever achieve dual reelection. His skill as an administrator was recognized by appointments to represent the state at an international exposition and his election in 1881 to become president of the National Education Association.

Smart's reputation and achievements did not go unrecognized in West Lafayette. The Purdue Board of Trustees was already in the process of looking for a strong leader to repair the damage done by the policies and problems of the White administration. Smart accepted the presidency of Purdue in August 1883.

Primary goals established by Smart and his administration included persuading people to care about higher education and overcoming public apathy about Purdue's state of affairs. By 1889, Smart had managed to reverse public opinion about Purdue and as a result, contributions to the University began to increase.

The years of Smart's presidency were marked by all-around University growth: new buildings were constructed, new academic programs were introduced, and student enrollment increased. His style of leadership was as brilliant as ever when the original Heavilon Hall burned to the ground four days after dedication, a day of tragedy for the University. His solemn pledge to students, "I tell you, young men, that tower shall go up one brick higher," still rings with assertion and strong leadership today, reminding current Purdue students of the strength of the University's past leaders.

During his presidency, Smart oversaw the introduction and establishment of the School of Pharmacy and the Schools of Civil and Electrical Engineering. From 1896 to 1900, Smart experienced a period of failing health that prevented him from providing the type of leadership for which he was known and for which he is still remembered; yet Purdue's physical plant and population still saw steady growth. His seventeen-year tenure saw a rise in enrollment to more than 700 compared with the 100 when he arrived. The value of buildings and equipment around campus doubled, and faculty increased from fifteen to well over seventy. Smart was instrumental in stabilizing University funding and led Purdue in gaining recognition not only in Indiana, but throughout the United States and in foreign lands. Smart remained Purdue president until February 21, 1900, when he died in office.

WINTHROP E. STONE
(PRESIDENT, 1900–21)

Winthrop E. Stone was born June 12, 1862, in Chesterfield, New Hampshire. At the age of sixteen, he entered the Massachusetts Agricultural College (now known as University of Massachusetts), where he received his BS in chemistry in 1882. Four years later—some records say—he received a similar degree from Boston University. Stone then traveled to Germany, where he studied at the University of Göttingen until 1888. After his return to the United States, he took a post as chief chemist at the State of Tennessee Agricultural Experiment Station.

In 1889, Stone came to Purdue as a professor of chemistry. Admired as a scholar and administrator, he was appointed the first vice president of Purdue in November 1892.

When President James H. Smart died in February 1900, the Board of Trustees named Stone acting president and soon after elected him president. His attention to detail was one of the qualities that marked his fruitful administration.

Noting the tremendous progress in the Schools of Engineering in the previous twenty years, Stone determined that the School of Agriculture needed to make similar advances. The construction of Agriculture Hall (now Pfendler Hall) in 1902

Winthrop E. Stone.

and the addition of several agricultural farms, including the Agricultural Experiment Station and other facilities, increased the stature of agriculture at Purdue. Stone, though, did not neglect other University needs; Eliza Fowler Hall, the Memorial Gymnasium, the original Civil Engineering Building, and the original Physics Building were among more than twenty buildings constructed during his tenure.

Academic programs were no less a priority than physical facilities. Stone presided over the development of the short-lived School of Medicine, the Department of Home Economics, and the Department of Education. During Stone's administration, insistence upon academic quality was a hallmark. Purdue's national reputation increased. His presidency, however, was tragically cut short in 1921 when Stone, an inveterate mountaineer, met his death in an attempt to conquer Mount Eon in the Canadian Rockies. He was almost at the summit when he fell 1,000 feet to his death. Today, Stone's presidency is remembered through Stone Hall, which houses various departments within the College of Liberal Arts.

Henry W. Marshall.

HENRY W. MARSHALL
(ACTING PRESIDENT, 1921–22)

Following the unexpected death of President Winthrop E. Stone, Henry W. Marshall was appointed acting president of the University on August 4, 1921. Marshall was a member of the Board of Trustees and chairman of its executive committee. While still publisher of the Lafayette *Journal and Courier*, he was appointed both vice president and acting president of the University.

Marshall served one year as acting president until Edward C. Elliott's appointment was announced in September 1922. As acting president, he handled the University's business matters while Stanley Coulter presided as chairman of the faculty.

EDWARD C. ELLIOTT
(PRESIDENT, 1922–45)

On December 21, 1874, just a few months after Purdue held its very first class, Edward C. Elliott was born in Chicago. His family moved to North Platte, Nebraska, in 1881, and he later attended the University of Nebraska. It was here that he received his bachelor's degree in chemistry in 1895 and his master's in chemistry in 1897. He taught chemistry in Leadville, Colorado for a year and was then appointed as Superintendent of Leadville schools. Elliott resigned in 1903 in order to continue his graduate work at Columbia University and the University of Jena, Germany. In 1905, he received a PhD in education from Columbia with the goal of educational administration as a career path. He joined the University of Wisconsin faculty in 1905, becoming a full professor in 1907 and education department head in 1909. In 1916, he left Wisconsin to become chancellor of the University of Montana system.

Elliott did not leave the University of Montana until May 1922, when he officially accepted the offer of Purdue's presidency. The Board of Trustees had conducted an extensive search, eventually finding Elliott, a man they believed would do well in the position. On September 1, 1922, Elliott officially took office as the sixth president of the University.

Elliott boldly led the University's growth from 1922 to 1945. Total value of the physical plant of the University increased fivefold under his leadership, eventually totaling $18.7 million dollars. Because the student body continued to grow, Elliott worked to develop a plan for future students. Matthews Hall, the Recitation Building, Ross-Ade Stadium, the Purdue Memorial Union, the Poultry Building, the Recreation Field, the Pharmacy Building, the Horticulture Building, the Agricultural Engineering Building, the Power Plant, the Chemistry Building, the Materials Testing Lab, the Chemical Engineering Building, the Electrical Engineering Building, the Mechanical Engineering Building, and part of Cary Quadrangle were among twenty-eight major buildings constructed during Elliott's term as president. Just as astonishing as the tremendous building program was the great increase in Purdue's assets. From 1929 to 1939, during most of the Great Depression years, Purdue's assets tripled.

More important than the material gains Purdue made during Elliott's tenure, however, was the fact that the enrollment increased from 3,000 to 7,121 students between 1922 and 1940.

Elliott proved himself to be a very people-oriented president. He frequently walked to campus from the president's home in Lafayette, greeting students he passed along the way. Many of his programs were directed toward an improved student life. He established freshman orientation, expanded course offerings, and enhanced the quality of instruction. It was Elliott who named Amelia Earhart as a

Edward C. Elliott.

consultant on women's affairs, though the appointment came only a short time before her tragic flight in 1937.

Among Elliott's countless other achievements were several that have yet to be mentioned. Purdue Research Foundation, an organization affiliated with Purdue that provides a means of fund development for the purposes of research. A master plan for campus facility growth was established and The Graduate School was organized. Additionally, the expansion of the School of Home Economics and construction of the Hall of Music, now named in his honor, were undertaken during his presidency, which included the chaotic times at the start of World War II.

After twenty-three years of service to Purdue, Elliott was forced to retire in 1945 due to a mandatory retirement age, a policy he had been instrumental in establishing. Elliott was named president emeritus of the University and moved to Washington, DC, where he directed a national survey of the pharmacy profession. His return to Lafayette, however, was inevitable and finally came to pass in 1948, when he began spending roughly two hours per day in his Purdue office.

In the fall of 1957, Elliott suffered a stroke that left him partially paralyzed. The Hall of Music that had been constructed during his presidency was officially renamed for him in January

President Elliott getting into his Packard, date unknown.

1958. It was a fitting tribute because he had originated the idea and obtained funding for the building. Elliott lived in Lafayette for the rest of his life, and he died on June 16, 1960, at the age of eighty-five.

ANDREY A. POTTER
(ACTING PRESIDENT, 1945–46)

Andrey A. Potter, engineer and educator, was born in Vilna, Russia, on August 5, 1882. Hoping for a prosperous future, he came to America in 1897 and became a citizen in 1906. He received a bachelor's degree in engineering from the Massachusetts Institute of Technology in 1903. He joined the Kansas State faculty in 1905 and was dean of the division of engineering and director of the engineering experiment station in 1920, when Purdue came calling.

Andrey A. Potter.

Potter was named dean of the Schools of Engineering and served in that position for thirty-three years. He served as acting president after Edward C. Elliott retired in June 1945 until Frederick Hovde assumed the presidency in January 1946.

Referred to by some as the "Dean of the Deans of Engineering Universities," Potter was close to the students. Teaching was the emphasis of the schools. Purdue's notable achievement as an educator of engineers can be ascribed in no small measure to the work, talents, philosophy, and humanity of Potter.

Potter retired from Purdue in 1953, beginning another "career" in bituminous coal research. He maintained his ties with Purdue by walking, almost daily, to his office from his Russell Street home. The Potter Engineering Center was named in his honor in 1977. He died on November 5, 1979.

FREDERICK L. HOVDE
(PRESIDENT, 1946–71)

Born February 7, 1908, in Erie, Pennsylvania, Frederick L. Hovde attended the University of Minnesota, where he epitomized the student-athlete. As quarterback of the football team, he received all-conference honors as well as numerous academic awards. After graduating from Minnesota in 1929 with a degree in chemical engineering, he attended Oxford University as a Rhodes Scholar from North Dakota, where he had lived since age five.

Frederick L. Hovde.

Hovde completed his education at Oxford in 1932 with a degree in physical chemistry. Following graduation, he returned to the United States and was named assistant director of the experimental General College of the University of Minnesota. He next became assistant to the president of the University of Rochester in 1936. Hovde returned to England in 1941 as a member of the newly formed U.S. National Defense Research Committee. Two years later, he was named Chief of the NDRC Division Three, the unit that researched and developed America's rocket ordnance. In order to honor his wartime services as a scientist-administrator in rocket research, Hovde was awarded the President's Medal of Merit and the King's Medal for Service in the Cause of Freedom by the British government.

In 1945, a member of the Purdue Board of Trustees contacted Hovde about the position of president of the University. He accepted that summer with the stipulation that he would stay in Washington to finish up his affairs as chief of rocket ordnance. On January 4, 1946, he went to work as president of Purdue and remained for twenty-five years, longer than any other president to date. Hallmarks of his presidency were his beliefs that Purdue's two principal tasks were to educate and to extend human knowledge through research, and that Purdue would achieve greatness only when its topflight scientific, engineering, and agricultural programs were accompanied by first-class undergraduate programs in the humanities and social sciences.

As the University shifted from a wartime training and research center to a peacetime educational facility, Hovde faced numerous problems. Instructional facilities were worn out or obsolete, faculty members had been recruited away to help wartime efforts, and enrollment with the GI Bill was booming. Hovde—and Purdue—made the most of the challenges.

As enrollment more than doubled from 6,000 in 1944–45 to 14,187 in 1946–47, the need for housing was an immediate challenge. Cary Quadrangle doubled its normal capacity; students were housed in the Agricultural Engineering Building, and temporary housing was constructed for GI Bill students and their families.

With the immediate problems of the post-war years mitigated, Hovde and his administration focused on building the University for the future. He was president during the years of Purdue's greatest growth in physical plant, budget, curricula, and students.

BOILER BYTE

DEDICATION TO BEAUTIFICATION

Purdue's first buildings were erected on a treeless expanse of farmland. Trustee Martin L. Peirce donated his annual salary as treasurer of the board—and his tireless personal attention—to the beautification of the University.

One of Peirce's projects was to plant a windbreak of evergreen trees around the campus. The old evergreens between Elliott Hall of Music and the Psychological Sciences Building are some of those original plantings. They date back to the 1870s.

In addition to the great influence Hovde had on the history and direction of Purdue, he also was active and influential in higher education on a national level. He retired in 1971 and the Executive Building was renamed the Hovde Hall of Administration to honor him in 1975. Hovde passed away on March 1, 1983, of emphysema.

ARTHUR G. HANSEN
(PRESIDENT, 1971–82)

Born February 28, 1925, in Sturgeon Bay, Wisconsin, Arthur G. Hansen was the first alumnus to hold the University's highest position. Had it not been for World War II and his entry into the U.S. Marine Corps, Hansen might never have come to Purdue.

Arthur G. Hansen.

He received a bachelor's degree in electrical engineering from Purdue in 1946 as part of the U.S. Marines' V12 program. He earned a master's in mathematics in 1948 and then took a post as an aeronautical research scientist at Lewis Flight Propulsion Laboratory in Cleveland. In 1958, Hansen received a doctorate in mathematics from Case Western Reserve University.

From 1959 to 1966, Hansen was a faculty member at the University of Michigan, where he chaired the Department of Mechanical Engineering. In 1966, he moved to the Georgia Institute of Technology. There he was dean of the College of Engineering and taught mechanical engineering. He was named president of Georgia Tech in 1969.

Hansen was named the eighth president of Purdue in 1971. During his administration came the construction of the Johnson Hall of Nursing, the Psychological Sciences Building, and the Potter Engineering Center. His time was also dedicated to building student confidence in administration and instituting a high-profile program raising private funds for the University. The Life Sciences Research Building—now named for him—was built with funds raised during his "Plan for the Eighties" campaign. He also supported the construction of a new Black Cultural Center. Hansen stayed at Purdue for ten years. In November 1981, he announced his resignation. Later, he was named chancellor of the Texas A&M University system.

Hansen passed away on July 5, 2010 due to complications from elective surgery in Fort Meyers, Florida, at age eighty-five.

He is fondly recognized now as the "students' president," and his achievements will always be remembered by the University.

JOHN W. HICKS
(ACTING PRESIDENT, 1982–83)

John W. Hicks was born in Sydney, Australia. Hicks was a graduate of the University of Massachusetts and held master's and PhD degrees from Purdue University. In 1950, the Purdue agricultural economics faculty saw the addition of Hicks, a man who would be an effective and popular teacher.

Hicks made an early move to the administrative side of the University, a move that would result in his announcement as President Hovde's assistant in 1955. By 1959, he was named to the additional role of legislative lobbyist for Purdue, a position he remained in for more than twenty years.

When Arthur Hansen resigned from the presidency, Hicks, then Hansen's executive assistant, was named acting president while the search began for a new president. As acting president, he participated in the Undergraduate Library's October 1982 dedication, the same library that would later be renamed in his honor. Hicks returned to his former administrative duties when Steven C. Beering was named president in 1983. He became senior vice president only one year later and eventually retired in 1987. Hicks died on December 20, 2002.

John W. Hicks.

STEVEN C. BEERING
(PRESIDENT, 1983–2000)

Steven C. Beering was born August 20, 1932, in Berlin, Germany. When he was fifteen, he immigrated to the United States with his family. In 1954, he received his bachelor's degree *summa cum laude* and, in 1958, his medical degree from the University of Pittsburgh.

During 1958–59, Beering served an internship at Walter Reed General Hospital in Washington, DC. From 1959 to 1969, he served as a resident, staff internist, director of education in medicine, and chief of internal medicine at Wilford Hall U.S. Air Force Medical Center in San Antonio, Texas.

After his U.S. Air Force career, he joined the faculty of Indiana University as assistant dean of the School of Medicine.

Steven C. Beering.

He was named dean in 1974 and also served as chief of medical staff at I.U. Hospitals and director of the I.U. Medical Center.

On July 1, 1983, Beering became the ninth president of Purdue University. During his tenure, he became an internationally respected presence in higher education, serving as chairman of the Association of American Universities and as an advisor to various federal and state leaders, private industry, and other institutions.

During his presidency, Beering emphasized recruitment of the best students, initiating the Presidential Honors Scholars and the Fellows Program, which provides a full undergraduate scholarship and fellowship for graduate studies. He also placed a high value on first-class faculty, increasing the number of distinguished and named professorships almost threefold during his tenure.

Infrastructure improvement was another priority. Buildings completed during Beering's administration included Knoy Hall of Technology, the Materials and Electrical Engineering Building, a major addition to the Civil Engineering Building, the Visitor Information Center, Mollenkopf Athletic Center, the Class of 1950 Lecture Hall, the Liberal Arts and Education Building, Hillenbrand Hall, Nelson Hall of Food Science, and several parking garages.

Beering also led the revival and updating of the campus master plan, originally developed in the 1920s. The update featured the addition of green spaces, including revamping the Purdue Mall into a people-oriented quadrangle. Auto traffic was eliminated and a new water sculpture was constructed to be

President Beering catching a ride on the back of the Boilermaker Special, date unknown.

41

the centerpiece. Also added were Founders Park near the Liberal Arts and Education Building and Academy Park north of the Purdue Memorial Union.

In September 1999, Beering announced his support of an $150 million plan to expand and modernize Purdue's engineering facilities. This plan would add 325,000 square feet of engineering space. Another major project that began during Beering's presidency was expansion of the Krannert complex with the addition of Jerry S. Rawls Hall. Ground was broken in spring 2001 and the project was completed in 2003.

On February 8, 2002, the Board of Trustees adopted a resolution to rename the Liberal Arts and Education Building in honor of President Emeritus Beering. Dedication of the Steven C. Beering Hall of Liberal Arts and Education took place in April that year.

MARTIN C. JISCHKE
(PRESIDENT, 2000–07)

Martin C. Jischke became the tenth president of Purdue University on August 14, 2000. A native of Chicago, he received his bachelor's degree in physics with honors from the Illinois Institute of Technology. His master's and doctoral degrees in aeronautics and astronautics were both awarded from the Massachusetts Institute of Technology.

A prominent American higher-education administrator and advocate, Jischke acted as president of Iowa State University from 1991 to July 2000 and had acted as chancellor of the University of Missouri at Rolla, and as a faculty member, director, dean, and interim president of the University of Oklahoma before that.

Jischke held numerous national leadership roles in service to colleges and universities. Among these roles were president of the Global Consortium of Higher Education and Research for Agriculture, chair and board member of the National Association of State Universities and Land-Grant Colleges, and board member of the American Council of Education. A Fellow of the American association for the Advancement of Science and American Institute of Aeronautics and Astronautics, Jischke was a recipient of the Centennial Medallion of the American Society for Engineering Education.

Jischke served on numerous civic, state, and corporate boards during his academic career. Additionally, he was a science

Martin C. Jischke.

adviser and consultant to a range of state and federal agencies, government officials, and corporations, including a term as a White House Fellow and Special Assistant to the Secretary of Transportation.

From the beginning of his tenure at Purdue, Jischke made one goal clear: he desired to "make a great university into a preeminent university." In order to accomplish this goal, Jischke met with the Board of Trustees in order to develop a strategic five-year plan, focused on construction plans and fundraising goals. His most notable accomplishment, apart from gathering impressive amounts of money for the University, is perhaps Discovery Park, a $100 million research and entrepreneurial complex.

On August 4, 2006, Jischke announced he would be stepping down from the presidency. He was awarded an honorary doctorate degree from the College of Engineering in 2007. On September 30, 2008, the Martin C. Jischke Hall of Biomedical Engineering was formally dedicated to honor the tenth president of Purdue University.

FRANCE A. CÓRDOVA
(PRESIDENT, 2007–12)

France A. Córdova.

France A. Córdova, Purdue's first female president, was born in Paris in August 1947, the oldest of twelve children. After spending a few early years in Germany, her family settled in California, near Los Angeles.

In 1969, as Neil Armstrong landed on the Moon, Córdova was graduating *summa cum laude* with a degree in English from Stanford University. That historic landing inspired her to set her sights on exploring the mysteries of the universe, starting with a doctorate in physics from California Institute of Technology in 1979. Córdova spent the next decade at Los Alamos National Laboratory where her research focused on observational and experimental astrophysics, multi-spectral analysis of X-ray and gamma ray sources, and space-borne instrumentation.

She headed the Department of Astronomy and Astrophysics at Penn State before joining NASA in 1993, becoming the first woman and youngest person to hold the position of NASA chief scientist.

Córdova joined the University of California at Santa Barbara in 1996 as professor and vice chancellor for research. She became distinguished professor and chancellor at U.C. Riverside in 2002.

President Córdova and the Silver Twins at the Indiana State Fair, 2010.

While there she initiated the first medical school to be established west of the Mississippi in forty years.

Córdova's first undertaking upon arriving at Purdue in 2007 was the development of a comprehensive strategic plan, New Synergies. The plan focuses on overarching concepts of "Discovery with Delivery," "Launching Tomorrow's Leaders," and "Meeting Global Challenges," and set in motion a period of significant advancement in student access and success, research delivery and marketability, and global outreach to benefit Indiana.

Under her guidance, Purdue launched a new College of Health and Human Sciences, a Global Policy Research Institute, and its first-ever West Coast Partnership Center in California. During her presidency, Purdue's national rankings and research funding reached record levels.

She is the winner of NASA's Distinguished Service Medal and recognized as a Kilby Laureate. Córdova has been named one of "America's 100 Brightest Scientists Under 40" by *Science Digest* magazine and one of the "100 Most Influential Hispanics" by *Hispanic Business Magazine*.

A fellow of the American Academy of Arts and Sciences and the American Association for the Advancement of Science, Córdova was appointed by President George W. Bush to the National Science Board in 2008 and to the Smithsonian Board of Regents by President Barack Obama in 2009.

Córdova finished her term as president of the University in July 2012.

TIMOTHY D. SANDS
(ACTING PRESIDENT, 2012–13)

Timothy D. Sands became the University's executive vice president for academic affairs and provost on April 1, 2010. The provost is responsible for oversight of all Purdue colleges and schools, the regional campuses, and related academic activities in coordination with the Office of the President. The position also oversees Purdue libraries, student services, and cultural centers. On July 20, 2012, Sands was ratified by the Board of Trustees as acting president of Purdue University in the interim period between France Córdova's retirement and Mitchell E. Daniels's accession to the post in January 2013.

Sands graduated with highest honors in engineering physics in 1980; received his master's degree in materials science and engineering in 1981; and completed a PhD in materials science and engineering in 1984, all at the University of California, Berkeley. Following his studies at UC Berkeley, Sands worked as a member and then director of a research group within Bell Communications Research Inc., now called Telcordia, in New Jersey. After nine years, he returned to California and joined the faculty at UC Berkeley in the Department of Materials Science and Engineering.

Sands arrived at Purdue in 2002 and was named the Basil S. Turner Professor of Engineering. In 2006, he was named director of the Birck Nanotechnology Center. He has published more than 240 papers and has received fifteen patents. He is co-inventor of a laser lift-off process that is used throughout the world in the making and manufacturing of high-performance blue and green LEDs. In 2009, he was named a fellow of the Materials Research Society (MRS).

Timothy D. Sands.

Purdue Acting President Timothy D. Sands greeting a graduate receiving her degree on the Elliott Hall of Music stage during the summer commencement ceremony, August 4, 2012.

Mitchell E. Daniels, Jr.

MITCHELL E. DANIELS, JR.
(PRESIDENT, 2013–)

Mitchell E. Daniels, Jr. was elected as the forty-ninth governor of the State of Indiana in 2004, in his first bid for any elected office. He was re-elected in 2008 to a second and final term, receiving more votes than any candidate for any public office in the state's history. On June 21, 2012, Daniels was unanimously elected as the twelfth president of Purdue University, beginning his term upon completion as governor in January 2013.

Before becoming governor, Daniels enjoyed a successful career in business and government, holding numerous top management positions in both the private and public sectors. His work as CEO of the Hudson Institute and as president of Eli Lilly and Company's North American Pharmaceutical Operations taught him the business skills he brought to state government. He also served as chief of staff to Senator Richard Lugar, senior advisor to President Ronald Reagan, and director of the Office of Management and Budget under President George W. Bush.

Many organizations have recognized the governor's leadership. In October 2010, Daniels received the Woodrow Wilson National Fellowship Foundation's inaugural Medal for Distinguished Service to Education for his efforts to reform education. In January 2011, the governor was one of three individuals selected to receive the first-ever Fiscy Award, presented for leadership and commitment to responsible financial stewardship by the non-partisan Fiscy Awards Committee. In May 2012, the Manhattan Institute presented the governor with its Alexander Hamilton Award for his achievements in state government, including healthcare improvements, landmark education reforms, and advancements in fiscal responsibility.

Daniels earned a bachelor's degree from the Woodrow Wilson School of Public and International Affairs at Princeton University in 1971 and his law degree from Georgetown University in 1979.

Indiana Govenor Mitchell E. Daniels talks with students outside Stewart Center following the announcement of his presidency, June 21, 2012.

BOILER BYTE

ONE OF THE ELITE AGAIN

During the latter part of World War II, the United States Maritime Commission constructed over 400 Victory cargo ships and over 115 Victory transports. After launching the SS *United Victory* in 1944, other ships were launched and named after Allied nations, American cities, and educational institutions. The SS *Purdue*, built in 1945, serviced the American soldier proudly along with the SS *M.I.T.*, SS *Berkeley*, SS *Cornell*, SS *Notre Dame*, and SS *Harvard*. During the Korean and Vietnam wars, the SS *Purdue Victory* (shown above) was reactivated to bring supplies to Far Eastern ports.

BRICKS AND MORTAR

AMONG THE PARKS AND PATHWAYS of the West Lafayette campus lie the buildings that so many have entered seeking higher education. The plaque found on the oldest building at Purdue, University Hall, states their purpose well: "In this structure built with bricks and cemented with aspirations, thousands of students have savored the finest that men have thought and felt throughout the ages: The wisdom of philosophers, the comprehension of scientists, the beauty of artists, the vision of dreamers, the realism of statesmen, for here nearly all the humanities and sciences have been taught—the hopes of its founders materialized. The exterior lined the past, the interior transformed into contemporary efficient space, may gifted teachers and talented students here learn together as they sift the wisdom of the centuries in search of the essentials for free men in the ageless future."

ACCELERATOR LABORATORY

Located beneath the Purdue Mall, the Accelerator Laboratory is a two-story building with 31,000 square feet of space and an entrance from the Physics Building. The laboratory was built to house an eight million volt FN Tandem Van de Graaf accelerator, provided to the University by the National Science Foundation in 1989. This subterranean structure is now called the Purdue Rare Isotope Measurement Laboratory, or PRIME, and is a dedicated research and service facility for accelerator mass spectrometry.

ARMORY

With military training compulsory during Purdue's early days, an armory was among the five original buildings on campus. Military Hall and Gymnasium was a one-story wooden structure large enough to accommodate a single company drilling at close formation. Located where Haas Hall now stands, the old armory was not only used for military purposes, but also served as a gym and hall for social functions. It also was the site of Purdue's first commencement in 1875.

On the morning of February 24, 1916, a fire of unknown origin destroyed the wooden building and all its contents. This unfortunate event was such a blow that the corps was disbanded for the rest of the year. Military training resumed in the fall of 1916.

Construction on a new armory began in June 1917. The new structure's unconventional roof, supported by eight large trusses, was designed by Professor Albert Smith, then of the Civil Engineering Department. More than 400 tons of structural steel were used.

Costing almost $200,000, the building was dedicated with appropriate services on April 26, 1918. At the dedication, President Winthrop E. Stone made the introductory address, in which he spoke briefly of the history of military training at Purdue.

ROTC students inside the Purdue Armory, date unknown.

The government immediately opened an auto mechanics training school at Purdue and used the new building as a barracks. About 500 men were quartered there a few days after it was finished.

In 1928, the ten-year-old Armory suffered considerable damage from a fire. It is believed that the blaze was probably caused by spontaneous combustion of refuse in the north end of the building. Gasoline and oil stored there immediately blazed up, and the fire gained headway before the fire department arrived. Although the north end of the building was destroyed, fire department efforts were successful in saving the remaining structure.

The Armory was pressed into "wartime" service again after World War II. As University enrollment swelled following the war thanks to the GI Bill, the demand for housing was tremendous. An assembly line was set up in the Armory where National Homes workmen fabricated the "black-and-whites," prefabricated homes constructed along State Street and Airport Road as faculty housing.

Although originally only Army Reserve Officers' Training Corps offices and classes were located in the Armory, now all ROTC units—Army, Navy, and Air Force—are housed there.

NEIL ARMSTRONG HALL OF ENGINEERING

Built as the flagship of the College of Engineering at Purdue, the design of Armstrong Hall hails the College's contributions to flight and the space program. This symbolism can be seen in the building's wing-like roof extensions that mimic the appearance of an aircraft.

Dedicated on October 27, 2007, the $53.2 million

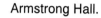

Armstrong Hall.

NEIL ARMSTRONG HALL OF ENGINEERING

building is itself a sculpture of steel and glass architecture. It is named for Purdue alumnus and astronaut Neil Armstrong. Hanging from the fifty-three-foot ceiling in the atrium is a replica of the Apollo I command module in which Robert Chaffee, Virgil "Gus" Grissom, and Ed White died during a training accident in 1967. In front of the building is a bronze sculpture of Armstrong as an undergraduate student during the 1950s.

Funding for the building came from $37.7 million in state funds, and the remaining balance was donated by private parties. Alumnus Bob Kirk and his wife Mary Jo donated the funds for the Armstrong sculpture by artist Chas Fagan of Charlotte, North Carolina. In recognition of their donation, the area in front of the building, where the statue sits, is named Kirk Plaza.

With more than 200,000 square feet to work with, Armstrong Hall houses teaching, research, and administrative offices on four floors. It is home to the School of Aeronautics and Astronautics, the School of Materials Engineering, and the School of Engineering Education. It also contains room for the dean of Engineering's office, Engineering Projects in Community Service (EPICS), the Minority Engineering Program, and the Women in Engineering Program.

STEVEN C. BEERING HALL

Formerly named the Liberal Arts and Education Building, the Steven C. Beering Hall of Liberal Arts and Education was completed in May 1993 at a cost of $28.5 million. Constructed during the tenure of the man it is now named after, Beering Hall stands as testimony to a physical growth spurt that Purdue's campus underwent during Beering's seventeen-year presidency.

The building is seven stories, towering over most of campus. It contains 214,000 square feet of computer rooms, classrooms, and offices. Beering Hall is home to the deans' offices for the College of Liberal Arts and the College of Education as well as several departments within each.

DELON AND ELIZABETH HAMPTON HALL OF CIVIL ENGINEERING

The Delon and Elizabeth Hampton Hall of Civil Engineering is located north of the Purdue Mall on Stadium Mall. The first phase of the current building, which houses the Purdue

School of Civil Engineering, was built in 1951 at a cost of $341,000. It was originally designed to be an experiment lab but, after an addition was completed in 1962, most of the Civil Engineering Department moved from its original home in Grissom Hall to the new building. Two departments, Materials and Geotechnical Engineering, stayed behind in Grissom Hall until a third addition was completed in 1988 at a cost of $16.9 million. This third addition not only had space for the two remaining areas left in Grissom, but also the Department of Earth, Atmospheric, and Planetary Sciences and the School of Health Sciences.

View of Beering Hall from a window in the Recitation Building.

There are several laboratory facilities located in the current Civil Engineering Building. The Department of Environmental Engineering makes use of two laboratories for its undergraduate and graduate education and graduate research.

The Karl H. Kettelhut Structural Engineering Laboratory is a 500-square-meter lab space built with a 226-square-meter strong floor that is designed to resist large vertical and horizontal loadings. It has a 1.8 square-meter grid of tie-down and lateral thrust anchors that can support loading frames used for component testing. Each anchor point in the grid has a forty-eight-ton capacity. The laboratory is equipped to handle structural models up to fifteen meters long.

The Christopher and Susan Burke Hydraulics and Hydrology Laboratory is the newest laboratory in the Civil Engineering Building. It was dedicated on October 16, 2010 and is named in honor of Christopher and Susan Burke for their donations that made the laboratory possible. The lab contains over 13,000 square feet of research, teaching, and outreach space.

CLASS OF 1950 LECTURE HALL

Purdue's Class of 1950 Lecture Hall first opened its doors in August 1990. Discussion about the development of the facility began as early as 1975, when a faculty committee of master teachers recommended that a large lecture hall be included as part of the new psychology building being planned at the time. The idea that funding for such a facility could be taken on as a class project was conceived one summer night in 1983, when local members of the class of 1950 gathered at the home of James F. Blakesley, now director emeritus of space management and academic scheduling.

Top: Class of 1950 Lecture Hall.

Bottom: "The Way It Was" sculpture located on the second floor of the Class of 1950 Lecture Hall. The statue is a depiction of two Purdue students of the 1950s discussing the events of the day.

The goal was to provide a first-class lecture facility with state-of-the-art audio/visual support systems. With demolition of most of old Peirce Hall complete and construction equipment at the ready, work on the structure began in May 1989. Eleven months later, the new facility was nearly completed. More than 100 members of the class of 1950 were on campus to witness and participate in the setting of the cornerstone on April 21, 1990. A time capsule containing memorabilia from the 1950s and the present was encased in the stone.

When the class bells rang at 7:30 a.m. Monday, August 20, 1990, all was ready as John W. Hatcher, assistant professor of management, stepped to the lectern to greet nearly 500 students in his Management 200 accounting class. The seven-year dream of the class of 1950 became a reality.

The lecture hall is the primary facility within the completed structure, accommodating 474 students. The building also holds three smaller classrooms, two discussion rooms, an audio/visual room, and a mechanical equipment room. The project cost about $3.5 million, of which more than $1 million was contributed by the Purdue class of 1950.

CULTURAL CENTERS

The three cultural centers located on Purdue's main campus provide opportunities for students to celebrate diversity and be exposed to different cultural experiences. Each cultural center offers different opportunities to students.

BLACK CULTURAL CENTER

The oldest cultural center on campus, the Black Cultural Center was established at Purdue in 1969. In a response to the turbulence of the times, the BCC was designed as a place where the black experience in America could be explored and celebrated.

Since its establishment, the Black Cultural Center has found a new home on the corner of Third and Russell Streets. Built in 1997, the nationally recognized BCC features architecture that alludes to African heritage. It houses a library, an art collection, and several performing arts venues.

LATINO CULTURAL CENTER

Established in 2003, the Latino Cultural Center is a resource for all Boilermakers to learn about and share Latino cultures. The LCC also serves as a place to provide the surrounding community with awareness of the diversity within the Latino community and is home to numerous organizations for students, staff, and faculty. The LCC houses a conference room, computer lab, book collection and study room, and there is an outdoor volleyball court.

NATIVE AMERICAN EDUCATION AND CULTURAL CENTER

The newest cultural center to call Purdue home, the Native American Education and Cultural Center, was established in 2007. It strives to foster an environment that can be a "second home" for Native American students on campus.

Black Cultural Center.

Located on Harrison Street, the NAECC houses two Native American student organizations, the American Indian Science and Engineering Society (AISES) and the Society for Advancement of Chicanos and Native Americans in Science (SACNAS).

DINING COURTS

Five facilities on campus are dedicated to feeding students with meal plans. Some are contained within residence halls, and some are freestanding dining courts. In 2000, Purdue launched a plan to consolidate all University Residence Dining Services. The $48 million project included renovation of the three existing dining courts, as well as the construction of two freestanding buildings. The goal of the plan was to create a modern dining experience while retaining the traditional design of Purdue's campus buildings. Every dining court project created won at least one citation from the *American School and University* or *College and University Planning* magazines.

EARHART DINING COURT

Contained within Earhart Residence Hall, the Earhart Dining Court is located on the lower level. Students are greeted by an eight-foot-tall bronze statue of Amelia Earhart, the pioneering female pilot. The statue is a recast of a sculpture made by California artist Ernest Shelton in 1969. The dining court is known for its "make it yourself" lines, where students can choose from a wealth of culinary options. The dining court opened with the residence hall in 1964, and it was renovated to meet modern standards in 2003.

FORD DINING COURT

Built as one of the freestanding projects outlined by the University Residence Dining Services consolidation project, the Fred and Mary Ford Dining Court opened in 2004. Both Fred and Mary are Purdue alumni, and Fred served as executive vice president and treasurer at Purdue for nearly twenty–five years. The dining court is located between Cary Quadrangle and Owen Hall, and its 62,325 square feet provide seating for 800 students.

Sculpture of former Purdue faculty member (1935–37) and famed pilot Amelia Earhart. The eight-foot-tall sculpture is at the entrance to Earhart Dining Court.

HILLENBRAND DINING COURT

The colorful, contemporary design of Hillenbrand Dining Court is the result of a 2003 renovation. Located on the first floor of Hillenbrand Residence Hall, the dining court opened in 1993. Features include an always-open quesadilla line, Thursday night steak specials, and brunch on Saturdays and Sundays. The Atrium, a banquet-style room full of long tables, plays host to movies on select nights.

WILEY DINING COURT

The newest of Purdue's dining courts, Wiley Dining Court opened in time for students returning to school in the fall of 2008. Its official dedication took place on October 2, 2008. Its open-concept design earned it recognition from the design world. It earned an "Outstanding Design" citation in the 2009 *American School and University* magazine. The building cost $19 million to construct and seats 500 in its 46,450 square feet. Like Hillenbrand Dining Court, Wiley has a weekly steak night on Tuesdays, and it is well-known for its wide selection of meat and other hearty menu items. The facility is adjacent to Wiley Hall, across the street from the Recreational Sports Center.

Wiley Dining Court won an "Outstanding Design" citation from the *American School and University* magazine.

WINDSOR DINING COURT

The smallest and oldest remaining dining court on campus went through an extensive $10 million renovation in 2003 to bring it into the twenty-first century. The 38,000-square-foot Windsor Dining Court, housed below the complex's Vawter Hall, was closed from 2003 until it reopened in August 2005. The result was an updated dining facility that retains the English Tudor architecture of Windsor Halls. Eight serving stations are surrounded by multiple seating areas, which can hold up to 500. The cuisine offers options from around the world, ranging from typical American to Southeast Asian and Italian. Beginning in the fall of 2010, Windsor Dining Court became the first and only dining court on campus to open its doors all day, from 9:30 a.m. to 7:30 p.m. Monday through Friday.

Aerial view of Discovery Park.

DISCOVERY PARK

Established in 2001, Discovery Park is an innovative, interdisciplinary research complex on Purdue's West Lafayette campus. Currently, the five buildings in the park provide 113,000 square feet of lab space that is shared by researchers from around the globe.

Discovery Park has created a collaborative environment in which global challenges such as sustainable energy supply, health care, economic competitiveness, homeland security, cancer, and the environment are studied objectively, generating new ideas and giving direction to future generations. In its first decade of operation, Discovery Park generated more than $600 million in sponsored program funding and more than $250 million in supporter gifts.

ELLIOTT HALL OF MUSIC

Originally dedicated as the Purdue Hall of Music on May 3 and 4, 1940, the building was renamed on January 16, 1958, to honor Edward C. Elliott, Purdue president from 1922 to 1945. Prior to the dedication, no building had been named for a man until at least ten years after his death. The Purdue University Board of Trustees met in 1958 and agreed to break this rule in honor of Elliott.

Located on a portion of Purdue's first athletic field, known previously as Stuart Field, the Hall of Music was the vision of President Elliott. His plans included a structure for the University that would accommodate cultural events as well as the commencement ceremonies. Funding for the project was secured by Elliott from the Public Works Administration, the Indiana

Elliott Hall of Music.

Sculptures on the south side of Elliott Hall of Music representing drama, music, and forensics (oration and debate).

General Assembly special session in 1938, a revenue bond issue, and other miscellaneous sources. The cost was $1,205,000.

With a seating capacity of 6,005 on three levels, Elliott Hall of Music is one of the largest theaters in the world. Designed by Walter Scholer of Lafayette, the auditorium offers unobstructed viewing of the 136-foot-wide by 37-foot-deep stage from all seats. In addition to facilities equipped to present almost any type of entertainment, the hall houses studios for WBAA, Indiana's oldest public radio station, University Bands, and Purdue Musical Organizations (PMO).

On the exterior of the building, figures carved on the north and south side symbolize drama, music, and forensics (oration and debate). Above the main stone cornice and below the wall coping are carved panels depicting the development of music, opera, radio, and cinema.

The Hall of Music has played host to such attractions as the Metropolitan Opera, *South Pacific*, Bob Hope, Bill Cosby,

Interior view from the stage in Elliott Hall of Music.

the Philadelphia Symphony Orchestra, the U.S. Marine Band, the German Obernkirchen Children's Choir, Blue Man Group, and various popular music artists including Elton John, Lady Gaga, and John Mellencamp. Speakers have included Dr. Martin Luther King, Jr., the Dalai Lama, and Eleanor Roosevelt. The popular Victory Varieties series, which began in the war years and continued through the late 1960s, brought such entertainers as Tommy Dorsey and his orchestra and Frank Sinatra. Regularly scheduled programs include commencement exercises, University convocations and lectures, many state and national conferences, and the annual PMO Christmas Show.

FELIX HAAS HALL (MEMORIAL GYMNASIUM)

First proposed by W. J. Jones of the U.S. Agricultural Experimental Station at Purdue, the Memorial Gymnasium is a lasting memorial to "those sons of Purdue who lost their lives on that fatal thirty-first day of October, 1903." That was the date of a train wreck in which a number of Purdue students and alumni died while traveling to a football game against Indiana University.

Seventeen steps leading into the gym correspond to the number of deaths; eleven steps for the eleven team members who died at the site of the accident, followed by a landing and six steps for the other students and alumni who died at the site or later from injuries.

The University wanted the building to be both a memorial and a useful building for students. It was first suggested that it include an auditorium, social and reading rooms, and a billiards room as well as a gym. Unfortunately,

Felix Haas Hall (Memorial Gymnasium), May 25, 1954.

funds fell short of what was needed for such an extravagant structure. A scaled-back version included a gym floor with a suspended running track/balcony combination. The track was the largest indoor track in the Midwest when it was built. The area under the entrance hall, which featured a trophy center and lounging area, contained a thirty-foot by sixty-foot swimming pool, showers, lockers, and team quarters. When completed in 1909, it was one of the finest athletic complexes in the country.

Ground was broken on May 30, 1908, and the building was dedicated in 1909. The building was home for the Boilermaker basketball team, which for many years dominated the Big Ten. It was also the scene of many formal dances as well as convocations and lectures.

With the completion of Lambert Fieldhouse in 1938, the Memorial Gym became the Women's Gymnasium. In 1985, Memorial Gym was remodeled to house the burgeoning Department of Computer Science. The renovated facility contains faculty and graduate student offices and laboratories. Four laboratories are for undergraduate use, two for computer science majors, and two for non-computer science majors.

Felix Haas Hall (Memorial Gymnasium) opening of the 1930 convocation ceremony with nearly 4,000 gathering to hear David E. Ross, president of the board of trustees; President Edward C. Elliott; Noble Kizer, athletic director; and Barton Gebhart, of Cincinnati, 1924 graduate representing alumni.

The facility also has two labs for graduate students and five research laboratories.

The building was renamed on June 2, 2006 to honor Professor Felix Haas, the first dean of Purdue's School of Science (1962–74) and University Provost (1974–86).

PHILIP E. NELSON HALL OF FOOD SCIENCE

Only fifteen years into its existence at Purdue, the Food Science Department found itself with its own building, dedicated on September 24, 1998. In 2010, the building was renamed after the department's founder, Philip E. Nelson, as he retired following a fifty-year career with the University. In addition to establishing the department at Purdue in 1983, he also campaigned tirelessly to raise $11 million of the building's $22 million construction cost.

A Purdue graduate, Nelson served as head of the Department of Food Science for twenty years and retired as the Scholle Chair in Food Processing. During this time, he received the 2007 World Food Prize based on his contributions to bulk aseptic processing technology.

The Philip E. Nelson Hall of Food Science houses food science faculty and the food process engineers from the Departments of Agriculture and Biological Engineering.

FORESTRY BUILDING

Built in 1912 as a horse barn, the Forestry Building was constructed at a cost of $23,000. It was converted to offices and classrooms and renamed Agricultural Experiment Annex and Agricultural Annex I before the forestry department made it home in 1973. The building was renamed to Forestry Building in 1976 upon the approval of the Board of Trustees.

Some of the laboratories housed in the building are: the Fish Ecology Research Laboratory, the Aquatic Molecular Biology and Analytical Laboratory, the Human-Environment Modeling Laboratory, the Wildlife Conservation Computer Lab, and the Wildlife Ecology Laboratory.

FOWLER HALL

On November 27, 1901, President Winthrop E. Stone announced a gift of $70,000 for a new auditorium. The gift had been presented by Eliza Fowler, the widow of Moses Fowler, the one-time business

BOILER BYTE

HORSING AROUND

The Purdue College of Veterinary Medicine's Equine Sports Medicine Center offers comprehensive evaluations designed to diagnose and treat the causes of poor performance in athletic horses. Opened in 1996, a computer-driven high-speed treadmill is the centerpiece of the center. The treadmill allows clinicians to recreate, in a laboratory setting, the conditions that a horse encounters in competition.

partner and lifelong friend of John Purdue. Finished in May 1903, it was a center of administrative activity, housing the office of the president, the Board of Trustees meetings, and an auditorium. Used for commencement exercises beginning in 1903, the hall also was a venue for plays, concerts, lectures, and readings.

The building was razed in 1954 to make way for Stewart Center. However, the tradition lives on in the Stewart Center auditorium, named Eliza Fowler Hall. A portrait of Eliza Fowler resides in the Hall's entrance to commemorate her generous donation.

Fowler Hall, interior view, 1911.

GRISSOM HALL

North of the Purdue Memorial Union, along Grant Street on Purdue University's main campus, stands Grissom Hall, originally called the Civil Engineering Building. Grissom Hall was the home of the Purdue Civil Engineering Department until 1962 when the Civil Engineering Building (now Hampton Hall of Civil Engineering) was completed. The first wing of Grissom, completed in 1906, was three stories tall and contained 45,450 square feet of classroom space. The second wing was completed in 1927 and makes up most of the building's total floor space.

The building was named after Virgil E. "Gus" Grissom, a 1950 Purdue Mechanical Engineering graduate and astronaut who tragically died in an Apollo training accident in 1967. President Hovde requested that it be named after Virgil Grissom because he had "helped establish his alma mater, Purdue, as the leading research and learning center in the field of space science and technology through his space exploration achievements."

HEAVILON HALL

In 1891, the state legislature appropriated $120,000 as a deposit toward the first mechanical engineering building at Purdue. Then, on October 31, 1892, President James H. Smart announced a significant gift: Amos Heavilon, a

We are looking this morning to the future, not the past . . . I tell you, young men, that tower shall go up one brick higher.

—President Smart

farmer and businessman from Frankfort, Indiana, gave property, notes, and cash worth $35,000 to the University. The Indiana General Assembly responded with another appropriation for the project.

The building was completed and dedicated on January 19, 1894. The building and its contents were valued at $180,000. At that time, it was considered the best engineering building in the country.

On January 23, just four days after its completion and just weeks before classes were scheduled to begin, Purdue suffered a great loss as fire, ignited by a boiler explosion, consumed the new engineering building. Only the tower remained standing, and it was brought down just a few days later to make way for reconstruction.

The morning after the fire, President Smart stood before the school's faculty and student body and claimed, "We are looking this morning to the future, not the past . . . I tell you, young men, that tower shall go up one brick higher." He also advised the seniors that if any of them desired to go to any other university to finish their courses, the faculty would aid them in making the change. Despite the offer, not one student went elsewhere to graduate.

Reconstruction of the building began almost immediately, and the first classes met in the new structure soon after it was

The first Heavilon Hall, dedicated January 19, 1894.

Just four days after its dedication, Heavilon Hall was consumed by fire caused by a boiler explosion, 1894.

completed in December 1895. Because of the generosity of manufacturers, most of the engines and laboratory materials were replaced free of charge. And, true to the word of President Smart, the tower did rise above campus once again—nine bricks higher. The 140-foot tower of the second Heavilon Hall was distinguished from its predecessor with the addition of a clock and four bells that rang on the quarter hour. Tradition had it that ladies got engaged under the tower at midnight.

The reconstructed Heavilon Hall, dedicated December 1895.

Weather and time took its toll on the building and the treasured tower that reigned over campus for sixty years. Plans were made to bring down the campus landmark in 1956—but not without protest. In 1959, the new Heavilon Hall was built where the former ones had stood, despite the fact that it would house liberal arts classes rather than engineering ones. Currently, the building is the home of the English; Speech, Language, and Hearing Sciences Departments; and the Purdue University Writing Lab.

HERRICK LABORATORIES

What used to be the Purdue Horse Barn became the research dream of two men, William E. Fontaine and Ray Herrick. Fontaine, a professor at Purdue in the 1950s, wanted to establish a facility for graduate students to work on industry projects for research subjects of their theses. He envisioned that the facility would be funded by industry so that students could lead the way in industry innovation. It was Herrick's sizable grant to Purdue University that transformed the Horse Barn into the Ray W. Herrick Laboratory in 1958. The facility was initially mainly focused on the refrigeration industry, since this is where Herrick had made his money.

During the mid-1960s, the building was renovated and expanded to better fulfill its role as a general research facility, and it was later expanded again to include transportation and machinery noise laboratories. After all of the expansions, the laboratories provide more than 15,000 square feet of research space and are home to many Mechanical Engineering students and faculty.

The majority of funding for the facility initially came from the refrigeration and air conditioning industries, but as research programs in engineering mechanics were added to research fields, other industries have contributed. The transportation industry has been especially generous. Some of the laboratories' research focuses have included: contributions to the understanding of what constitutes irritating noise, smart sensing for machinery diagnostics and damage detection, and contributions to the science of indoor air quality, especially in airplanes.

MARTIN C. JISCHKE HALL OF BIOMEDICAL ENGINEERING

The dedication of the Jischke Hall of Biomedical Engineering, on August 30, 2008, celebrated the tenth anniversary of the biomedical engineering program at Purdue. The $25 million building, which opened for operation in the fall of 2006, was named in honor of former Purdue President Martin C. Jischke, who was pivotal in the program's creation during his tenure as president.

Containing 91,000 square feet, the hall provides spaces for specialized laboratories and integrated educational facilities for undergraduate, graduate, and research work. The building was specially designed to meet the needs of biomedical engineers, and optics laboratories were constructed on individual concrete slabs in the basement level to ensure instrument accuracy without vibration interference from other laboratories.

Funds for Jischke Hall were obtained from the state, the Whitaker Foundation, alumni, and other private donors. The three-story building is home to the Weldon School of Biomedical Engineering, the first named school in Purdue engineering.

KRANNERT BUILDING AND RAWLS HALL

The relationship that led to the Krannert Building was established in 1960 when Herman C. Krannert approved a management development program for his executives that was to be taught by Purdue faculty. In 1962, Krannert and his wife, Ellnora, donated $2.73 million as an endowment to form the Krannert Graduate School of Industrial Administration. At the same time they also provided funds for the construction of a new management building, which would later become the Krannert Building.

The Krannert Building was completed in 1964, and in 1965, classes moved from the Stanley Coulter Annex to their new home on the southeast side of Purdue's campus. The building is used for classrooms, teaching and administrative offices, and the Krannert

Roland G. Parrish Library of Management and Economics.

Library, which was renamed the Roland G. Parrish Library of Management and Economics in 2012. Roland G. Parrish is a former Boilermaker student-athlete who provided a $2 million leadership gift to support the $4.2 million renovation project.

In 2003, the Krannert Building got a new neighbor, the Jerry S. Rawls Hall, which was built to further accommodate the Krannert School of Management. Located on the opposite side of Grant Street and connected by subwalks and an overhead bridge, the 126,000-square-foot addition houses thirteen classrooms, a career center, auditorium, breakout rooms, distance learning facilities, and computer labs.

Jerry S. Rawls, a 1968 Krannert master's alum, spearheaded the latest addition when he pledged $10 million to the Krannert Frontier Campaign in 2000. His gift remains the largest in the Krannert School's history and among the largest at Purdue. For his generosity the new facility was named after him.

RICHARD AND PATRICIA LAWSON HALL OF COMPUTER SCIENCE

The Richard and Patricia Lawson Hall of Computer Science was dedicated on September 15, 2006 and cost a total of $20 million. It was named after alumnus H. Richard Lawson and his wife, Patricia A. Lawson, and it is the first and only building constructed specifically for the Department of Computer Science at Purdue. The Department of Computer Science is now split between two locations, Lawson Hall and Felix Haas Hall (also known as Memorial Gymnasium). Lawson Hall contains classrooms, instructional and research laboratories, meeting spaces, and office spaces for faculty, graduate students, and research assistants.

Richard and Patricia Lawson Hall of Computer Science.

H. Richard Lawson received his master's degree in Computer Science from Purdue in 1968, received an honorary doctorate from Purdue in 2006, and is the co-founder of Lawson Software, a leader in the field of enterprise research planning. Lawson donated $4.7 million to the Department of Computer Science so that it could bring its operations into a more consolidated space.

LILLY HALL OF LIFE SCIENCES

Grant funds from pharmaceutical company Eli Lilly and Company helped complete the construction of Lilly Hall of Life Sciences. The building's original plan was deemed too small by Purdue President Frederick Hovde and Head of Agronomy J. B. Peterson. As a result, the space was expanded by 50 percent. Lilly Hall contains 750 rooms in 499,877 square feet, and the separate east and west wings are connected to the main building with aluminum slip joint thresholds.

The west wing was built first, in 1951, and the Agronomy Department moved there in 1955. The main building began construction in 1957, and in 1959, the Biology and Animal Sciences Departments moved into the east wing. The building as a whole was dedicated June 16–18, 1960.

With its nearly half a million square feet of space, the Lilly complex is the largest building on campus. Lilly houses the Life Sciences Library and corresponding classrooms, laboratories, and offices for the departments of Agronomy, Botany and Plant Biology, Animal Sciences, and Biological Sciences.

CHARLES J. LYNN HALL OF VETERINARY MEDICINE

Housing Indiana's only veterinary school, the Charles J. Lynn Hall of Veterinary Medicine was dedicated on October 12, 1960. The naming was the result of a unanimous vote among the Board of Trustees.

Charles Lynn had a fifty-year career with pharmaceutical company Eli Lilly, beginning as a salesman in 1895 and working his way up to vice president and member of the board of directors. Along with his wife, Dorothy, he had an interest in animal breeding that he turned into a philanthropic project, to the benefit of Purdue University. After establishing Lynwood Farms just north

BOILER BYTE

FLYING MACHINES AND BASEBALLS

During the 1911 Gala Week, two events were of great interest to the seniors who had returned to campus for commencement ceremonies after the undergraduates had departed. The Purdue baseball nine played a Japanese team from Waseda University, and thousands of people saw for the first time "machines able to convey man through air, circling about, and finally coming to earth again." (*Debris*, 1912)

This state-of-the-art building brings to our program one of the most comprehensive, innovative, and user-friendly facilities in the nation. And it offers upgraded and updated dining options for the Purdue campus and Greater Lafayette community.

—Richard Ghiselli, head of Hospitality and Tourism Management, Marriott Hall Dedication

of Indianapolis, he deeded the property to Purdue University in 1942 for use as an experimental station. Later he established the Lynn Fund in the Purdue Research Foundation. Lynn was inducted into the Indiana Livestock Breeders Hall of Fame sometime prior to 1955, and he served on the Purdue Board of Trustees from 1945–53.

Lynn Hall houses the Small Animal Clinic and the Large Animal Clinic, both of which are available to the general public for animal treatment. Nearly all of the College of Veterinary Medicine is located in the building, along with the veterinary medical library.

MARRIOTT HALL

Marriott Hall was dedicated Tuesday, April 17, 2012. Marriott houses the School of Hospitality and Tourism Management. The J. Willard and Alice S. Marriott Foundation made the lead gift of $5 million for the $13 million building at State and University streets. The 40,000-square-foot facility includes a 95-seat demonstration classroom, restaurants, classrooms and conference areas, a career center, and student services center. Restaurants in Marriott Hall include:

- The John Purdue Room, a fine-dining restaurant in which students prepare and serve the food

Marriott Hall.

and manage the kitchen and dining room. Through windows, diners can watch what is happening in the kitchen.

- Boiler Bistro, a quick-service restaurant where the food is cooked to order, giving students another type of operation to experience.
- Lavazza, an innovative coffee bar.

Marriott Hall is the second Purdue building to receive LEED Gold certification (the Gatewood Wing of the Mechanical Engineering Building was first) as a green building. The LEED (Leadership in Energy and Environmental Design) certification is awarded through the U.S. Green Building Council to building owners who implement practical and measurable green design, construction, operations, and maintenance solutions.

The atrium of the new LEED-certified Gatewood Wing of the Mechanical Engineering Building.

MECHANICAL ENGINEERING

Mechanical Engineering was first housed in Heavilon Hall; however, it was moved to the Mechanical Engineering Building after the building's dedication and the completion of its main wings in 1932. By 1942, the southeast wing of the current building was completed, which became the Aeronautical Lab. A connection between the lab and the main part of the current building was finished in 1948, completing the structure of the Mechanical Engineering Building.

In 1975, the southeast wing was renovated for $1.5 million, and it was renovated again, along with the main wing, in 1980 for just over $2.5 million. Another addition, more than fifty years in the making, was recently completed.

Preliminary plans for a third addition to the Mechanical Engineering Building began in 1955, when Scholer Architects presented a plan for an addition to the building's west side.

LEED certification identifies the Roger B. Gatewood Wing of Mechanical Engineering as a pioneering example of sustainable design and demonstrates Purdue's leadership in transforming the building industry.
—Rick Federizzi, USGBC president, CEO, and founding chairman, Gatewood Wing Dedication

However, due to lack of funding, the project never progressed. Finally in 1999, President Beering approved the School of Engineering's master space plan, which included an expansion of the Mechanical Engineering Building. After a committee was formed in 2000 to plan and fund the addition, ground was broken in the summer of 2009 on the Roger B. Gatewood Wing. Gatewood, a 1968 graduate of the School of Mechanical Engineering, made the leadership gift for the $34.5 million project in 2003 and again donated funds in 2007 to cover the cost of building it to LEED certification standards.

The green wing houses an atrium, classrooms, research laboratories, instructional laboratories, and offices for faculty, staff, and students. The atrium is also the new home of the clockworks from Purdue's original Bell Tower, which were previously located in the older portion of the building. Construction was completed in April 2011.

PFENDLER HALL

Originally known as Agricultural Hall and then Entomology Hall, Pfendler Hall first opened its doors in 1902 thanks to funding provided by the Indiana General Assembly. The building's construction marked the beginning of an expansion of the campus' agricultural infrastructure. The first presidential reception room on campus was located in this building's lobby.

In the 1960s, the Department of Entomology moved to Agricultural Hall and, in order to reflect its new purpose, the building was renamed "Entomology Hall." Along with faculty and classes came the department's noted insect collection, one of the largest in the United States.

The hall closed for renovation in 2000. In 2001, it was renamed in memory of David C. Pfendler, a staff member of the School of Agriculture for thirty-eight years, who retired as associate dean in 1974.

Pfendler Hall again underwent renovation in 2003. In April of 2004, the hall was reopened following a $16 million facelift that turned it into a state-of-the-art teaching and research facility. The John S. Wright Fund for the Promotion of Forestry in Indiana provided a major financial gift for the project. Fittingly, faculty and graduate students of the Department of Forestry and Natural Resources now occupy the building.

PHYSICS BUILDING

In 1941, the Department of Physics found a new home in the current Physics Building. Dedicated in 1942, the oldest section of the building was dedicated as the Charles Benedict Stuart Laboratory for Applied Physics, thanks to funding raised by Alice Earl Stuart, the widow of Charles Benedict Stuart, former member of the Purdue Board of Trustees.

The winter of 1948 saw the completion of the building's second phase, a small addition to house an electron synchrotron. The first major addition was completed in the summer of 1962, which included research space as well as a lecture hall. Finally, in 1968 the Karl-Lark Horovitz Laboratory of Nuclear Structure was opened, which houses the tandem Van de Graff accelerator.

Today, the Physics Building contains state-of-the-art research equipment, classrooms, lecture halls, offices, and laboratories.

PURDUE MEMORIAL UNION

The class of 1912 gave the union building its financial start. From 1903 to 1910, each class gave a $5 assessment per person toward the construction of the Memorial Gymnasium. When the gym was completed in 1909, the classes of 1911 and 1912 wanted to find another worthwhile project to invest in rather than break the tradition of the class gift to the school.

These two classes eventually decided to build an appropriate gateway at the entrance to Stuart Field. However, early in 1912, a proposal to construct a union building on campus

Construction of the Purdue Memorial Union, 1929.

The Purdue Union embodies more than any other agency, of the present or the future, the inner moving spirit of the University. Here, in this building to be, life will be lived, enriched, and humanized by enduring and understanding friendships. This stone, placed in this building today, is at once a symbol of our faith in yesterday, a mark of our might of today, an unfailing sign to the men of tomorrow of duty ever unfulfilled.

—President Elliott, cornerstone speech

was given to the student council. The council then referred it to a special committee charged with studying union buildings at other universities. The class of 1912 then voted that its assessments be directed toward constructing a home for student, alumni, and faculty activities. Instrumental in initiating the student fund drive for the union was undergraduate student George O. Hays, a member of the class of 1912.

On April 17, 1912, a mass meeting of students and faculty approved the first Union Constitution. Before being interrupted in 1917 by World War I, $17,800 had been collected for the project. In 1918, alumnus O. M. Booher, who later served as executive director of the Purdue Alumni Association, suggested that the union be built in honor of the Purdue students who served in the war. A subscription plan was started in 1920 for this purpose. With this idea of a memorial to the 4,013 who had served and those sixty-seven Purdue students who had died for their country, the name "Purdue Memorial Union" came into being.

Groundbreaking ceremonies took place in June 1922, and the building was ready for partial use by September 1924.

Purdue Memorial Union, south doors, featuring an eighty-five-foot by forty-two-foot reflecting pool which was installed in the 1950s (removed in 2004), 1995.

Purdue Memorial Union, front view in the spring of 2008.

The building was used in an unfinished condition until 1929. It was then that the first section was completed and dedicated on November 26. The original section included the Great Hall, lounges, a ballroom, billiard room, barber shop, cafeteria, and meeting rooms.

Additions to the building have continued the Purdue Memorial Union's purpose of providing a home for student, faculty, and alumni activities. In 1929, the first wing of the Union Club hotel was added. In 1936 came the East Wing, which included the bowling alley, Browsing Room, and Anniversary Drawing Room. The West Wing was opened in 1939 along with the North Ballroom, and a second Union Club Wing. In 1955, the North Union Club opened. And in 1959, the massive Memorial Center (now Stewart Center) was built adjacent to the PMU. The Memorial Union today continues to pursue its original goal of "Bringing People Together" with a variety of food service areas, recreational activities, ballrooms, meeting rooms, offices for student organizations, and lounges. Additionally, it remains a standing tribute to those Boilermakers who have served our country with several memorials within the Great Hall.

[The] large solid columns and the plain but beautiful interior symbolized the ruggedness, sincerity, and individualism of Purdue students. The upswept arches of the windows in the Great Hall symbolize the youth and the spirit of the students of all creeds and races within its walls.

—Irving Pond about the Great Hall

The Memorial Cross in the Great Hall of the Purdue Memorial Union, date unknown.

THE GREAT HALL

Just inside the Purdue Memorial Union's south entrance is the Great Hall. In reflecting on the great hall, architect Irving Pond said that the "large solid columns and the plain but beautiful interior symbolized the ruggedness, sincerity, and individualism of Purdue students. The upswept arches of the windows in the Great Hall symbolize the youth and the spirit of the students of all creeds and races within its walls."

Set into the floor of the Union's Great Hall is the Gold and Black Memorial Cross. Originally dedicated to the students and alumni who died in World War I and later rededicated to all the students and alumni involved in foreign wars, tradition dictates that no one shall walk on the cross. Located near the Memorial Cross stands a plaque inscribed with the names of those University faithful who gave their lives during World War I. A similar plaque located nearby lists those who died in World War II. Close to these plaques stand two others that honor the service of Purdue alumni and students involved in the Korean and Vietnam conflicts. A third plaque titled "Global Memorial" states, "In memory of Purdue students, faculty, and staff who have given their lives in military service to the United States in wars, security conflicts, and other military actions since the Vietnam War." Below this statement are individual name plates that state the name, military branch, war, and date of death of each of those who gave their lives in military service.

A glass-encased model of the West Lafayette campus is on permanent display in the Great Hall, just past the Memorial Cross.

STAINED GLASS WINDOW

The stained glass window adorning the southwest entrance to the Purdue Memorial Union is dedicated to the memory of James H. Smart, president of Purdue from 1883–1900. It was donated in 1940 by Alice Earl Stuart, wife of Charles B. Stuart (president of the Board of Trustees during Smart's tenure).

The theme, shown at the top of the window, is taken from the words of Abbé Suger, a distinguished twelfth-century churchman and builder. It says, "Our poor spirit is so weak that it is only through the use of materials that it can rise to the truth." The glass window consists of four separate panels, with four main figures: Mother Earth, Sister Water, Brother Fire, and Brother Wind. These four representations can be seen in the medallions placed in the upper part. Below the four main figures are twelve others holding various items depicting disciplines offered by Purdue, including a train, a bridge, an airplane, a dynamo, a tractor, a rabbit, and a tulip. The window symbolizes the love and wisdom that characterized Smart's presidency. The bright colors of blue, red, yellow, green, and purple symbolize the mixing of students of all creeds and races within its walls.

Purdue Memorial Union stained glass window.

PURDUE AIRPORT

First established in November 1930, the Purdue University Airport was created when David Ross donated 360 acres of land southwest of campus to be used as an airstrip. Purdue thus became the first college in the United States to own and operate an airport. Since then, the airport has offered commercial and charter services as well as flight training and aircraft sales and service.

Though the airport no longer offers commercial flights, it now encompasses over 516 acres of land. Prior to the end of commercial flights, it served the University and Greater Lafayette with scheduled flights to major airline destinations such as Chicago, St. Louis, and Detroit. The airport is

Purdue Airport, March 21, 1937.

capable of handling large transport planes such as an Airbus 320 or a Boeing 757 as well as smaller private and general aviation aircraft.

FRANCE A. CÓRDOVA RECREATIONAL SPORTS CENTER

The France A. Córdova Recreational Sports Center (RSC) was the first university building in the United States built solely to serve students' recreational sports needs. Completed in 1957, the building was expanded in 1981 to accommodate growing interest in its various programs. Facilities included space and courts for archery, fencing, general exercise, handball, racquetball, riflery, squash, wallyball, weightlifting, swimming, basketball, volleyball, table tennis, tennis, badminton, and jogging. Outdoor facilities include horseshoe tossing areas, volleyball nets, tennis courts, and playing fields.

In the fall of 1999, the two outdoor basketball courts were torn down to make room for the new Aquatics Center. In this center, the Purdue men's and women's swimming and diving teams have their meets. The new Boilermaker Aquatics Center addition, opened in fall 2001, features a fifty-meter competition pool and a separate diving well. The center is home for the intercollegiate, educational, and recreational swimming activities held on the West Lafayette campus.

Due to the growing number of students eager to utilize the facility, construction began in spring 2010 on a 127,000-square-foot expansion to enlarge the current facility into a contemporary student fitness and wellness center. The new facility was completed in fall 2012. More than 355,000 square feet—not including the aquatics or outdoor space—is now available for use by students, faculty, and staff. With the completion of the new rennovations, the RSC was renamed in honor of France A. Córdova, the University's eleventh president.

PURDUE RESEARCH PARK

Just north of the Purdue University West Lafayette campus lies a 725-acre park dedicated to the development and growth of starter companies. More than 160 organizations call the Purdue Research Park home, and nearly 100 of them are technology-related. As the state's first designated certified technology park, it contains 52 buildings and employs more than 3,000 people.

One of the highlights of the Purdue Research Park is its incubation program, which has received national recognition. Beginning businesses are able to set up in the Purdue Research Park's 400,000 square feet of high-tech incubation space, where they are assisted though business development support.

The Purdue Research Park located in West Lafayette is one of four campuses around the state. The Purdue Research Park also has parks located in Indianapolis, Merrillville, and New Albany. Expanding to other locations around the state has allowed Purdue University to fulfill its commitment to promote economic growth in Indiana's high-tech sector, launching nearly sixty ventures, several of which have focused on drug development, tissue engineering, and medical device development.

The success of the Purdue Research Parks has earned both the establishment and the University recognition at both state and national levels. Purdue University was named in the top eight universities for startup companies by Innovation Associates in 2005, was the 2004 Outstanding Science/Research Park Award winner, and was placed in the top twelve universities for economic development in 2001.

In West Lafayette, the Research Park continues to grow. In a partnership between the University, the Purdue Research Park, and the City of West Lafayette, commercial lots are available for purchase or land-lease by high-tech firms to establish and develop their business.

An outdoor concert at the Slayter Center for the Performing Arts, date unknown.

SLAYTER CENTER FOR THE PERFORMING ARTS

A gift from former bandsman R. Games Slayter and his wife, Marie, Slayter Center is an outdoor concert facility and band shell located at the bottom of Slayter Hill.

A 1921 chemical engineering graduate, Slayter played tuba in the Purdue "All-American" Marching Band. He went on to a prominent career developing numerous products and materials, including fiberglass. Slayter died on October 15, 1964, five days after attending an open house for the center.

The contemporary structure was formally dedicated on May 1, 1965. The University commissioned Vittorio Giannini's "Variations and Fugue" to commemorate the completion of Slayter Center.

The hill seats up to 4,000 for a show. The stage, with risers, is designed for optimum seating of a 110-piece symphony band.

Slayter Center was constructed at the foot of a natural hill on the Purdue West Lafayette Campus. The architect, Joseph Baker, found his inspiration in the prehistoric Stonehenge in England. He believed that the dignity and quietness of Stonehenge would lend itself well to the outdoor programs presented in Slayter Center. The side and back walls are made up of stele that relate to the stone monoliths of Stonehenge. The spaces between the stele are filled with encapsulated shattered French glass of several hues.

To maintain an outdoor feel to the structure, the ceiling of Slayter Center does not touch the sides of its stage. The amphitheater's "flaring horn" design compresses the sound and projects it out to the audience, rather than merely reflecting the sound.

Students preparing to sled down Slayter Hill.

SMITH HALL

Gifted to the University by W. C. Smith, Smith Hall was built on the University's campus in 1913 at a cost of roughly $63,000.

Originally, the building housed Purdue's Commercial Creamery and Dairy Department. Purdue's Commercial Creamery operated continuously for more than fifty years, providing food for many of Purdue's own food-service facilities. Many of the developments that led to the innovations of current dairy technology were developed from the research conducted in this department and through these programs.

Currently, Smith Hall houses the Entomology Department of the University. The Boilermaker Butcher Block, operated by students studying animal science, also operates out of Smith Hall. Students butcher animals to learn about high quality cuts of meat and how to process it, and the meat is available for sale to the public.

STANLEY COULTER HALL

Dedicated on May 17, 1917 as the biology building, Stanley Coulter Hall is now home to the School of Languages and Cultures (formerly the Department of Foreign Languages and Literatures). Its transition from biology to foreign languages included a 1960 remodeling, during which the interior was completely gutted and redone. In 1961, it was reopened as Stanley Coulter Hall, named for the first dean of the School of Science.

In 1998, Stanley Coulter Hall underwent another renovation, with a price tag of $4 million. This consisted of an extension of the north side of the building, which added thirty offices and seven computer labs to the facility.

University Hall.

UNIVERSITY HALL

Originally called the Main Building, the ornate Victorian-style structure was the fourth major building on campus. Now it is the oldest building still standing. University Hall dates back to the third year of Purdue's existence. Disputes between John Purdue and the Board of Trustees about

the building's location initially delayed construction of the hall. Dedicated in 1877, the building was designed to be the main college building housing a chapel (also known as an assembly hall) with galleries on three sides, an academy hall, a library room, three cabinet rooms, eight recitation rooms, and four well-lit basement rooms.

The office of President Emerson E. White was housed in the building, as well as the bursar's and registrar's offices and academic offices. The library located in University Hall consisted of 800 volumes on the east half of the first floor; by 1895, the library shelves had taken over much of the second floor. Today, Purdue's thirteen libraries offer more than 2.5 million volumes and over 60,000 current periodicals. Rooms for the school's two literary societies—the Irving Literary Society for young men and the Philalethean for young women—were also located in University Hall.

In 1923, a major renovation of University Hall was completed. The third floor of the building was made into rooms for the English Department and the chapel was completely rebuilt. The out-of-date heating system was then upgraded and gaslights were replaced with electric ones, modernizing the entire utility system.

In 1960 the interior of the building was gutted, leaving only the brick facade behind. A contemporary interior was built—

The old University Hall Library.

gone were the creaky oiled floors and curving staircases; for all practical purposes, a new building was erected.

In 2006 a project to make University Hall more accessible was initiated. This project included the installation of an elevator, an updated fire alarm system, an exterior ramp into the building, and by reworking existing bathrooms and drinking fountains for ADA compliance.

In University Hall a plaque commemorating the remodeling relates the campus infrastructure to the learning that goes on inside: "In this structure built with bricks and cemented with aspirations, thousands of students have savored the finest that men have thought and felt throughout the ages: The wisdom of philosophers, the comprehension of scientists, the beauty of artists, the vision of dreamers, the realism of statesmen, for here nearly all the humanities and sciences have been taught—the hopes of its founders materialized. The exterior lined the past, the interior transformed into contemporary efficient space, may gifted teachers and talented students here learn together as they sift the wisdom of the centuries in search of the essentials for free men in the ageless future."

UNIVERSITY RESIDENCES

With thirteen residence halls and two apartment complexes, Purdue Residences is the largest on-campus housing system in the nation among universities where students are not required to live on campus. Roughly 30 percent of all students live in on-campus housing.

Purdue Residences are located along the edge of campus, from the west side near the airport, to the north end in close proximity to athletic facilities, to Hawkins Hall on the south side behind the Krannert Building and Young Hall. As student enrollment has increased with the years, the University has met housing needs by building more residence halls, the latest having been completed in the fall of 2012.

University Residences, including dining services, is entirely self-supporting and receives no tax or tuition funds.

CARY QUADRANGLE

In memory of their son, Franklin Levering Cary, after his passing in the summer of 1912 before entering Purdue as a freshman, Franklin

Cary Quadrangle.

M. and Jessie Levering Cary donated $50,000 to the University in 1927 for the initial construction of the residence hall for male students now known as Cary Quadrangle. The Cary beneficence enabled the University to construct the first of what eventually became the five-unit dormitory system on Spitzer Place.

The tract of land that adjoins Ross-Ade Stadium, known as Spitzer Place, was donated to the University by Professor and Mrs. George Spitzer in 1889. The first unit, called Franklin Levering Cary Memorial Hall, opened in 1928, and today is known as Cary East. A second contribution from Franklin Cary partially funded a second unit, Cary North (now known as Cary Northeast), which opened in 1931. Construction began several years later on two new units—Cary Northwest and West. The latter was completed in 1938. The final unit, Cary South, did not open until 1939.

A major remodeling project began the summer of 2000 and was completed in the summer of 2006. The renovation upgraded the electrical, plumbing, heating and ventilation, and telecommunication utility services in all rooms and common spaces in every building of Cary Quadrangle. Additionally, Cary East, Northeast, West, and Northwest converted all student rooms into air-conditioned suites complete with a bathroom between every two rooms. Cary currently houses over 1,000 male students.

Among its more infamous traditions, Cary was home of the annual "Nude Olympics," where residents and other students raced in the nude around Spitzer Court on the coldest day of the year. On a more educational note, Cary is home of the WCCR, the first residence hall radio station.

EARHART HALL

Earhart Hall opened in 1964 and was named after Amelia Earhart. Earhart came to Purdue University in 1936, when there was only one residence hall for women and enrollment was only 4,700 students. She resided in Duhme Hall in the Windsor complex, working in a dual role as a consultant in careers for women and as a technical advisor for the Department of Aeronautics. Earhart was a member of Purdue faculty until her disappearance in 1937.

The residence hall was originally named H-8, for its shape and its eight floors of rooms. Earhart Hall also has a self-contained dining court, and in front of its doors is an eight-

First Street Towers.

foot-tall bronze statue of Amelia Earhart, holding an airplane propeller. The statue is a recast of a sculpture made by California artist Ernest Shelton in 1969.

FIRST STREET TOWERS

Built to provide upscale independent living with the benefit of meal plans, First Street Towers are the latest addition to the Purdue Residence Halls. The first two buildings were completed in time for students to move in for the fall 2009 semester, and their construction cost $52 million. The residence hall provides 365 single-student rooms with private baths, air-conditioning, and community rooms with flat-screen televisions.

After testing out the popularity of the residence hall, the University proceeded with construction on a third building in 2010. Completed and move-in ready in fall 2012, the addition provides 174 more rooms.

HARRISON HALL

Built in the traditional H-shape that defines many of Purdue's residence halls, Harrison Hall opened in 1966 and is named for arguably the most famous man to serve on the Purdue Board of Trustees. Benjamin Harrison was a lawyer, soldier, United States senator, and president of the United States from 1888–92. Following his term in the White House, he served on the Board of Trustees from 1895 until his death on March 13, 1901.

Harrison Hall is located on the southwest part of campus and is home to the Harrison Grillé, a late-night restaurant located on the building's main floor.

HAWKINS HALL

Hawkins Hall was originally named Graduate House II when it was completed in fall 1968. However, it soon became apparent that its name was too easily confused with the first Graduate House, so it was altered to Graduate House West until 1981. At this time the building was renamed Hawkins Graduate House (now Hawkins Hall), after George A. Hawkins, a Purdue graduate who went on to dedicate forty-four years to his career at Purdue.

Following his graduation from Purdue in 1930, Hawkins served as an engineering teacher and researcher, vice president for academic affairs, and dean of the School of Engineering. During his early years on staff with the University, he also completed his master's degree in 1932 and doctorate in 1935.

Hawkins Graduate House is located on the south side of campus and was originally set up to provide an environment specifically for graduate students. Undergraduate students are also allowed to live in Hawkins Hall. Unlike typical undergraduate residence halls, Hawkins Hall is open 365 days a year and students are always living in the building.

HILLENBRAND HALL

Dedicated on October 7, 1993, Hillenbrand Hall offers suite-living space for 800 students. In 2010, the residence hall made floors co-ed, with suites of all-male and all-female students. Hillenbrand Hall was named for a father and son who both served on the Purdue Board of Trustees. John Hillenbrand served from 1913 to 1946, while his son William served from 1967 to 1975.

Hillenbrand Hall contains its own dining court, which has been renovated to reflect the contemporary, state-of-the art design that is evident through the entire building.

HILLTOP APARTMENTS

Originally built as married student housing in 1946, Ross-Ade Project I consisted of 22 buildings providing apartments for 200 families. In 1956, Ross-Ade Project 2 added another 54 apartments, and in 1969, Ross-Ade Project 3 was built, with 140 apartments. Prior to 1976, all 32 buildings were used as married housing, but in 1976, buildings 11, 21, and 22 housed a total of 99 male undergraduate students and three resident assistants. Students had the option of signing up for board contracts from Owen Hall.

The following year, ten buildings housed single male students. In 1978, the entirety of Ross-Ade I was converted to single-student undergraduate housing. All 22 buildings housed single undergraduate men. In 1993, the name was changed to Hilltop Apartments and all buildings are open to all undergraduates.

McCUTCHEON RESIDENCE HALL

Opened in 1963, the John T. McCutcheon Hall rises eight stories as the western-most residence hall on campus. The residence hall's namesake was an 1889 graduate of Purdue who went on to garner international fame as a world traveler, war correspondent, cartoonist, and writer. At the pinnacle of his success, he was awarded the Pulitzer Prize for a cartoon in 1931 during his time working for the *Tribune* in Chicago.

MEREDITH HALL

Meredith Residence Hall was once known by the name X-Hall, for its distinctive shape. Opened to students in 1952, the hall has been through phases where it housed only men or only women, until its present-day status as a co-ed residence hall where alternating floors house men or women. The four-floor hall also houses one of campus' two mini-marts, Boiler Crossing.

The hall was renamed for Virginia Claypool Meredith, dubbed the "Queen of American Agriculture" due to her support of farmers and farm life. After her husband's death ten years into their marriage, Meredith took full responsibility of their business and made it her life's work to discover and implement good agricultural practices, particularly in Indiana. In 1921, she became the first woman to serve as a trustee of Purdue University.

OWEN HALL

Owen Hall opened in 1947 and is home to over 700 students. It was originally named H-1 for its shape but was later renamed for Richard Owen, the first president of Purdue University. The residence hall is located on the north side of campus, making it ideal for students who attend varsity athletic events, as it is a short walk from the hall to Mackey Arena, Ross-Ade Stadium, or the Intercollegiate Athletic Facility.

PURDUE VILLAGE

Formerly known as Married Student Housing, the Purdue Village now provides housing for both married and single students. As the demography of the student population shifted to include fewer and fewer married students, the occupancy in Married Student Housing was on a steady decline, falling to only 75 percent occupancy in 1997. The demographic change to Purdue Village was made in 1998.

Built during the late 1950s and early 1960s, the apartments are located southwest of campus. Of the 1,500 apartments (including Hilltop Apartments) that were once dedicated to married students, 644 are still in use for their original purpose. There are either twelve or sixteen apartments to a building, and units for families are unfurnished, while those for single graduate and undergraduate students come furnished.

In 2008, a new 12,000-square-foot Community Center for Purdue Village was opened.

SHREVE HALL

Named for Eleanor Burns Shreve and her husband, Randolph Norris Shreve, Shreve Hall first opened its doors to students in 1970. Eleanor made her living as an author, educator, world traveler, musician, and constructive activist. Much of her writing focused on scenarios for radio, which was at its peak during this time period. The Taiwan College of Engineering in Formosa was established with the help of both Eleanor and her husband. Much of their interest also lay in stone carving and gems. The Shreve Jade collection currently resides in the Indianapolis Museum of Art.

Their devotion to higher education did not go unnoticed. The Board of Trustees named the residence hall in honor of the couple and in recognition of their contributions to education and Purdue University.

TARKINGTON HALL

Opened in 1958 as "H-2," Tarkington Hall houses 710 male Purdue students. The building is divided into four directional units—Northeast, Southeast, Northwest, and Southwest.

Tarkington Hall also houses Boiler Junction, one of two mini-marts located within Purdue Residence Halls and operated by University Residences Dining Services. Its name was changed in 1965 in memory of Newton Booth Tarkington, who attended Purdue University for only one year but never forgot his Boilermaker roots as he went on become a Pulitzer Prize-winning author in 1919 and 1922. Although he finished his education at Princeton University, he donated numerous gifts to Purdue before his death in 1946.

WILEY HALL

Built in conjunction with Tarkington Hall, Wiley Hall was completed in 1958. Only a wall separates Tarkington's southwest wing from Wiley's northwest one, and from the street the two appear to be a single building.

Wiley Hall was named for Harvey W. Wiley, the first professor of chemistry at Purdue. His call to the necessity for safe foods and work with sugar-producing crops led to his acclaim as the "father" of the United States beet sugar industry.

WINDSOR HALLS

The oldest women's residence hall at Purdue, Windsor Halls, was originally named Women's Residence Halls (WRH). Windsor Halls, is made up of five all-female accommodations built over a period of about twenty years. Duhme Hall (originally South Hall) was opened in 1934, Shealy (North Hall) in 1937, Wood (West Hall) in 1939, and Warren (D Hall) and Vawter (E Hall) in 1951. Subwalks that are accessible to students connect all of the halls. In 1969, the name Windsor was selected to recognize the English Tudor architecture of the halls.

Walter Scholer, architect for many buildings on the West Lafayette campus, also designed Windsor. The design is such that nearly every room in each hall receives sunlight sometime during the day. Four of the brick and Indiana limestone halls align in

Aerial view of Windsor Halls.

Windsor Halls crest, symbolizing graciousness and refinement.

such a way that if someone were to open the lobby doors in Duhme, Shealy, Warren, and Vawter, he or she would be able to shoot an arrow in a straight line through all of them.

A number of unique items can be found in the Windsor complex:

- The Memorial Bench in the Duhme-Shealy courtyard was dedicated in May 1964 in memory of Judith Ann Montgomery, a Duhme resident who was killed in a plane crash a few miles from Purdue in May 1963. Montgomery loved the outdoors and was quoted as saying, "The courtyard was like one's private garden."

- Mrs. Charles W. Hickox of Michigan City, Indiana, donated the "Tired Boy" statue in Windsor Circle to Purdue. The sculptor of the "Tired Boy" statue, L. Bracony, was inspired by an incident during World War I. He had noticed two people, a small boy and a woman, who had stopped in the midst of the bombing to rest. He was touched by the confidence that the tired child placed in the woman. The statue stands as a symbol of faith.

- A wise old owl perches atop the gable of Duhme Hall to brood over all latecomers to that hall.

- Those who pass the front door of Duhme can view a colored glass depiction of the Little Lady on the WRH crest, symbolizing graciousness and refinement.

- Duhme's cornerstone contains copies of *The Purdue Exponent*, plans and photographs of the hall, and a Bible.

- Warren's cornerstone contains a 1948 "Guide to Purdue University," a pictorial album of Purdue, a photograph of a 1950 physical education class in tennis, and a home economics newsletter.

- Some interesting contents of Vawter's cornerstone are 1949 issues of the "Co Edition," three WRH dance programs, a Little Lady lapel pin, a WRH guest meal ticket, a "yellow" slip, a WRH weekly menu, and 1950 *Mademoiselle* fashion magazine.

- The "Windsor Round Table," located in the Wood reading room, once graced the dining room of Hazelden, the estate of George Ade.

Top: Purdue Hall, built 1874, was the first dormitory on campus, which housed approximately 125 men. It was remodeled in 1902 as a recitation building and later was demolished in 1961.

Bottom: Purdue Ladies Hall, located on the current site of Stone Hall, was the first residence hall for women. It was built in 1874 and demolished in 1927.

The interior design of Windsor was created by the same artist who decorated rooms for King Edward VIII. The living rooms are furnished with eighteenth-century English furniture. Each of the formal living rooms contains a grand piano; the one located in Duhme was the only musical instrument on display at the Chicago World's Fair. Windsor has hosted several famous people, including Amelia Earhart, who lived in Duhme while working as a career consultant for two years, and Lillian Gilbreth, a resident of Wood Hall while teaching industrial engineering. The mother of twelve children, Gilbreth was featured in the book *Cheaper By the Dozen*. The most recent famous resident was astronaut Janice Voss Ford, who lived in Duhme Hall.

WESTWOOD

On June 12, 1971, R. B. and Lillian V. O. Stewart presented the University with their home, Westwood, located on the west edge of campus. New Purdue President Arthur G. Hansen moved into the house in September of the same year. Stewart served as vice president and treasurer of the University, retiring in 1961.

Over the years, the home has been remodeled and enlarged so that Purdue presidents can host University constituencies in a home setting. Westwood continues to be the home for the University president's family.

Westwood.

Yue-Kong Pao Hall.

YUE-KONG PAO HALL

Built in 2003, Yue-Kong Pao Hall is a $47 million facility for the Patti and Rusty Rueff Department of Visual and Performing Arts. The two theatre venues in Pao Hall are the 300-seat proscenium Nancy T. Hansen Theatre and the flexible-seat Carole and Gordon Mallet Theatre. Also in the building are classrooms, studios, and workshop space.

Sir Yue-Kong Pao was a Chinese businessman and shipping mogul whose two daughters both graduated from Purdue. Anonymous donors gave $4 million for the building's construction on his behalf.

BOILER BYTE

SENIOR CORDS

In the fall of 1904, two seniors noticed a sample of corduroy in the window of Taylor Steffen Company in Lafayette and decided to have a pair of trousers made out of it. Other seniors liked them so much that the next year they were adopted as the official garb of the senior class. Only the seniors were allowed to wear them, and they made sure that underclassmen did not take over this fashion. Over the years seniors started painting pictures on their cords to represent their major areas of study, extracurricular activities, housing units, and other college experiences.

Along with the cords, seniors also wore derby hats and carried bamboo canes. Freshmen tried to steal and deface these items. However, they were always given back by the first home football game, in time for the senior parade. During the first game, the seniors would throw their derbies after the first touchdown or at the end of the game if no touchdowns were scored.

The Senior Cord tradition has come and gone over the years. Most recently, in the fall of 1999, a dozen student organizations began to bring back senior cords, wearing them to home football games. The effort has survived in only a few groups. *Photo courtesy of Janet Stephens, THGphotography.*

LANDMARKS

YOU'VE WALKED PAST THEM hundreds of times. You might not be familiar with their history, but you are definitely familiar with their images. They are our Purdue landmarks. Some are as simple as a plaque in a courtyard; others can be seen from a far distance. Each has a purpose and a place in Purdue's history, whether it is the Stone Lions Fountain, Purdue Bell Tower, or Freedom Square. Built to honor individuals and events, erected in memory or as a testament to the strength and innovation of Purdue's community, our landmarks are unique reminders of our past and continuing links to our future.

Academy Park.

ACADEMY PARK

Academy Park, located north of Stewart Center and the
Memorial Union, honors Purdue faculty and celebrates academic
excellence. Designed with outdoor teaching in mind, it is a
twentieth-century interpretation of the site where Plato founded
a school in ancient Greece. At the northwest corner of the Union
is an obelisk inscribed with quotes of Plato, Aristotle, Socrates,
and Diogenes:

> The direction in which education starts a man will
> determine his future life. —Plato, 428–348 B.C.E.

> Education is the best provision for old age.
> —Aristotle, 384–22 B.C.E.

> There is only one good, knowledge, and one evil,
> ignorance. —Socrates, 469–399 B.C.E.

> The foundation of any state is the education of
> youth. —Diogenes, 400–325 B.C.E.

An honor roll, the Book of Great Teachers, is displayed
in the Union as part of Academy Park and its dedication to
outstanding teaching.

The 245,000-square-foot outdoor area provides plazas,
seating areas, and a large shaded lawn. It was dedicated April 26,
1997 as a part of the year's Gala Week festivities.

THE ACRES

Located west of campus, the Acres, once called Tower Acres, is an area where nearly twenty fraternities and sororities are located. Development of the area began in the 1960s, and in 2006, the last lot was purchased by the Phi Kappa Tau fraternity for $1 million.

BOILERMAKER STATUE

On Friday, November 4, 2005, a new structure was erected on Purdue University's campus in the form of the Boilermaker Statue. Weighing in at 5,400 pounds and standing eighteen feet tall, the statue is located on John Wooden Drive on the east side of Ross-Ade Stadium. The Boilermaker Statue project was commissioned by an anonymous donor and was sculpted by Jon Hair of Cornelius, North Carolina. He began work on the statue in 2003 and the entire project cost over $500,000. Hair is one of the most commissioned sculptors in the United States and is a member of the National Sculpture Society. In addition, the statue also honors the Eugene R. Grotnes family for their ties to the University. Eugene Grotnes graduated from Purdue with a mechanical engineering degree in 1951. His father, Carl C. Grotnes, and grandfather, Charles Grotnes, developed at their company some of the first machines for producing rims for the automobile, truck, and agricultural industries. The Boilermaker Statue will forever stand as a symbol of true Boilermaker spirit, hard work, and dedication.

Purdue Boilermaker Statue.

CENTENNIAL TIME CAPSULE

The last chapter of Purdue's centennial observance closed September 11, 1970, with the sealing of a time capsule containing memorabilia from the 1969 observance and a letter from President Frederick L. Hovde to the Purdue president of 2069.

The capsule, a rectangular copper box measuring nine by twelve by twenty-five inches, was sealed without fanfare in the base of the Centennial Marker on the Purdue Mall. The capsule was welded tightly before being sealed, coated with two layers of epoxy enamel, and placed in the underground chamber in the base of the marker. It was closed with nearly a foot of concrete and then covered by a limestone cap. When the mall was reconstructed in 1989, the Centennial Marker and time capsule were moved to the east side of the Materials and Electrical

BOILER BYTE

GOLD JERSEYS

During the Purdue-IU Old Oaken Bucket football game on November 23, 1986, an old tradition was revived. This was the wearing of the Gold Jerseys. Gold Jerseys had not been worn since the late 1940s. It was a pleasant surprise to the fans, and it helped motivate the Boilermakers to a 17-1 victory.

Engineering Building. A ceremony was conducted in October 1989 when the time capsule was reburied.

In addition to President Hovde's letter, the capsule contains a 1969–70 University course catalog, a 1969 *Debris*, publications of the University, copies of various proclamations recognizing the University's centennial and its hundred years of contributions, news clippings of University centennial activities, copies of programs from University events, copies of year-end newspapers highlighting University events, a centennial flag, the summer issue of the *Purdue Alumnus*, and similar programs, bulletins, and materials used throughout the year. A tape recording of President Hovde's address at the centennial kickoff luncheon on January 15, 1969 is also included.

The Centennial Marker, installed and dedicated in 1968, was a gift of Purdue benefactors William J. Hale and Robert Ingalls, Jr., Bedford, Indiana businessmen.

CLASS OF 1939 WATER SCULPTURE

The Class of 1939 Water Sculpture, also known as the Purdue Mall Fountain, was dedicated at Homecoming on October 29, 1989. The fountain was commissioned by the class of 1939 as a fiftieth anniversary gift. The fountain was sculpted by Robert Youngman and cost about $350,000 to construct.

Class of 1939 Water Sculpture at night.

Located in Purdue Mall, the fountain stands thirty-eight feet tall and is made of 228 tons of concrete. It sprays 588 gallons of recycled water per minute. It runs from the second week of April to the end of October, weather permitting.

Originally, the spout of water was unprotected as it shot straight into the air; however, due to injuries caused by the jet, the University installed a metal cylinder around the jet. The cylinder has not stopped students from participating in fountain runs on hot days after class or after ceremonies.

CLASS PILLARS

The original entrance to the University stood just south of Stewart Center on the east side of Memorial Mall at the entrance to what is now Memorial Mall Drive. Two pillars were added to the entrance in 1891 along with wrought iron fences connecting them.

In April 1923, members of the class of 1897, during their twenty-fifth reunion, carved their graduating year into the two pillars. The gateway in between was widened to allow an automobile to pass through. During the mid-1950s when Memorial Mall Drive was widened, the gateway and pillars were removed.

In fall 1991, the pillars were relocated to the east side of the Memorial Mall across from Stewart Center. Children and grandchildren of the class of 1897 and the class of 1936 raised

Close up view of the Class of 1939 Water Sculpture with Hovde Hall in the background.

Class of 1897 pillars, in their original location south of Stewart Center, 1927.

Class of 1897 pillars, in their current location at the entrance to the Hello Walk.

the money to refurbish and install the pillars, which had been in storage.

During 1929 and 1930, the senior classes presented limestone pillars that created a new entrance to the University off Northwestern Avenue. The pillars now stand between the Electrical Engineering and Materials and Electrical Engineering buildings.

Another set of pillars, between the Materials and Electrical Engineering and Physics buildings, were a gift from the class of 1905, marking the twenty-fifth reunion of the group.

Continuum sculpture.

CONTINUUM SCULPTURE

The spirit of veterinary medicine at Purdue is captured by a forty-five-foot-long bronze sculpture in front of the Lynn Hall of Veterinary Medicine. Commissioned in 1998 and dedicated during Homecoming weekend on September 23, 2000, the sculpture is made up of seven pieces depicting a variety of humans and animals. The sculpture is led by a boy running with his dog, followed by a female veterinary professional holding a stethoscope up to a calf. Close behind her is a man in a lab coat holding up and examining a rack of test tubes. Following are a horse, a pig, and a cat, whose sculptures respectively show their skeletal, circulatory and nervous systems in relief. Bringing up the rear of the procession is a nine-foot-tall by sixteen-foot-wide cave wall that depicts prehistoric animal drawings, with animal shapes cut out in cookie-cutter style.

The Continuum Sculpture was created by Washington sculptor Larry Anderson over eighteen months. He got the commission as a result of entering an art contest by the School of Veterinary Medicine in 1996, which Anderson won. The project was funded entirely by private gifts.

FREEDOM SQUARE

Freedom Square, located on the south lawn of the Purdue Armory, was dedicated Sunday, September 11, 2011, just prior to the Purdue 9/11 Tenth Anniversary Commemorative Ceremony. The base of the flag pole is in the shape of a pentagon, each side with a seal representing the branches of the armed forces: Army, Marine Corps, Navy, Air Force, and Coast Guard. Engraved in the top section of each side are the words honor, service, courage, leadership, and education. The purpose of Freedom Square is to celebrate the freedom U.S. citizens have earned and preserved. The Order of the Iron Key, a Purdue student society devoted to service-oriented leadership, was in charge of the project and fundraising. More than 190 individuals and Purdue student organizations contributed $55,650 toward the project.

A little girl traces the engraved letters on the Freedom Square sculpture after the dedication ceremony, September 11, 2011.

The dedication of Freedom Square on the south lawn of the Purdue Armory was held just prior to the Purdue 9/11 Tenth Anniversary Commemorative Ceremony, September 11, 2011.

Gateway to the Future .

FLAGPOLE

During the Spanish-American War, the need for a flagpole on campus became evident. G. W. Munroe, then a student and later a professor, made a speech in chapel appealing for funds. The students donated $43 (not a paltry sum then), which Munroe took to President James H. Smart. The cost of the flagpole exceeded that sum, but Smart accepted the money and appropriated the rest of the money needed to purchase the flagpole. Although it has been replaced once, the flagpole still stands on Memorial Mall today.

GATEWAY TO THE FUTURE

The Gateway to the Future is located near the intersection of Stadium Avenue and University Street and was dedicated in October 2008 as combined gift from the classes of 1958 and 1959. The archway consists of two twenty-seven-foot-tall columns constructed of Indiana limestone, which are crowned with brass lanterns. Each lantern is nearly five feet tall. A steel arch running between the columns displays "Purdue University" in black, uppercase letters.

HELLO WALK AND MEMORIAL MALL

The Hello Walk has been an institution at Purdue since 1893. It is tradition to say "hello" to anyone who passes there. The walkway once began at the old entrance to campus at State and Marsteller streets and continued along the west side of what is now Memorial Mall, once called the Oval. When the Oval was altered in the 1950s, the Hello Walk was changed to include the crosswalks in Memorial Mall. The plaque on Hello Walk reads, "Smile and say hello to everyone you meet."

The Hello Walk and the Memorial Mall sidewalks were renovated during the 1998–99 academic year, and a new plaque was installed. Renovation of the Hello Walk was a gift of the class of 1951.

HORTICULTURE PARK

Horticulture Park was originally created for education and research purposes. Students can use the park to learn the identities of a wide array of trees and shrubs. Located on McCormick Road and Third Street, the park is adjacent to Stewart Woods, and together they create a thirty-five-acre plot of wooded land conducive to photography, nature observation, and relaxation. The park is open to visitors year-round during daylight hours.

JOHN PURDUE'S GRAVE

John Purdue, who gave monies and land for the founding of the University, had requested that he be buried on campus after his death. In keeping with this wish, the University interred his remains in a grave just east of University Hall, which was under construction when he passed away in 1876. The class of 1894 donated funds for the Memorial Fountain next to John Purdue's grave.

The gravesite area and fountain were restored and rededicated during Gala Week 1996 with funds donated by the class of 1946.

Smile and say hello to everyone you meet.
— Hello Walk plaque

Memorial Fountain next to John Purdue's grave.

Loeb Fountain.

LOEB FOUNTAIN

In 1959, Purdue installed its first major fountain, directly in front of the Executive Building (now Hovde Hall of Administration). The fountain was added, along with a large set of steps, to serve as a glorious front entrance to both Hovde and Elliott halls. The fountain was moved in 1988, in anticipation of the construction of the Purdue Mall Fountain, to its present location in Founders Park, just south of the Steven C. Beering Hall of Liberal Arts and Education. During the move, the retaining wall around the fountain was removed, thus eliminating the standing water portion of the fountain.

Named to honor Solomon Loeb, a Lafayette merchant in the early years of the city, the fountain was donated by the Bert E. and June Loeb Foundation. Loeb Fountain can recycle up to 2,200 gallons of water per minute.

Loeb Fountain became the centerpiece for Founders Park, a beautifully landscaped pedestrian mall. Dedicated April 23, 1994, during Purdue's 125th anniversary year, the park is larger than two acres and includes walks, trees, tables, seating, lighting, and retaining walls. Founders Park is dedicated to the students, faculty, administrators, trustees, and benefactors who helped nurture the University in its early years.

Replacement of the Old Pump as part of the Gala Week Celebration. Left to right: John Henderson, M. Booher, Mrs. Edwin S. Anderson, William Anderson (small child), Vice President R. B. Stewart, George A. Ross, Edwin S. Anderson (partially hidden), Mrs. Frances McLaughlin Shirk, J. H. Carnine, W. Carl Furnas, and Paul Spotts Emrick, May 3, 1958.

OLD PUMP

The Old Pump, originally located just southeast of Ladies Hall, was a historic meeting site for men and women. Resourceful co-eds used the pretense of getting water to supplement their dating with "chance meetings" by the Old Pump.

It is believed that the well was originally dug in the 1860s for a farm family before the University was built. It is said to have worked until 1906, but eventually was forgotten about when a water system was installed on campus.

The Old Pump itself was an all-wood, cistern-type well, painted vivid green with yellow trimmings. After the University grew and earlier dormitories were abandoned, the class of 1893 placed a stone well platform bearing the class numerals in the place of the pump to keep the old meeting place sacred.

When Ladies Hall was torn down in 1927, President Edward C. Elliott had the pump, a symbol of romance, reconditioned and placed south of University Hall. The Purdue Reamer Club spring pledge class of 1958 was responsible for its resurrection at the southeast corner of the new Home Economics Building, now known as Stone Hall.

Old Pump.

PURDUE BELL TOWER

On January 19, 1894, Purdue dedicated Heavilon Hall, an engineering laboratory with a tower that stood tall and proud above the modest skyline of the young campus. Four days later, the building lay in ruins, destroyed by explosion and fire. Students, faculty, and administrators watched helplessly as flames devoured their new campus landmark. Purdue President James H. Smart brought the campus back together and rallied the spirits of the students and staff after the fire by claiming "We are looking this morning to the future, not the past . . . I tell you, young men, that tower shall go up one brick higher." Almost immediately, construction on the new Heavilon Hall was begun and the tower did rise again—nine bricks higher than the original.

The new Heavilon Hall Tower, completed in December 1895 and standing 140 feet tall, had the same powerful presence as the original but with its own special features: a clock and four bells. On April 8, 1896, the new clock and chimes were dedicated, capping the long struggle to build the tower. The four bells, which had been paid for by various campus alumni and community groups, including the class of 1895, were cast in Troy, New York, and weighed twelve hundred, six hundred, three hundred, and two hundred pounds. The Howard Watch and Clock Company of Boston donated the clock, which served as a campus landmark for sixty years.

By 1956, time and weather had taken their toll on the building and its tower; Heavilon Hall was demolished and a new building—for humanities rather than engineering—was built bearing the same name. The tower clock and bells, not part of the new building's design, were placed in storage.

The Purdue Bell Tower is located in the Special Places Garden, which was a donation of the class of 1949. Sinninger Pond can be seen behind the Bell Tower on the left.

Beginning in 1990, the "movement," the heart and primary working mechanism of the clock, was painstakingly restored under the direction of John Fessler, a clocksmith and Purdue professor of veterinary clinical sciences. The restored clockworks are now displayed in the atrium of the Roger B. Gatewood wing of the Mechanical Engineering Building.

A century after the dedication of the second Heavilon Hall and forty years after the building and its tower had been removed from campus, the tower bells regained their spot above campus in the new Purdue Bell Tower. The new tower is located next to Sinninger Pond in the "Special Place Garden," which was a gift from the class of 1949. Dedicated at Homecoming on October 14, 1995, the 160-foot spire of red brick trimmed in limestone is a modern architectural interpretation of the old Heavilon Hall tower.

Electric "clappers" strike the hour, half-hour, and end of classes. The tower also is equipped with an electronic carillon that plays recorded songs at various times during the day and evening and for special occasions on campus. Members of the class of 1948 provided a leadership gift for the $1.45 million tower.

Purdue Bell Tower.

PURDUE MALL

The Purdue Mall, sometimes referred to as the Engineering Mall due to the number of engineering buildings nearby, is surrounded by the Electrical Engineering Building, Mechanical Engineering Building, Materials and Electrical Engineering Building, and Forney Hall of Chemical Engineering, as well as the Physics Building, Schleman Hall, and Hovde Hall. Within the area of the mall are the Varsity Walk, the Awards Obelisk, and the Class of 1939 Water Sculpture.

The Varsity Walk runs west of the Materials and Electrical Engineering Building, with the Awards Obelisk located at the southeast corner of the Forney Hall of Chemical Engineering. This pillar shows the recipients of the Flora Roberts, G. A. Ross, Special Boilermaker, Distinguished Alumni, and Varsity Walk awards.

The Class of 1939 Water Sculpture was built from funds donated by the class of 1939 in observance of their fiftieth anniversary. The water sculpture was designed by Robert Youngman. Van Phillips, a Purdue professor of theater, designed the lighting system. The fountain was dedicated on October 28, 1989.

Purdue Mall.

THE PURDUE RAILROAD

In the late 1800s, the railroad industry was plagued with technical problems that were expensive to correct. In 1892, Purdue built a test site and laboratories to help overcome the engineering problem of the railroads, while allowing students to gain valuable experience from the research. The first of its kind ever built, the Purdue Locomotive Testing Plant carried out the first test of a full-scale locomotive in a laboratory in 1892. This plant was a significant influence in American locomotive development. Significant, too, was the recognition that the testing facility established the University as a leader in transportation research. Some of the equipment included in the building were a dynamometer, on which a train engine rode and was tested while stationary, and a brake testing machine.

The first steam engine was ordered from the Schenectady Locomotive Works, and appropriately called the *Schenectady*. Transporting and installing the locomotive in its campus home was an engineering feat in itself. When *Schenectady* arrived at a switch in the tracks near the present Purdue Airport, an all-campus holiday was called so that faculty and student volunteers could help move the engine to campus. Three teams of horses and a group of adventurous students dragged several wooden skids with rails to the switch. The 85,000-pound *Schenectady* was lifted off the tracks and placed on the first skid. As the engine was pushed forward, the skids were pulled around to the front so that the train could be moved without stopping until it reached its test building, one and a half miles away. It reached the plant eight days after the arduous moving process began.

From 1892 to 1894, many tests were conducted on the *Schenectady*. On January 23, 1894, the test building, along with the newly dedicated Heavilon Hall, was destroyed by fire. The *Schenectady* was pulled out of the rubble and sent to Indianapolis to be repaired. In the meantime, the specially constructed Locomotive Laboratory was built just north of the Heavilon laboratories. When the refurbished *Schenectady* returned to campus, the engine did not have to be dragged across farmland to the main line of the railroad. The new Purdue Railroad had been constructed, with the Locomotive Laboratory as its terminus.

At the time, the one and a quarter-mile Purdue Railroad was considered the shortest in the world. The line spurred off the main Monon Rail Line near what is now the Purdue Airport and proceeded north then eastward toward campus along what is now Harrison Street. The tracks turned north, heading diagonally through the agricultural campus and crossed State Street between Matthews and Stone Halls. The tracks proceeded north, turning east over the ground that is now the Class of 1950 Lecture Hall. In its later years, the Purdue Railroad was used primarily to haul coal to the North Power Plant and was later extended for experimental traction car use to the present Electrical Engineering Building.

Over the years, a number of locomotives were tested—*Schenectady II* and *III* followed the original as well as the *Vauclain*, *Purdue No. 4*—as were railway parts such as brakes, axles, and draft gears.

Several major advances in railroad technology were developed at Purdue. An air brake system designed at the University was eventually required on all trains in the United States. The system enabled all cars of a train to brake at the same time, preventing some parts of a train from stopping sooner than others, possibly causing a derailment. The other innovations were draft gears that were tested and redesigned in the Draft Gear Laboratory, now the American Railway Building. Draft gears are special shock absorbers placed at the ends of railroad cars to prevent the cars from bumping or crashing into one another.

BOILER BYTE

NEVER SAY NEVER
Edward C. Elliott, the sixth president of Purdue, was not afraid to change his mind. When Al Stewart asked for funding for a mixed choir, Elliott reputedly hollered: "Never! Never, as long as I am president will this university ever spend one damn penny on music on this campus, young man! Get that through your head!" Elliott came to be a great fan of Stewart's famous Varsity Glee Club and spearheaded construction on the Purdue Hall of Music. It was later named the Edward C. Elliott Hall of Music, after the man who didn't want to spend "one damn penny" on music.

Another building associated with the important railway research, the Locomotive Museum, housed many important pieces of railroad history. The building, just east of the North Power Plant, was conceived in 1900 by Engineering Dean W. F. M. Goss to preserve properly some of the more valuable old locomotives. He made arrangements with various railroad companies to display steam engines that had made some contribution to the advancement of the industry. One of the more interesting relics housed in the museum was a wooden model of the *Tornado*, the second locomotive to be used on the Seaboard Air Line and built in 1840. Also in the museum was the old coach used on the Boston and Providence Railroad around the year 1835. It was first drawn by horses, had four wheels, leather springs, and probably carried eight passengers inside. The museum also contained an interesting collection of old types of railway track and full-sized, cross-sectioned models of locomotive cylinders and front ends, illustrating the working of steam through the simple piston valve and cylinder and through compound cylinders. Over the years, many of the aisles were almost impassible from the clutter and the collection was virtually forgotten. When the building was razed in 1930, items on loan were returned to their owners or to other museums where they could be cared for properly. Much of the outstanding collection is now housed at the National Museum of Transportation in Kirkwood, Missouri.

Railway testing continued at Purdue though 1938, when the *Vauclain, Purdue No. 4* boiler was declared unsafe. At that time, many railroad companies had stopped funding research and development. Also, fewer students were enrolled in the research program. As a result, most of the equipment was unused for several years until it was sold for scrap during World War II. The original test facility behind Heavilon Hall was turned over to the Department of Chemistry for use in the Manhattan Project. By 1953, the test buildings were removed to allow for construction of new buildings.

SMOKESTACK

The giant smokestack on the University's North Power Plant once could be seen thirty miles away and was one of the tallest and biggest in the state. Thirteen men took eighty-four days to construct the stack from March 27 to June 19, 1924, at the

BOILER BYTE

MISS IU

Before the annual Purdue-Indiana football game, Purdue students used to make a bonfire to rally fellow fans. At the bonfire, they would burn a coffin containing a mannequin dressed as an IU cheerleader, known as Miss IU. The Purdue Reamer Club was responsible for procuring the mannequin and placing her in her coffin for display in the Great Hall the week before the annual football game. In the early 1980s, some students protested that it was sexist to use a female cheerleader; that year they put IU memorabilia inside of the coffin instead. The tradition has since been discontinued.

Smokestack, 1924.

cost of $15,000. When the crew finished they constructed a similar smokestack, at the University of Michigan, which has since been demolished.

The Purdue smokestack originally rose 250 feet above the ground. A story in a 1937 *The Purdue Exponent* reported the exact number of bricks in the chimney to be 194,445.

A number of legends were told about the smokestack. One says that a band was placed on the stack for every year that the administration promised to cut enrollment. Another states that the number of bands corresponds to the number of virgins who have graduated from Purdue.

Eighteen feet had to be removed off the top of the structure in 1972, because of deterioration from sulfur. In 1984, an additional sixteen feet were removed to safeguard against falling debris from the weather-ravaged top of the chimney.

The Purdue landmark was torn down in 1991. The North Power Plant remains standing but unused. Before being taken out of service, the facility served only as a source of heat generation for the University; electricity generation had been taken over by the Wade Utility Plant and Public Service Indiana.

When the smokestack was torn down, many suggested ideas for a new towering landmark for the campus resulting in the new Purdue Bell Tower.

SMOKING FENCE

During the old days when smoking was forbidden on campus, students would congregate for a smoke along the iron rail fence that surrounded much of the main campus. Students would lean over these fences so that they were officially "off campus" and could smoke without breaking any rules. Parts of the original fence remain along Grant Street. A smoking ban was reintroduced in 2011.

STONE LIONS FOUNTAIN

A gift from the class of 1903 to the University, the Stone Lions Fountain, manufactured by the Charles C. Blake Monument Company of Chicago, was dedicated in 1904. It is believed that its current location, just off Oval Drive at the southeast corner of Stanley Coulter Hall, is its original location on campus.

The Stone Lions Fountain features a decorative stone top, a plain stone base, and a stone midsection containing four lion faces,

Stone Lions Fountain.

on each of the four sides. Each face projects out of this midsection, appearing as though the lions are beginning to leap out of the stone. Drinking water once spouted from each of their mouths into a small basin below each lion face. The landmark ceased functioning as a fountain sometime between 1923 and 1931. That has changed, though, thanks to the Purdue Reamer Club.

As a seventy-fifth anniversary project, the Reamer Club, in collaboration with the University Development Office, raised funds over three years to renovate and restore the Lions Fountain. More than $48,000 was contributed by Reamer Club alumni, friends, and corporations for the effort to restore the landmark as a true fountain. Renovation began in March 2000; the rededication ceremony took place on April 22, 2001.

Stone Lions Fountain before its renovation in 2000–01.

Much campus folklore focuses on the Lions Fountain. One story claims that each time a virgin walks by the Lions, they will roar. Another once insisted that if a man and woman were to first kiss under the bell tower of the old Heavilon Hall and then walk past the Lions, the couple would get married. A variation of that story that is used today replaces the phrase "the bell tower of the old Heavilon Hall" with the phrase "the Purdue Bell Tower."

The Purdue Reamer Club helps keep the tradition of the Lions Fountain alive by singing assortments of Purdue songs and cheers that have been handed down throughout the years. They sing around the Lions Fountain during the pledge process each semester.

STUART FIELD

In 1892, at the suggestion of Board of Trustees member Charles B. Stuart, seven acres of land were set aside for an athletic field. The field was located just east of the Armory, where Elliott Hall of Music now stands. The field was named in honor of Charles Stuart and his brother William V. Stuart, who served on the Board of Trustees from 1899 to 1921.

In 1910, the size of the field was doubled. Stuart Field was used as an all-purpose facility until 1923, when construction of Ross-Ade Stadium and the Recreation Field made it possible to have tennis courts, a football field, and an outdoor track available in more spacious surroundings.

Stuart Field was then used as a baseball field by the Athletic Department until 1939. The north end of the field was still used for football practice and intramural, interclass, and inter-

"Transformation" by Faustino Aizkorbe, a gift from the class of 1952, towers on the east end of Agricultural Mall near the Yue-Kong Pao Hall of Visual and Performing Arts.

fraternity games. Stuart Field also hosted the Purdue Circus between 1913 and 1922 as well as many other programs.

TRANSFORMATION SCULPTURE

The Transformation Sculpture is a forty-foot-tall bronze sculpture by Spanish artist Faustino Aizkorbe on the east end of Agricultural Mall, near the Yue-Kong Pao Hall of Visual and Performing Arts building. Aizkorbe was approached by the class of 1952 to create the sculpture as their class gift to the University.

Transformation is based on the common architectural pillars of Spain and symbolizes Purdue's continual growth and development, even as it remains a sound pillar of learning. Mounted underground on a footing that is sixteen feet square, the sculpture appears to be emerging directly from the earth. It was dedicated on April 20, 2002.

TREES OF PURDUE

About 8,000 trees of 257 varieties populate Purdue's West Lafayette campus. Among these are one national champion and two state champion trees. The national champion smoke tree, which shares the designation as the largest tree of its species in the United States, stands on the south part of campus near South Russell Drive. The state champion trees are a jack pine and a hawthorn. Purdue's largest tree, a burr oak, stands west of the band practice field just off of Third Street.

The greening of the Purdue campus, built on flat farmland, began early on when Trustee Martin Peirce donated funds for plantings and to begin a nursery. Some original pines donated by Peirce in 1874 remain north of the Psychological Sciences Building. Another stand of nineteenth-century trees are the chinquapin oaks south of Windsor Halls. The trees were standing before construction began for the original portion of campus.

The sycamore tree standing in front of Lilly Hall that was planted in 1990 by alumnus and astronaut Jerry Ross and his wife, Karen, to commemorate the impact 4-H experiences had on their lives.

Other notable trees on the Purdue landscape are a number of sweet gum trees, referred to as shuttle gums; a "space tree"; and a unique cedar of Lebanon. Taken to space in 1984 by Purdue alumnus and astronaut Charles Walker, 200 sweet gum tree seeds were germinated before returning to Earth. The shuttle gums are located on the south side of the Forestry Products Building, on the northwest corner of Grissom Hall, on the northwest corner of the Electrical Engineering building, on the southeast corner of Forney Hall of Chemical Engineering, and in Pickett Park. Called the "space tree," a sycamore tree standing in front of Lilly Hall was planted in 1990 by alumnus and astronaut Jerry Ross and his wife, Karen, to commemorate the impact 4-H experiences had on their lives. The cedar of Lebanon located south of the Nelson Hall of Food Science is better known as the Purdue Hardy Cedar of

Purdue Gardens.

Lebanon. Normally a native of the country of Lebanon, this hardy cedar has slightly different genetic material, making it possible for the tree to withstand temperatures colder than a normal cedar of Lebanon.

The Purdue Grounds Department, in cooperation with the Indiana Department of Forestry and Natural Resources, has developed three trails that look at the variety of trees on the West Lafayette campus. Brochures and information on the Internet are available to visitors.

In addition, the Purdue Arboretum was established in 2008. The Arboretum is a collection of woody plants—trees, shrubs, woody ground covers, and climbing vines—that serves as a resource for classes, research, and community outreach programs. The entire campus is included in the Arboretum and new collections of woody ornamentals will be added as time and money permit.

Unfinished Block P being unveiled at its dedication, October 23, 2008.

UNFINISHED BLOCK P

The Unfinished Block P is an eight-foot-tall bronze sculpture in Academy Park meant to symbolize that one is always learning, even after graduation, as well as being a monument to students who could not complete their degrees. Cast by sculptors Rick and Rita Hadley, it was designed to appear like an incomplete Block P carved out of stone. Funding for the statue came from Rex Sebastian, a 1951 alumnus of Purdue, and an anonymous donor. Many student organizations also contributed to the project, led by efforts from the members of Iron Key.

Golden Taps, a ceremony to honor students who have passed away during the year, now takes place at the Unfinished Block P.

The Unfinished Block P sculpture will serve as a reminder that even after you've left Purdue, the educational experience is never complete. All students become lifelong Boilermakers and lifelong learners and should strive to always continue to learn and grow throughout their lives.

— President France A. Córdova

BOILER BYTE

POTS AND PLEDGE BOARDS

Hats that have been worn through the years by Purdue students and organizations:

- Alpha Lambda Delta pots, white with a candle on them, were worn by freshmen coeds receiving a 5.5 index at the end of the semester or a 5.5 graduation index at the end of the year when the University was on a 6.0 scale.

- Freshmen wore green beanies or pots during orientation and burned them at the pep rally before the Old Oaken Bucket game.

- Gimlets, junior and senior Greek men who had distinguished themselves in activities, wore gold sailor-like pots with a black "G" on the front.

- Gold Peppers wore gold pots with a pepper outlined in black and carried golden peppers dangling from gold and black ribbons.

- Green pots were worn by men in the Green Guard Honorary, and white pots were worn by female students who participated actively in the Green Guard counseling program.

- The Reamer Club wear billed pots that are black and carry a pledge board in the shape of an "R" and a wooden reamer.

- Skull and Crescent had gold and black pots with a skull and crescent on top. They were worn by sophomore fraternity men who had made outstanding contributions in activities.

- Tomahawk pots are maroon and gold and were worn by independent sophomores active in student organizations. They also carried tomahawk-shaped pledge boards and a goofboard, which is a mammoth tomahawk.

STANDING TALL

PURDUE ALUMNI have included some of the most significant and innovative people in their fields. Throughout Purdue's history, alumni and staff have consistently been relied upon to originate and inspire new ideas and inventions. Purdue's influence reaches well beyond the state of Indiana, stretching into the farthest regions of our world and literally beyond. Whether the person is faculty, staff, alumnus, or student, all have earned their place on Purdue's historical roster. Purdue is proud to have fostered in them the inspiration that they continue to kindle in all Boilermakers.

George Ade.

GEORGE ADE

George Ade was born on February 6, 1866, in Kentland, Indiana. He entered Purdue in 1883, a time when "every student had to go to chapel every morning and answer 'here' or 'present' when his name was called." Ade recollected that a student then could be fed for $2.50 a week and go to school for the entire year on about $200.

Ade graduated from Purdue in 1887 with a Bachelor of Science degree. After graduation, he got a job at the *Lafayette Morning News* and the *Lafayette Call*. In 1890, he took a job at the *Chicago Record*. While there, he developed his literary skills, writing twelve plays, two musicals, ten books, and numerous stories. A best-selling writer, nationally read columnist, and author of smash Broadway musical comedies, he became a friend of playwrights and presidents.

But Ade never forgot Purdue. His play called *The College Window* was based on college life and the game of football—the college being Purdue and football being the infant sport at the University at the time.

Old maids adopt cats and canaries. Dave Ross and I adopted Purdue.

—George Ade

In 1909, Ade was named to the Purdue Board of Trustees, serving until 1916, when he resigned in protest over President Winthrop Stone's lack of support for intercollegiate athletics, among other things.

A Purdue philanthropist, Ade donated money and the land for the football stadium with David Ross as well as funds for the Memorial Gymnasium and the Sigma Chi house. Ade, who briefly served as editor of the *Purdue Alumnus*, died May 23, 1944. He was inducted into the Indiana Journalism Hall of Fame in 1982.

NEIL ARMSTRONG

Neil Armstrong was born on August 5, 1930, in Wapakoneta, Ohio. His interest in flying came at an early age. His father took him to the National Air Races in Cleveland, Ohio, when Armstrong was only two years old. The passion intensified when he took his first plane ride in a Ford Tri-motor, a "Tin Goose," at the age of six. He began flying lessons at age fifteen and had his student pilot's license by the next year.

In 1947, Armstrong received a scholarship from the U.S. Navy and enrolled in Purdue to study aeronautical engineering. His studies at Purdue were cut short in 1949, when the U.S. Navy called him to active duty in the Korean conflict. He flew seventy-eight combat missions and was stationed on an aircraft carrier, the U.S.S. *Essex*. Armstrong flew U.S. Navy Panther jets.

In 1952, Armstrong returned to Purdue and graduated with a Bachelor of Science degree in aeronautical engineering in 1955. He went on to receive a Master of Science degree in aerospace engineering from the University of Southern California.

In 1962, Armstrong was accepted by NASA as an astronaut, one of nine astronauts in the second group of astronauts to be chosen. In March 1966, Armstrong flew his first space mission as command pilot of Gemini VIII, which completed the first successful docking of two vehicles in space.

Neil Armstrong. *Photo courtesy of NASA.*

Armstrong's last and most famous mission began on July 16, 1969, when he, Michael Collins, and Edwin "Buzz" Aldrin began their trip to the Moon. As commander of Apollo 11, Armstrong piloted the lunar module to a safe landing on the Moon. On July 20, 1969, at 10:56 p.m. EDT, he became the first man to walk on the Moon. At that time he made the statement he is most famous for: "That's one small step for man, one giant leap for mankind." After the successful flight, Armstrong was awarded the Medal of Freedom, the highest award given to a U.S. civilian.

After resigning from NASA in 1971, Armstrong was on the aerospace engineering faculty at the University of Cincinnati until 1980. Armstrong became a fellow of the Society of Experimental Test Pilots and the Royal Aeronautical Society and an Honorary Fellow of the American Institute of Aeronautics and Astronautics and the International Astronautical Federation. He was a director of the Cincinnati Gas and Electric Co., Cincinnati Milacron, Inc., the Eaton Corporation, RMI Titanium Company, Thiokol Corporation, UAL, Inc., and USX Corporation. He was a member of the National Academy of Engineering and the Academy of the Kingdom of Morocco. He served as a member of the National Commission on Space (1985–86), as vice-chairman of the Presidential Commission on the Space Shuttle *Challenger* Accident (1986), and as chairman of the Presidential Advisory Committee on the Peace Corps (1971–73).

The Neil Armstrong Hall of Engineering was dedicated in 2007 as the flagship building of the Purdue University College of Engineering. Neil Armstrong passed away on August 25, 2012.

HERBERT C. BROWN

Herbert C. Brown.

Born in London to Ukrainian parents in 1912, Herbert C. Brown and his family moved to the United States when he was two years old. He received his bachelor's and PhD degrees from the University of Chicago in 1936 and 1938, respectively.

Brown married Sarah Baylen, a fellow student, in 1937. They had met at Crane Junior College and went to Wright Junior College together. In his yearbook, Sarah penned a prediction: "To a future Nobel Laureate." Sarah was also instrumental in Brown's interest in boron, giving him Alfred Stock's book *Hydrides of Boron and Silicon* as a graduation present.

Brown completed a postdoctoral program at the University of Chicago and then was named to the faculty. He joined Wayne State University in 1943 and was appointed to the Purdue faculty in 1947.

Brown was named R. B. Wetherill Distinguished Professor in 1959, and in 1960 was named Wetherill Research Professor of Chemistry. He officially retired in 1978, and in 1979, holding true to Sarah's prediction, he earned the Nobel Prize for chemistry. Two of Brown's former postdoctoral students, Ei-ichi Negishi and Akira Suzuki, also went on to win the 2010 Nobel Prize in chemistry.

As R. B. Wetherill Research Professor Emeritus of Chemistry, Brown published five books as well as more than 1,200 scientific publications. He won essentially every major award in chemistry and in 1998 was recognized by the American Chemical Society with the establishment of the Herbert C. Brown Award for Creative Research in Synthetic Methods.

In 2000, the Browns established the Herbert C. Brown Center for Borane Research at Purdue to focus on boron compounds and their chemical reactions. The Center continues to carry on the important work Brown started more than six decades ago. The Herbert C. Brown Laboratory of Chemistry at Purdue was named in his honor. On December 19, 2004, Brown passed away at the age of ninety-two.

EUGENE A. CERNAN

Born in Chicago on March 14, 1934, Eugene Cernan is a 1956 graduate of Purdue with a bachelor's degree in electrical engineering. An ROTC student and commissioned in the U.S. Navy, he was selected for the astronaut program in 1963. Cernan was the pilot of the Gemini IX mission and performed a two-hour, ten-minute space walk, becoming the second American to walk in space. Cernan was lunar module pilot of the Apollo 10 mission that journeyed to the Moon but did not land. He commanded the Apollo 17 mission—the last scheduled manned mission to the Moon. When Cernan stepped off the lunar surface to reenter his spacecraft, he became the last astronaut to leave his footprints on the Moon.

Neil Armstrong (left) with Eugene Cernan (right) after the dedication of Armstrong Hall of Engineering, 2007.

In 1973, Cernan was named special assistant at the Johnson Space Center and was senior U.S. negotiator in the discussion with the Soviet Union on the Apollo-Soyuz Project. After retirement from the navy in 1976, he entered industry and is now president of Cernan Corporation, a management consulting and research firm in the commercial aerospace industrial field.

Roger B. Chaffee.

ROGER B. CHAFFEE

Roger B. Chaffee was born in Grand Rapids, Michigan, on February 15, 1935. He earned his BS in aeronautical engineering from Purdue in 1957 and entered the U.S. Navy that same year. He was married to Martha Horn Chaffee, and they had two children, Steve and Sheryl.

He logged more than 2,000 hours of flight time on jet aircraft and received the Navy Air Medal. In 1963, he was selected by NASA to be a member of the third group of astronauts.

Chaffee was killed in an Apollo training accident in January 1967, one that also claimed the lives of Purdue graduate Virgil "Gus" Grissom and Ed White. At the time of his death, he was only a few weeks away from becoming the twentieth American to

fly in space. He was laid to rest in Arlington National Cemetery, at a ceremony attended by then President Lyndon B. Johnson. Chaffee Hall on the Purdue campus is named in his honor.

STANLEY COULTER

Stanley Coulter.

Stanley Coulter was born in Ningpo, China, on June 2, 1853, the son of American missionaries. A graduate of Hanover College, he taught for nine years, then left the profession to become a lawyer. Five years later, he returned to education. Coulter was on vacation and in the middle of a lake fishing when he received a telegram from Purdue President James H. Smart, calling on him to teach at Purdue. He became a professor of zoology and assistant principal of the preparatory academy. He went on to spend thirty-nine years at Purdue in various influential roles at the young University.

Coulter was named first dean of the newly established School of Science in 1907 and later became the first dean of men in 1919. He was chairman of the faculty in 1921–22.

Coulter retired in 1926 and received an honorary PhD from Purdue in 1931. He died in 1943 and Stanley Coulter Hall, originally the Biology Building, is named in his honor.

DAVID CROSTHWAIT, JR.

Born in Nashville on May 27, 1898, David Crosthwait, Jr. set a new precedent for African Americans in science with his many inventions. After growing up in Kansas City, Missouri, Crosthwait attended Purdue University, where he received a Bachelor of Science degree in 1913 and a Master of Engineering degree in 1920.

Following the receipt of his bachelor's degree, Crosthwait relocated to Marshalltown, Iowa, where he began his professional career with the C. A. Durham Company, now Marshall Engineered Products Co. In this position he designed heating installations, and by 1925, Crosthwait was named director of the research department.

During the 1920s and 1930s, Crosthwait invented an improved boiler, a new thermostat control, and a new differential vacuum pump, which improved the heating systems in larger buildings. His reputation for innovative solutions earned him the commission to design the heating system for Radio City Music Hall in New York City.

From 1930 to 1971, Crosthwait served as technical advisor of Durham-Bush, after the Durham Company merged with the Bush Manufacturing Company in 1956. During his career, Crosthwait received thirty-nine U.S. and eighty foreign patents related to the design, installing, testing, and service of heating, ventilating, and air-conditioning (HVAC) power plants and systems.

After his retirement from industry in 1971, Crosthwait returned to Purdue to teach a course on steam heating theory and control systems. In 1975, the University awarded him with an honorary doctorate. Crosthwait died on February 25, 1976.

AMELIA EARHART

One of the most famous people to have been associated with Purdue, Amelia Earhart was renowned for her flights across the Atlantic, from Hawaii to California, and from Mexico City to Newark, New Jersey. The first woman, and only second human being, to fly solo across the Atlantic, she also was the first woman to make a nonstop transcontinental flight.

Earhart served as a part-time career counselor for women at Purdue from 1935 until the time of her disappearance. She was also an advisor in aeronautics. While at Purdue, she resided in Duhme Hall, the south unit of Windsor Halls.

BOILER BYTE

MODEST BEGINNINGS
Purdue's world-renowned College of Pharmacy has its genesis in a casual conversation in an Indianapolis drugstore in 1883. The school opened with seven students; today, it has one of the largest pharmacy graduate programs in the nation, with more than 8,500 alumni on record. Nationwide, 20 percent of all pharmacy deans are either Purdue alumni or former faculty members.

Ameila Earhart.

Gebisa Ejeta, director of the Purdue Center for Global Food Security, surrounded by a crop of sorghum. Ejeta earned the 2009 World Food Prize for his work in developing sorghum varieties resistant to drought and the parasitic weed Striga.

The Lockheed Electra plane Earhart flew on her last, ill-fated journey was financed through Purdue Research Foundation sources. She disappeared in July 1937 while attempting an around-the-world flight.

Earhart Hall was named in her memory. The Purdue University Libraries Archives and Special Collections Division is home to the George Palmer Putnam Collection of Amelia Earhart Papers, which is the world's largest and most comprehensive collection of Earhart memorabilia. The collection includes thousands of items ranging from books to a flight suit, photos, maps, and hundreds of telegrams and medals. The entire collection has been digitized and is available online.

GEBISA EJETA

Gebisa Ejeta was born in a remote Ethiopian village with no school. His mother, recognizing the value of an education, was determined to help him find a better way of life. He walked twenty kilometers to the nearest elementary school every Sunday evening and walked the same distance back home again on Friday afternoon. Through hard work and discipline he was able to earn a scholarship to a boarding school, which later allowed him to enter Alemaya College of Agriculture, where he earned his bachelor's degree in plant science in 1973. He graduated with highest distinction and at the top of his class.

In 1974 Ejeta came to Purdue University, where he earned his master's and PhD in plant genetics and breeding. After completing his degrees at Purdue in 1978, he returned to Africa where he joined the International Crop Research Institute for the

Semi-arid Tropics (ICRISAT) and conducted seminal sorghum research in Sudan for five years. In January 1984 he returned to Purdue to join the faculty, where he has since stayed.

Ejeta received the 2009 World Food Prize for his work in developing sorghum varieties resistant to drought and the parasitic weed Striga. His research dramatically increased the production and availability of sorghum for hundreds of millions of people in Africa, where it is a major crop. Sorghum is among the world's five principal grains. Ejeta is Purdue's second World Food Prize laureate. Philip E. Nelson received the award in 2007 for his aseptic processing innovation.

Ejeta was appointed a science envoy for the U.S. Department of State in September 2010. Science envoys collaborate on programs that develop new sources of energy, create "green" jobs, digitize records, clean water, and grow new crops in developing countries. In April 2011, President Barack Obama appointed Ejeta to the Board for International Food and Agricultural Development for three years. As a member of the board, he advises the administrator of the U.S. Agency for International Development on agricultural development priorities and on U.S. universities' involvement in Title XII (Famine Prevention and Freedom from Hunger) issues worldwide. This appointment to USAID is personally significant because a predecessor to this program built the high school and college that he attended in his native Ethiopia.

Ejeta is the executive director of the Purdue Center for Global Food Security and serves on boards of the Consortium of the Consultative Group on International Agricultural Research, the Sasakawa Africa Association, and the Chicago Council on Global Affairs Agricultural Development Program.

Purdue's impact can be seen and felt, from the earliest days of space travel and discovery, to current efforts to feed our hungry world and achieve global food security. I would like to believe that Purdue's global impact has been generated not serendipitously, but by design— through leaders with the wisdom to encourage and value a culture of research with purpose, educating and nurturing each new generation of leaders, and building a community of students, faculty and staff with a collective commitment to the pursuit of excellence in the advancement of knowledge suffused with service to humanity.

—Gebisa Ejeta,
Spring 2010 Commencement Speech

RAY EWRY

Ray Ewry was born in Lafayette, Indiana, in 1873. At the age of five he became an orphan, and at seven he contracted polio. Although most doctors offered little hope that he would ever walk again, one therapist encouraged him to try special strengthening exercises. The conditioning was similar to today's plyometrics—exercises that improve muscle power and quickness.

By 1890 when Ewry entered college at Purdue, he was strong enough to excel in track and field. He specialized in the standing jump, which involved no run-up. He also played football and joined the Sigma Nu fraternity. He earned his bachelor's and master's degrees in mechanical engineering.

After college he continued to participate in track and field at the Chicago Athletic Association and later the New York Athletic Club. His first opportunity to compete in the Olympics came in Paris in 1900—the second games of the modern era. He won three gold medals in the standing high jump, standing long jump, and standing triple jump (also called the hop). He set the world record in the standing high jump at five feet and five inches. From this Olympic experience he gained the nickname the "Human Frog." At the 1904 Olympics in St. Louis, Ewry again earned three gold medals in the same events. Ewry went on to earn two more gold medals in Athens, Greece, during the 1906 Intercalated Olympic Games, and he won his last two gold medals in the 1908 London Olympics. He probably would have earned three at the 1906 and 1908 Olympics, but the standing triple jump was eliminated after the 1904 games.

Until the 2012 Olympic Games, once again in London, Ewry still held the record for the most individual gold medals of any male U.S. Olympian. His record was beaten by swimmer Michael Phelps. Some record books give Ewry just eight golds, not counting the two medals won in the 1906 Athens event. Many sport historians rank that competition at the

Ray Ewry during the 1904 Summer Olympics in St Louis, Missouri.

same level as regular Olympic Games, but the International Olympic Committee doesn't recognize the Intercalated Games, a discontinued competition that was intended to occur between the regular Olympics.

On July 19, 2012—seventy-five years after his death in 1937—a granite monument to honor Ewry was erected in Lafayette.

ELIZA FOWLER

In 1901, Eliza Fowler began a tradition of support for Purdue with her family. The Fowler family's association with the University actually started with a friendship born in Ohio. Friends John Purdue and Moses Fowler came to Lafayette together in 1839. They briefly owned a business together, then parted ways, each becoming successful entrepreneurs.

Moses Fowler invested in Benton County farmland. In 1872, Fowler and his wife, Eliza, platted the town that bears their name in the middle of their Benton County holdings. At the time of his death in 1889, Fowler was one of the richest men in Indiana, and he passed that fortune on to his widow and heirs.

The Fowler family and the University first came together a year after the death of Moses, when James Madison Fowler, the son of Moses and Eliza, became treasurer of Purdue. The first gift came from Eliza, $70,000, used to build the first assembly hall on the West Lafayette campus. This gift was the largest contribution made to the University since John Purdue gave $150,000 in 1869.

Eliza Fowler Hall was used for orientations, convocations, lectures, and for the first indoor commencement exercises, which were previously held outside on Memorial Mall. The building also housed the office of the University president and included several other meeting rooms for faculty and trustees. Eliza died in May 1902, just as work on the building was starting.

Because of a pressing need to establish a campus conference center, Fowler Hall was demolished in 1954. But the tradition and the name live on in the Stewart Center auditorium that bears Eliza Fowler's name. The 400-seat theater was built in almost the same location as the original structure.

BOILER BYTE

TANK SCRAP

This rough-and-tumble battle originated when the class of 1889 painted a large "89" on the steeple of the old Ag Building. Faculty objected to the defacing of hallowed halls, so the students moved off-campus.

The West Lafayette Water Company's fifty-foot water tower at the top of Salisbury Street hill was the ideal venue, and the scrap became traditional. Freshmen would paint their numerals on the tank, and the sophomores would try to remove them.

Formal battle ensued, with the freshmen at the bottom of the hill, while the sophomores surrounded the tank and charged the freshmen. The class that tied up all the members of the other class won. They would then strip the losers to their underwear, dump paint on them, and parade them through town.

The Tank Scrap continued until 1913, when a participant died due to a broken neck. On September 20, 1913, the classes voted to discontinue the scrap.

Lillian M. Gilbreth.

LILLIAN M. GILBRETH

Often called the "mother of modern industrial management," Lillian E. Moller was born in Oakland, California, on May 24, 1878. Born into a large German family, she was schooled at home. Although her father disapproved of her quest for higher education, she attended the University of California at Berkeley while living at home and maintaining her household duties. She earned two degrees from the University of California, a bachelor's in literature and a master's in English.

In 1903, a trip to the East Coast led her to her future husband, Frank B. Gilbreth. They married in 1904, intent on both careers and having children—twelve to be exact. A contractor, Frank had made motion studies of workers as they performed their tasks. He was eager to have Lillian join him in his work.

After having three children, Lillian started her thesis for her PhD in psychology from Brown University. The subject of her thesis was the psychology of management. Frank and Lillian chose to fuse their backgrounds to work for a common goal, the study of management as a science. The couple created a consulting firm. While Frank focused on the manual aspects of getting the job done efficiently, Lillian dealt with psychological aspects of management and why people should want to get the job done efficiently. In the summer of 1913, the Gilbreths were an integral part of the creation of the first of four Summer Schools of Management, where they taught professors about the current advances in management and the new field of industrial engineering.

In efforts to create less fatigue and more free time, Frank and Lillian created and tested their theories within their family. Frank would take pictures of the children as they washed dishes so he could figure out how to reduce their motions. Lillian set up the Family Council, which included a purchasing committee, a budget chairperson, and a utility committee, which fined wasters of water and electricity.

Lillian continued the work and the consulting firm after Frank's sudden death in 1924. In 1926, she was named the first female member of the American Society of Mechanical Engineers.

Gilbreth continued her work in industry until she received a call from President Edward C. Elliott and Dean Andrey Potter of the Purdue Schools of Engineering inviting her to become a visiting professor in the School of Industrial Engineering and Management. At Purdue she continued work on time and motion studies and taught those advanced management ideals in the classroom. She worked to improve Purdue's motion study labs and was able to make them accessible to the local agricultural industry.

In her later years at Purdue, Gilbreth worked with the former Department of Education and Applied Psychology and served as a consultant on careers for women.

When she retired in 1948, Gilbreth was awarded an honorary doctorate in industrial psychology from Purdue. She left the University an impressive collection of works, the Gilbreth Collection, which includes 1,500 volumes plus many original research notes related to her and Frank's time-and-motion studies and investigation of worker fatigue.

Two of the twelve Gilbreth children recounted family life in the books *Cheaper by the Dozen* and *Belles on their Toes*, which were both made into movies. Gilbreth returned to campus numerous times until her death in January 1972.

VIRGIL "GUS" GRISSOM

Virgil "Gus" Grissom was born in Mitchell, Indiana, on April 3, 1926, and earned his BS in mechanical engineering at Purdue in 1950. He became a U.S. Air Force pilot in 1951 and flew 100 combat missions in Korea. He received the Distinguished Flying Cross and Air Medal with Cluster, among other decorations.

In 1959, Grissom was one of the original seven Mercury astronauts selected by NASA. As a pilot of the *Liberty Bell 7*, he became the second American in space. In 1965, he was command pilot of the first manned Gemini flight and thus became the first person to fly more than one mission in space. He was killed in a fire during an Apollo training accident in January 1967 that also claimed the lives of fellow astronauts Ed White and Roger Chaffee, who was also a Purdue alumnus. Grissom Hall, located north of the Purdue Memorial Union, was named in his honor.

Virgil "Gus" Grissom.

LEROY KEYES

From 1966 to 1968, Purdue football was defined by the presence of Leroy Keyes. Playing on both sides of the ball as a running back and defensive back, his career with the Boilermakers set records that remain untouched today.

Leroy Keyes, 1968.

Born February 18, 1947, in Newport News, Virginia, Keyes attended George Washington Carver High School where he was a three-sport athlete in football, basketball, and track. As a result of a successful high school career, Keyes was made offers by elite football schools such as Notre Dame and the U.S. Army but chose to be a Boilermaker. During his time at Purdue, he was a member of Omega Psi Phi fraternity and was selected for Iron Key.

While pursuing a degree in physical education with a minor in biology, Keyes ran his way into the record books. In 1966, he played mostly defensive back and picked up three interceptions, helping the Boilermakers earn a trip to the Rose Bowl, where they defeated Southern California 14–13. In a televised game against Notre Dame earlier that year, he grabbed a Notre Dame fumble and ran it ninety-five yards to find the end zone, which stands as the longest return of a fumble recovery in school history. During the 1967 season, he amassed 1,003 rushing yards and became the first player in Purdue history to rush for more than 1,000 yards. In the same season he tied the school record with fourteen rushing touchdowns. Keyes was the first Boilermaker to score over 200 points, with 222, and set a school record for touchdowns at thirty-seven.

Keyes' performance on the gridiron earned him two consensus All-American awards, in 1967 and 1968, and he finished third and second in the race for the Heisman Trophy. In 1967, he was also named Most Valuable Player of the Big Ten Conference after leading the Boilermakers with 1,870 total offensive yards, the most in a season at Purdue.

Following his career at Purdue, Keyes was drafted to the Philadelphia Eagles in 1969. He stayed with the Eagles until 1973, when he was traded to the Kansas City Chiefs, where he played his last year of professional football.

In 1987, Keyes was selected as Purdue's "All-Time Greatest Player" as he was named to Purdue's All-Time Football Team as both an offensive and defensive back. He was inducted into the Virginia Sports Hall of Fame in 1987, the College Football Hall of Fame in 1990, and the Purdue Hall of Fame in 1994.

WARD "PIGGY" LAMBERT

On May 28, 1888, Ward Lambert was born in Deadwood, South Dakota. At the age of two, his family moved to Crawfordsville, Indiana, where he was to spend the rest of his childhood. As a boy, he frequently went sledding and wore a stocking cap, which had a large tassel on it. His friends started calling him "Pig-Tail." As the years went on, the nickname was changed to "Piggy."

He attended Crawfordsville High School, where he played basketball. His coach, Ralph Jones, never started Piggy because of his small size. Piggy did, however, learn the skills that would stay with him the rest of his life.

After graduating from high school, Lambert attended Wabash College, where he played baseball, basketball, and football, even though he weighed only 114 pounds. When he graduated, he was awarded the Shevlin Scholarship to the University of Minnesota, where he studied chemistry. In 1912, he accepted a position as a chemistry and physics teacher at

Lebanon High School. He quickly guided Lebanon to two consecutive state titles in basketball before accepting a head coaching position at Purdue in 1916.

In 1917, Lambert enlisted, serving in World War I as a lieutenant in field artillery. In 1919, he returned to Purdue, where he coached basketball and baseball, his first love. As a basketball coach, he guided Purdue to a 371–152

Ward "Piggy" Lambert talking with his basketball players.

record in his twenty-nine years as a head coach. With his fast-break offense, he guided Purdue to eleven Big Ten titles and four second-place finishes. In 1945, he received *Esquire's* Award for the Most Outstanding Coach in the country.

Among the players he coached were the legendary John Wooden, a three-time All-American; three-time All-American Charles "Stretch" Murphy; and All-Americans Don White, Ray "Candy" Miller, George Spradling, Norm Cotton, Emmett Lowery, Robert Kessler, Jewell Young, and Paul Hoffman.

In twenty years as the Boilermaker baseball coach, he compiled a .508 winning percentage.

In 1946, Lambert retired from Purdue and took the post of commissioner of the National Pro Basketball League. He missed coaching, however, and returned to Purdue in 1949 and coached both freshman baseball and basketball. He held this position until his death on January 20, 1957. Purdue named the fieldhouse and gymnasium to honor his memory. The baseball field is also named in his memory as Lambert Field.

GUY "RED" MACKEY

Guy "Red" Mackey was born on December 14, 1905, in Glasgow, Kentucky, and spent his boyhood in New Albany, Indiana. He came to Purdue in 1925 and participated in football, wrestling, baseball, and track. He played on the Big Ten Championship football team in 1929 and was named to the Intersectional Coaches All-American Honorable Mention as an end. He graduated from Purdue in 1929 in agricultural education.

Guy "Red" Mackey. *Photo courtesy of Purdue University Athletics Communications.*

He then joined the Purdue staff as assistant freshman football coach. In 1932, he was named wrestling coach, and in 1941, he became assistant athletic director.

In 1942, Mackey became athletic director of Purdue University. Among his challenges was to ensure the financial stability of intercollegiate athletics. His plan was simple but was met with consternation from some. He said, "We must put the money into the sports that pay their own way. Build football and basketball to where they can support the rest of the programs, where possible, but not to the point where they have hurt the money-making sports." Mackey worked to put football and basketball on a sound basis and give them the best facilities.

Enlarging Ross-Ade Stadium was a primary goal. Seating was increased to more than 51,000 in 1949 and to 67,332 by the end of Mackey's tenure. Today, Ross-Ade Stadium is the second-largest football stadium in the state.

Other facility improvements under Mackey were the construction of the Purdue Arena, now Mackey Arena; a ten-lane, all-weather track; and the Recreational Gymnasium, the first facility of its kind in the United States.

While Mackey was athletic director, Purdue became a power in football and basketball circles. The fulfillment of a Mackey dream came in 1966 when Purdue won the right to represent the Big Ten in the Rose Bowl on January 2, 1967.

In late 1970, health problems, including two strokes, began to plague Mackey. On February 22, 1971, he died, ending a forty-five-year association with Purdue. A member of the National Football Foundation and Hall of Fame, Iron Key, Gimlet, Reamer, and Sigma Pi fraternity, he was recipient of the Distinguished Alumni Award for meritorious service to the University.

President Emeritus Fredrick L. Hovde paid tribute to Mackey by saying, "He has brought honor to his institution and was truly one of the great men of his profession." A plaque with Hovde's quote and tributes to Mackey are displayed in Mackey Arena, which was renamed in his honor in 1971.

BOILER BYTE

OCTOBER 31—AN IMPORTANT DATE FOR PURDUE UNIVERSITY

- John Purdue's birthday (1802)

- Amos Heavilon's $35,000 gift to Purdue (1892)

- Purdue Train Wreck (1903) en route to football game with Indiana University

MARY LOCKWOOD MATTHEWS

Mary Lockwood Matthews was born in Louisville, Kentucky, on October 13, 1882. When her mother died in the mid-1880s, she and her brother were adopted by Virginia Claypool Meredith, a pioneer in agricultural education and the first woman appointed to the Purdue Board of Trustees (1921).

Matthews received a bachelor's degree in home economics from the University of Minnesota in 1904. She was an instructor of clothing in the Lafayette Industrial School from 1904–08, and at the University of Minnesota the following year. She joined the Purdue faculty in 1910 as an extension home economics instructor. In 1912, she was named head of the Department of

Mary Lockwood Matthews.

George Ade (left) and John McCutcheon (right), about 1894.

Household Economics. In 1926, this became the School of Home Economics, and Matthews was appointed the founding dean.

After serving on the Purdue staff for more than forty years, she retired in June 1952. Upon retirement, she was named dean emeritus. Matthews died on June 5, 1968. The Home Economics Building was renamed Matthews Hall in her honor.

JOHN T. McCUTCHEON

John T. McCutcheon was born in Tippecanoe County on May 6, 1870. While at Purdue, he was art editor of the 1889 *Debris*, the first volume of Purdue's yearbook. He also came up with the name. An 1889 Purdue graduate, he became a cartoonist and writer with the *Chicago Morning News* and its successors the *Record* and the *Record Herald*. In 1903, he joined the *Chicago Tribune* staff, where he was editorial cartoonist, winning the Pulitzer Prize in 1931.

A world traveler, McCutcheon served as a war correspondent at the Battle of Manila Bay, the Boer War in South Africa, and World War I.

While at Purdue, McCutcheon and fellow wit George Ade began a friendship that would continue through their lives. After graduation, they collaborated on several projects, including "Stories of the Streets and the Town," which Ade wrote and McCutcheon illustrated. Purdue honored McCutcheon, naming one of the high-rise residence halls for him. When he died in 1949, his widow gave Purdue originals of many of his cartoons, which are housed in the Purdue University Libraries Archives and Special Collections Division. His fraternity, Sigma Chi, also displays some of his original drawings.

VIRGINIA CLAYPOOL MEREDITH

Virginia Claypool Meredith, a descendant of English pioneers, was born near Connersville, Indiana, on November 5, 1848. She graduated from Glendale College near Cincinnati in 1866 and the same year married Henry Clay Meredith, a graduate of Indiana University and member of the Indiana State Board of Agriculture.

All who had the privilege of working with her were constantly the beneficiaries of her kindly and farsighted wisdom.
—President Elliott about Meredith

When her husband died only twelve years after they married, Meredith assumed active charge of their 400 acre livestock ranch, successfully handling and managing the farm and its prize cattle. Meredith's involvement with Purdue began in 1889, when she became a speaker for the Farmers' Institutes, held throughout the state to educate farmers on the latest science and technology in agriculture. The origins of home economics education can be found in these Farmers' Institutes of the late nineteenth century.

"Long before home economics became a subject of instruction, farm women attended institutes and appropriated whatever pertained to the farm home, the farm family, and farm income," Meredith wrote in an unpublished history of Indiana agriculture, completed 1930. "So they were ready and eager to hear those speakers who came later to discuss, first, domestic science and afterward home economics."

She frequently petitioned Purdue presidents to introduce a home economics curriculum at the University. But it was not until 1905 that Purdue developed a Department of Home Economics. The University of Minnesota called before then, in 1897, appointing her "preceptress of the Girls' School" and charging her with establishing a home economics curriculum. Although she frequently returned to Indiana to supervise her farm, Meredith spent six years in Minneapolis.

In 1921, the State of Indiana recognized Meredith by naming her a trustee of Purdue—the first female member on that board. In addition to her work at Purdue, Meredith was a contributor and editor of *Breeder's Gazette* and an organizer of the Indiana Federation of Women's Clubs.

Beginning in 1890, when she was named "Queen of American Agriculture" after a speech in Vicksburg, Mississippi, and continuing through 1930, when the State of Wisconsin honored her for "eminent service" in agriculture, Meredith was praised again and again for her work.

At the time of her death in 1936, President Edward C. Elliott said of Meredith: "Thus comes to an end a brilliant

Virginia Claypool Meredith.

career of devoted service to the nation, the state, the University, and above all to the advancement of the place of women in our civilization. All who had the privilege of working with her were constantly the beneficiaries of her kindly and farsighted wisdom. She was an ideal trustee. The best of her life was built into the University she loved so well." X Hall, a women's residence, was renamed Meredith Hall in her memory.

JACK MOLLENKOPF

Jack Mollenkopf.

Kenneth "Jack" Mollenkopf, born in Ohio on November 24, 1905, was Purdue's most winning football coach until former coach Joe Tiller took the title in the 2008 season. An outstanding high school athlete in football and baseball, he attended Bowling Green College. An assistant coach from 1947 to 1955, Mollenkopf succeeded Stu Holcomb as head coach in 1956.

In his fourteen-year career with the Boilermakers, he suffered only one losing season, with a 3–4–2 record in 1956. Overall, his record was an impressive 84–39–9. He took Purdue to its first Rose Bowl in 1967, where the team beat USC 14–13. During his tenure, he produced fourteen All-American players, ten of them in his last five years, when the team went 40–10–1. Mollenkopf was known as "Jack the Ripper" and was seen as a father-figure by his players, stern and strict, yet very honest. In 1969, Mollenkopf retired as head coach from Purdue. Six years later, he died at age seventy-two of intestinal cancer. The indoor athletic practice facility was named in his honor and dedicated June 2, 1990.

NATIONAL SOCIETY OF BLACK ENGINEERS

Founded in 1975, the goal of the National Society of Black Engineers is "to increase the number of culturally responsible Black Engineers who excel academically, succeed professionally and positively impact the community." The society is one of the largest student-governed organizations in the country, encompassing more than 29,500 students at more than 394 chapters on five continents.

The National Society of Black Engineers emerged from a Purdue organization called the Black Society of Engineers, started in 1974 by undergraduate students Edward Barnette and Fred Cooper. Six men, dubbed "The Chicago Six," brought the movement to a national level: Anthony Harris

(ME '75), Brian Harris (IE '75), Stanley L. Kirtley (CE '75), John W. Logan, Jr. (CE '75), Edward A. Coleman (ME '75), and George A. Smith (EE '76).

EI-ICHI NEGISHI

A former student of 1979 Nobel Laureate Herbert C. Brown, Ei-ichi Negishi was named Nobel Laureate in chemistry on October 6, 2010.

Negishi was born on July 14, 1935 as a Japanese citizen in Changchun, China. In 1943, at age eight, he and his family fled to South Korea during World War II, returning to Japan at its conclusion. He spent the rest of his childhood in Japan and received his bachelor's degree from the University of Tokyo in 1958. Following his graduation he briefly worked with a Japanese pharmaceutical company, Teijin, before coming to the United States to pursue a PhD at the University of Pennsylvania in 1960 (graduating in 1963). He again joined Teijin, but soon decided an academic career suited him better.

In 1966, he joined Professor Brown's laboratories at Purdue as a postdoctoral associate, and by 1968, he was appointed assistant to Professor Brown. In 1972, Negishi left to be an assistant professor at Syracuse University, where he began the work that would lead to his Nobel Prize. From 1976 to 1978, he published several papers describing cross-coupling reactions of various organometals. His work involving zinc, aluminum, and zirconium is now called Negishi coupling. In 1976, he was promoted to associate professor at Syracuse, and in 1979, he returned to Purdue as a full professor, the same year that Brown was awarded his Nobel Prize.

While Negishi continued his research, he was appointed as the first H. C. Brown Distinguished Professor of Chemistry in 1999. He has also received many other accolades, including the Guggenheim Fellowship in 1987, the A. R. Day Award and a Chemical Society of Japan Award in 1996, the ASC Organometallic Chemistry

Ei-ichi Negishi teaching class the morning his Nobel Prize award was announced.

Award in 1998, a Humblodt Senior Researcher Award from 1998–2001, the Royal Society of Chemistry's Sir E. Frankland Prize Lectureship in 2000, and the Person of Cultural Merit and Order of Culture Awards in 2010.

Negishi has produced over 400 publications, including two books. His works have been cited over 17,000 times. His Nobel Prize in chemistry was awarded in recognition of his development of palladium-catalyzed cross-coupling during the 1970s. The 2010 Nobel Prize was shared among three chemistry researchers, Negishi, Akira Suzuki, and Richard Heck.

In 2011, Purdue announced the establishment of the Negishi-Brown Institute. The institute will support basic research in catalytic organometallic chemistry through graduate and postdoctoral fellowships, regular workshops and symposia, and establishing new relationships with industrial partners. Negishi is the center's inaugural director.

Negishi continues to conduct research and teach graduate and doctoral students at Purdue. He has a wife, Sumire, and two daughters.

PHILIP E. NELSON

Philip E. Nelson is from Morristown, Indiana. He received his bachelor's degree at Purdue in agriculture in 1956. After completing his degree, he returned to Morristown to become the plant manager of the family-owned tomato cannery, Blue River Packing Co. When the cannery was closed in 1960, he worked on his family farm for a while before returning to Purdue to become an instructor in horticulture in 1961. He earned his PhD in 1967 with a concentration on the volatility of flavor in canned tomatoes. He became a professor of food science in 1975. He served as the director of the Food Science Institute from 1975 to 1983, and then he served as the chairman of

Philip E. Nelson speaking on Friday, July 9, 2010, during a Purdue Board of Trustees meeting after board members approved a facility name change to create the Philip E. Nelson Hall of Food Science. Nelson ended a fifty-year career at Purdue with his retirement in May 2010. He was the Department of Food Science's first chairman when it was created in 1983, and he served in that position for twenty years.

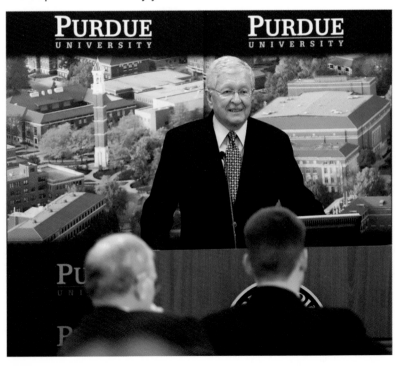

the Department of Food Science from its creation in 1983 to 2003. Nelson retired from Purdue in May 2010 at the age of seventy-five, completing a fifty-year career at the University. After his retirement, the Board of Trustees approved a facility name change to create the Philip E. Nelson Hall of Food Science. Nelson was the president of the Institute of Food Technologies 2001–02, a professional organization within the food science profession and food industry. He served on prestigious committees of the U.S. Department of Agriculture, the Food and Drug Administration, and the National Academy of Sciences. In 2007, Nelson was the first Purdue faculty member to receive the World Food Prize. He earned the award through his aseptic processing innovation, which revolutionized food trade by reducing postharvest waste and making seasonal fruits and vegetables available year-round and easier to transport worldwide.

His research and accomplishments in bulk aseptic processing are well-known worldwide. His career epitomizes the mission of Purdue University: education, research and engagement.

—President Jischke about Nelson

In 2008, Indiana Governor Mitch Daniels created the Philip E. Nelson Innovation Prize to recognize scientists annually for their discoveries, research, and inventions. Nelson has co-authored three textbooks, published in excess of seventy peer-reviewed articles, and created twelve U.S. patents and twenty-eight international patents, mostly through his research in aseptic processing.

ORVILLE REDENBACHER

Orville Redenbacher turned a childhood passion into an industry phenomenon. Born in 1907, the Brazil, Indiana native developed a passion for perfecting popcorn while in 4-H during his childhood.

Redenbacher graduated from Purdue University with a degree in agronomy in 1928. While at Purdue he was a member of the agricultural fraternity Alpha Gamma Rho and the "All-American" Marching Band. In 1988, he was awarded an honorary doctorate degree from Purdue's College of Agriculture.

After graduating from Purdue, Redenbacher worked as an agent for the Farm Bureau and managed the 12,000-acre

Orville Redenbacher.

Princeton Farms in Princeton, Indiana. Though he worked with fertilizer, he was unable to shake his obsession with popcorn, and in 1951, he teamed up with partner Charlie Bowman to buy the George F. Chester and Son seed corn plant near Valparaiso, Indiana. They renamed the company Chester Hybrids. While selling farm products for income, Redenbacher and Bowman tried thousands of hybrid strains of popcorn before finding success.

In 1970, they launched their popcorn, and by the mid-1970s, Redenbacher and Bowman had taken hold of a third of the unpopped popcorn market. In 1976, Redenbacher sold the company to Hunt-Wesson Foods, which was a division of Norton Simon, Inc. Over the next several years the company went through many ownership changes, before being finally bought by ConAgra in 1990. During this time Redenbacher moved to Coronado, California, and continued to promote his product through appearance and television commercials.

In 1979, the city of Valparaiso began the Popcorn Festival, in honor of Redenbacher and Bowman. The partners often served as grand marshals of the event.

In September 19, 1995, Redenbacher passed away suddenly from a heart attack.

DAVID ROSS

David Ross was born near Brookston, Indiana, on August 25, 1871. While growing up in Brookston and Lafayette, he evidenced a fascination for machines. On his first trip to Lafayette in 1879, his parents took him for a steamboat ride on the Wabash River. During the ride, the boy disappeared and was later found in the ship's engine room. Clearly, Ross was destined to be involved with machines.

In 1889, against his father's wishes, Ross enrolled at Purdue. The elder Ross believed college to be a waste of time, while David thought it the key to success. He studied electrical engineering, but graduated with a mechanical engineering degree because Purdue did not yet grant degrees in electrical engineering. Ross put his degree to work, founding the Prairie Telephone Company in the late 1890s, which provided the first telephone service to Brookston. He returned to his father's farm after graduation, but his real passion was for the relatively new automobile. While at the farm, Ross designed a steering gear for wagons and the new "horseless carriage." A Cleveland company wanted him to move there and develop it, but he decided to stay in Lafayette.

David Ross.

In October 1906, Ross and Jack Kneale formed the Ross Gear and Tool Company. The company also produced differentials and axles for automobiles. The company still exists today as part of TRW Commercial Steering. In all, Ross patented eighty-eight devices, most related to automobile steering and building structures and materials.

In 1921, Ross was voted as the first alumni trustee of Purdue and was later elected president of the board. He served in that capacity from 1933 until his death in 1943. During his board tenure, Ross accomplished many things for his alma mater, including:

- With the help of George Ade, Ross bought an old dairy farm north of campus and made initial contributions toward building a new stadium. Ross-Ade Stadium was dedicated during the football game between Indiana and Purdue on November 22, 1924.

- In keeping with his belief that Purdue should be one of the best engineering schools in the country, Ross purchased land on which later would be constructed the Purdue University Airport and "the Hills," the civil engineering surveying camp.

- Ross also noticed that there was not a pension fund set up for faculty at Purdue. He donated 4,000 Ross Gear and Tool shares to the University, which yielded $380,000 to set up the first pension fund.

- In 1920, Ross was asked to serve on an alumni committee that had been trying to make money for a student union since 1911. At that time, only $50,000 had been collected to build a student union. Through Ross's efforts, more than another $500,000 was raised by the time of completion of the first phase of the Memorial Union in 1924.

- Ross's dedication to Purdue is also the reason for the 1930 establishment of the Purdue Research Foundation to support research and scholarly activities of the faculty and graduate students.

Ross continued to be a major force in the community until his death on June 28, 1943. His grave is just west of the Slayter Center of Performing Arts atop Slayter Hill—part of the many acres he donated to the University. Appropriately, the epitaph on his grave reads: "David Ross, 1871–1943. Dreamer. Builder. Faithful Trustee. Creator of Opportunity for Youth."

BOILER BYTE

THE DIGNITY OF A PROFESSOR

Harvey Washington Wiley, known as the father of the United States Pure Food and Drug Act, was a professor of chemistry in Purdue's early years. At age thirty, he was the youngest member of the faculty, and he shocked the community by acquiring a bicycle and learning to ride it. Hauled before the Board of Trustees, he was told by a somber member: "Imagine my feelings and those of other members of the board upon seeing one of our professors dressed up like a monkey and astride a cartwheel riding along our streets. Imagine my feelings when some astonished observer says to me, 'Who is that?' and I am compelled to say, 'He is a professor in our university!'" Wiley offered his resignation, but it was not accepted.

Jerry Ross looking into the space shuttle during a spacewalk on the mission STS-37. Dr. Ross, Purdue's record breaking spacewalker, is also shown in the chapter opening image on page 118. *Photo courtesy of NASA.*

JERRY ROSS

Jerry Ross was born on January 20, 1948, in Crown Point, Indiana. When Ross was in fourth grade, the Russians launched *Sputnik 1* on October 4, 1957. After the launch of *Sputnik 1*, Ross started to collect any newspaper articles he could find about space work. From these articles he learned that scientists and engineers were the ones doing the work within the space program, and he decided in fourth grade that he would attend Purdue University and become an engineer.

Jerry Ross attended Purdue from September 1966 to January 1972. Ross earned his bachelor's and master's in mechanical engineering. He also met and married his wife, Karen, during his time at Purdue.

After graduating from Purdue, he entered active duty in the U.S. Air Force at Wright-Patterson Air Force Base in Ohio. In August 1975, he transferred to Edwards Air Force Base in California to attend the Flight Test Engineer course at the USAF Test Pilot School. After finishing Test Pilot School, he served as a flight test engineer on the B-1 bomber Joint Flight Test Team. In February 1979, he joined NASA and transferred to the Johnson Space Center in Houston, Texas, to work as a U.S. Air Force detailee, helping integrate military payloads into the Space Shuttle.

In May 1980, Ross's dream of going up into space became a reality when he was selected as a NASA astronaut. His first Space Shuttle flight, STS-61B, launched on December 3, 1985. During this mission they launched three communications satellites, and Ross performed his first two spacewalks to evaluate manually building structures in space.

After STS-61B, Ross had several more mission opportunities and was the first person to launch into space seven times. He is one of only three astronauts to support the U.S. Space Shuttle program from its first launch through its final landing. He is tied for third among spacewalkers worldwide and second in the United States for most spacewalks performed, with nine spacewalks. He helped to develop and create the facilities, tools, techniques, and training to build the International Space Station. He also led the team of spacewalkers who began the assembly of the ISS and was among the first to enter it on-orbit.

Ross was awarded two Defense Superior Service Medals, the Air Force Legion of Merit, four Defense Meritorious Service Medals, two Air Force Meritorious Service Medals, the National Intelligence Medal of Achievement, and fifteen NASA medals. He is the only three-time recipient of the American Astronautical Society's Victor A. Prather Award for spacewalking achievements and the only four-time recipient of the Society's Flight Achievement Award. He was named to the Purdue University Air Force ROTC Hall of Fame and was a recipient of the Honorary Doctor of Science from Purdue University in 2000. He also received the Distinguished Engineering Alumni Award from Purdue's College of Engineering in 2004. In 2003, his hometown school system, Crown Point Community School Corporation, named Jerry Ross Elementary School in his honor.

Today, Ross lives with his wife, Karen, in Houston, Texas, and he is retired. He travels often, speaking at various venues with the hope of inspiring children to follow their dreams.

Jerry Ross showing his patches from his seven missions, he was the first person to launch into space seven times. *Photo courtesy of NASA.*

SALTY DOGS

In 1947, a group of seven students formed a New Orleans-style jazz band called the Original Peerless Jazz Band. They later settled on Salty Dogs as their name, taken from an old jazz tune.

Original members of the group were Darrel Guimond, a trumpet player from Oakland City, Indiana; Tom Bartlett, a trombone player from Geneseo, Illinois; Bob "Ace" Lord, a drummer from Kewanna, Indiana; Larry "The Professor" Wilkins, a clarinet player from New Albany, Indiana; Steve Key, a tuba player from Hobart, Indiana; Brent "Knuckles" Dickson, a piano player from Hobart, Indiana; and Lynn "Obie" Oberholtzer from West Lafayette, Indiana.

Quite popular on campus and elsewhere, the Salty Dogs were once asked to play for Barry Goldwater at a Republican rally. Their early popularity grew with the help of the Purdue Reamer Club, which sold their records to help raise scholarship money.

The Salty Dogs went through several personnel changes as the students graduated. While the Salty Dogs left Purdue's campus in the early 1960s, a contingent continued to play at Purdue. Alumni members of the Salty Dogs returned to campus on occasion to play before the crowds in the Memorial Union on football weekends.

HELEN B. SCHLEMAN

In 1934, Helen B. Schleman began her tenure at Purdue as director of the first women's residence hall built after Ladies Hall was razed in 1927. She oversaw Duhme Hall, which later became part of Windsor Halls. During World War II, she took a four-year leave of absence to serve in the women's reserve of the U.S. Coast Guard where she earned the rank of captain.

Schleman returned to Purdue in 1947 as dean of women, succeeding Acting Dean Clare A. Coolidge, who had served since 1942 when Dean Dorothy C. Stratton left to direct the women's reserve of the U.S. Coast Guard. As dean, Schleman fought for the rights of women at Purdue, overseeing the end of curfew and starting a freshman conference program.

Born in Francesville, Indiana, on June 21, 1902, Schleman lived in Valparaiso, Indiana, while growing up. She earned a bachelor's degree in English from Northwestern University in 1934, a master's degree in hygiene and physical education from Wellesley College in 1928, and a master's degree in psychology and

Helen B. Schleman.

education from Purdue in 1934. Before joining the Purdue staff, she served on The Ohio State University staff from 1926 to 1932.

Schleman retired as dean of women in 1968. She went on to be the founder and first director of Span Plan, a program to encourage adult students to continue or start a college career. After retirement, she was an active member of the community, continuing her efforts in working for the rights and opportunities for women. In 1990, the student services building was named in her honor as the Helen B. Schleman Hall of Student Services.

Schleman passed away February 5, 1992, at the age of eighty-nine, leaving behind a legacy of rights and hope for all.

CAROLYN E. SHOEMAKER

Born in Lafayette, Carolyn E. Shoemaker received her bachelor's degree from Purdue in 1888 and her master's one year later. She was appointed an instructor of English in 1900 and was a professor of English literature in 1913 when appointed the first dean of women. She served until 1933, when she died of nephritis.

A major leader in the organization of the Purdue Union and the drive to raise funds for the building, Shoemaker was a Purdue

Carolyn E. Shoemaker.

Purdue was not a part of her life; Purdue was her life.
—Stanley Coulter about Shoemaker

stalwart. In giving her eulogy, Stanley Coulter, dean of men and dean of science emeritus, said of her, "Purdue was not a part of her life; Purdue was her life." Shoemaker Cooperative House is named in her memory.

ROBERT B. STEWART

Robert B. Stewart, first vice president, is credited by many as being the single most significant force in determining the character and shape of Purdue University. He was, among other things, an inveterate builder. Stewart, who came to Purdue in 1925 as chief business officer, spent thirty-six years building the University both physically and fiscally.

The list of Stewart's achievements in building and carefully structuring Purdue—and then in extending that excellence to other areas of education—is staggering. Among his many accomplishments: he developed the fiscal management system for the University, which many of the nation's colleges and

Robert B. Stewart.

universities then adopted; he helped shape the philosophy and funding of Purdue's undergraduate residence hall system; he helped develop the Purdue Research Foundation from its original seed monies of $50,000 to its present preeminence as the research arm and real estate manager for the University; he devised new ways of financing buildings through trust gifts and interest-free bonding, and enabled Purdue to purchase land and grow as needed; he headed the national committee that set up and administered the World War II military training programs on college and university campuses across the country; he established the Purdue Student Housing Corporation to administer the cooperative housing program to provide lower-cost housing to students; he helped acquire land and gifts to develop the regional campuses in Fort Wayne, Hammond, Michigan City, and Indianapolis; and he helped develop the Purdue Calumet Development Foundation to promote urban renewal.

Born March 31, 1896, Stewart grew up in the harsh cold of northern Minnesota. His father died when he was five, and his mother supported the family by running a small farm. He attended high school in Wrenshall, completing its two-year curriculum at age sixteen, and then enrolled in Central Business College in Duluth, Minnesota. He earned his diploma in 1914, then taught in Wisconsin and studied penmanship in Ohio. He then returned to Duluth to teach penmanship at Central Business College, where he met Lillian Victoria Olssen, a local teacher who was a student in his class. They married in 1918.

They both entered the University of Wisconsin in 1919, Lillian in fine arts and R. B. in economics and finance. They attended university classes in the morning and taught classes in the public schools in the afternoon. Both were elected members of the Phi Beta Kappa national scholastic honor society, the first married couple to be elected at the same time. Although he wanted to study law, R. B. accepted a position with Albion College in Michigan instead because money for law school was not available. He was hired to put the financial affairs of the small college in order.

Three years later, in 1925, Stewart received a telegram from Edward C. Elliott, president of Purdue, inviting him to interview for the position of controller. Elliott chose Stewart over two others, making Stewart, at that time twenty-nine years old, the youngest chief financial officer of any state university.

The Purdue University Stewart joined in 1925 had just celebrated its semi-centennial the year before. The enrollment was a little more than 3,200 students with a faculty and staff of 300. The campus consisted of 744 acres, 9 research farms, 31 major buildings, and 50 minor ones—including chicken houses. The entire physical plant was valued at just under $5 million.

The physical appearance of campus changed drastically during Stewart's tenure. Old, unsafe buildings, such as Ladies Hall, were torn down, and dozens of new buildings and complexes were erected. Stewart helped secure the gift and presided over the building of Cary Quadrangle. Among other major buildings completed during his watch were residences Windsor Halls, Married Student Housing (now Purdue Village), X Hall (Meredith Hall), Harrison Courts, State Street Courts, Ross-Ade Apartments (now Hilltop Apartments), Terry Courts, and three H halls (Owen, Tarkington, and Wiley) as well as the Recreational Gymnasium, the Student Hospital, Memorial Center (which now bears his name), Elliott Hall of Music, Physics Building, Civil Engineering Building, Lilly Hall of Life Sciences, Chemistry Building (Wetherill Laboratory of Chemistry), Mechanical Engineering Building, Executive Building (Hovde Hall), Lambert

He was a giant among higher education's financial administrators. Purdue would simply not be the great university it is without the tremendous influence wielded by R.B. Stewart during the 1930s, '40s, and through the '50s. He built a fiscal structure here that became the model for universities throughout the country.

—President Beering about Stewart

149

Fieldhouse and Gymnasium, Home Economics Administration (Stone Hall), Veterinary Science and Medicine (Lynn Hall of Veterinary Medicine), and the new Heavilon Hall.

Among Stewart's contributions nationally was his leadership of the committee that set up the programs to educate veterans. The Servicemen's Readjustment Act of 1944, or GI Bill, provided returning World War II veterans with money for education and job training and guaranteed loans for homes, farms, and businesses. In 1964, the United States awarded Stewart a special certificate of appreciation for his work with the GI Bill.

In 1932, Stewart purchased land on which to build his home, a forty-acre wooded tract west of campus. During the depression, his Tudor-style home was one of the few being built in the community; he often helped out the workmen by giving them advances on their wages during those hard times. In 1971, when he moved to Florida permanently, Stewart donated the home, named Westwood, to the University. It is now used as the president's residence.

Stewart died June 10, 1988. On his death, President Steven C. Beering said, "He was a giant among higher education's financial administrators. Purdue would simply not be the great university it is without the tremendous influence wielded by R. B. Stewart during the 1930s, '40s, and through the '50s. He built a fiscal structure here that became the model for universities throughout the country."

Dorothy Stratton.

DOROTHY STRATTON

Dorothy Stratton was born in Brookfield, Missouri, on March 24, 1899. She received her bachelor's degree from Ottawa University. She then pursued a master's degree in psychology at the University of Chicago and a PhD in student personnel administration from Columbia University. She also studied at Northwestern University, the University of Washington, and the Berkeley and Los Angeles branches of the University of California.

Stratton became the first full-time dean of women at Purdue in 1933. During her tenure at Purdue, the enrollment of women students increased from 500 to more than 1,400. She also saw the construction of three modern residence halls for women; the creation of a liberal science program for women in the School of Science; and the institution of an employment placement center for Purdue women. She was instrumental in establishing the Housemother's Training School that gave intensive instruction to several hundred fraternity and sorority housemothers from all parts of the country.

Dorothy Stratton was one of the truly great people in the history of Purdue University, higher education and indeed our nation. In each of [the positions she served] Dr. Stratton was a trailblazer in helping to create opportunities for women. All of us are indebted to Dr. Stratton for her courageous leadership and vision. Her 107-year lifespan touched three centuries and she was blessed to live to see many of the changes she advanced come into reality. She counted great people in history such Amelia Earhart and Lillian Gilbreth among her friends. We were indeed fortunate to count her among ours.

—President Jischke about Stratton

In 1942, she was commissioned as a senior lieutenant in the U.S. Navy. Later in 1942, she was transferred to the U.S. Coast Guard, where she became the creator and first director of the U.S. Coast Guard Women's Reserve during World War II. Upon being named director, she was promoted to lieutenant commander, then commander in January 1944, and finally to captain one month later. She was awarded the Legion of Merit Medal for her contributions to women in the military upon retirement in 1946. From 1947 to 1950 she was director of personnel at the International Monetary Fund. She next served ten years as national director of the Girl Scouts of America.

Stratton was a member of numerous organizations: John Purdue Club, President's Council, Virginia Gildersleeve International Fund, National Association of Deans of Women, American Association of University Women, Business and Professional Women's Club, National Education Association, American Association for the Advancement of Science, and associate member of the American Psychological Association, to name a few. She was the last survivor of the original women's service directors who volunteered in World War II. She died September 17, 2006 at the age of 107.

Don Thompson.

DON THOMPSON

Don Thompson was born in 1963 in Chicago. Thompson graduated from Purdue with a bachelor's degree in electrical engineering in 1984. He began his career with McDonald's as an electrical engineer in 1990. Since then, he has moved within the company, serving in positions such as president of McDonald's USA, U.S. chief operating officer, executive vice president, and division president. Thompson is also a director of Exelon Corporation, a utility service company located in Chicago.

In an article in *Black Enterprise*, he was recognized as the first African American chief operations officer. In his current role as president and chief executive officer of McDonald's Corporation, Thompson directs global strategy and operations for the 32,000 McDonald's restaurants in 117 countries.

In addition, Thompson serves on several boards for philanthropic organizations, including the Johnnetta B. Cole Global Diversity and Inclusion Institute, the Salvation Army Steering Committee for the Ray and Joan Kroc Community Centers in San Diego, and is a former board member of the San Diego Ronald McDonald House Charities.

Thompson has received recognition for his work, with both McDonald's and other leadership roles. In 2007, *Black Enterprise* magazine recognized him as Corporate Executive of the Year; in 2008, Thompson was awarded the Corporate Executive Award from the Trumpet Foundation; and in 2009, he received the Distinguished Civic Leadership Award from the Access Community Health Network. From his alma mater, Thompson was awarded the Purdue University Outstanding Electrical and Computer Engineering Award and was named a Purdue Old Master Fellow in 2006. He joined the Purdue Board of Trustees in July 2009. In 2008, Excelsior College in Albany, New York presented him with an honorary doctorate of science.

JANICE VOSS

The first female Purdue graduate to fly in space, Janice Voss received a bachelor of science in engineering from Purdue in 1975. A South Bend, Indiana native, Voss was born on October 8, 1956. Her family moved to Rockville, Illinois during her childhood and then to Wilbraham, Massachusetts, where she graduated from high school.

She continued her higher education at the Massachusetts Institute of Technology, earning a Master of Science degree

Astronaut and former Kepler mission science office director Janice Voss inspects a printout depicting the star field as seen through Kepler's eyes. *Photo courtesy of NASA.*

in electrical engineering in 1977 and PhD in aeronautics and astronautics in 1987. In addition, Voss took correspondence courses at the University of Oklahoma from 1973 to 1975, and she attended Rice University from 1977 to 1978 for graduate work in space physics.

Voss worked for NASA early in her career, at the Johnson Space Center. From 1973 to 1975, she worked for the Engineering and Development Directorate, and in 1977, she returned to work as a crew trainer, teaching entry guidance and navigation. After receiving her doctorate in 1987, Voss moved to work for with Orbital Sciences Corporation with mission integration and flight operations support. During this time she garnered recognition from the space and flight community, being awarded the Zonta Amelia Earhart Fellowship in 1982, the Howard Hughes Fellowship in 1981, and the National Science Foundation Fellowship in 1976.

Following her extensive education and work experience, NASA selected Voss for the space program in 1990, and she became an astronaut in July 1991. She flew into space on five missions from 1993 to 2000, logging over 49 days in space, 18.8 million miles, and 779 Earth orbits. Voss was awarded NASA Space Flight Medals in 1993, 1995, 1997, and 2000.

After her time in space, Voss followed technical assignments with NASA, which included mission development, robotics issues, and research. From 2004 to 2007, she served as the science director for the Kepler spacecraft at NASA's Ames Research Center in Mountain View, California. The Kepler Space Observatory, a telescope and observation spacecraft, launched on March 6, 2009, on a four-year mission to detect planets similar to Earth. Voss most recently served as the payloads lead of the Astronaut Office's Station Branch.

Voss died of breast cancer on Monday, February 6, 2012.

MARY WEBER

One of only two female Purdue graduates to become an astronaut, Mary Weber is the most recent. She received her Bachelor of Science in chemical engineering from Purdue in 1984. In 1988, she received her PhD in physical chemistry from the University of California, Berkley, and in 2002, a master's of business administration from Southern Methodist University.

Born on August 24, 1962, in Cleveland, Ohio, Weber grew up in Bedford Heights, Ohio, where she graduated from high school. After earning her doctorate, she joined Texas Instruments to research new processes for making computer chips. During her time with Texas Instruments, she received one patent and also published eight papers in scientific journals. Additionally, she is an avid skydiver, completing over 3,500 dives since 1983.

In 1992, Weber was selected by NASA to be a part of the fourteenth group of astronauts. She held many positions during her ten-year career with NASA, including working with a venture capital firm to develop a business venture leveraging space technology, chairman

Mary Weber. *Photo courtesy of NASA.*

of the procurement board for the Biotechnology Program contractor, part of a team that revamped the $2 billion plan for International Space Station research facilities, participating in critical launch, landing, and test operations at the Kennedy Space Center, testing shuttle flight software, and developing the training protocols and facilities for experiments aboard the International Space Station.

In July 1995, barely ten years after graduating from Purdue, Weber was on a flight to space, aboard *Discovery* on a ten-day mission to conduct research and deliver to orbit a NASA communications satellite. At thirty-two, Weber was one of the youngest American astronauts to go to space.

She returned to flight in May 2000 aboard *Atlantis* for work on the construction of the International Space Station. Between the two flights, Weber accumulated 450 hours in space, 7.8 million miles, and 197 orbits around the Earth.

In December 2002, Weber resigned from NASA. She is currently working as vice president at the University of Texas Southwestern Medical Center in Dallas, where she lives with her husband, Jerome.

JOHN R. WOODEN

More than eighty years after his graduation from Purdue, John Wooden remains well known as one of the greatest collegiate basketball players of all time. During his career as a Boilermaker, he became the first to earn three All-American Awards and was a three-time, first-team All-Big Ten and All-Midwestern selection. His prowess on the court, developed by legendary coach Ward "Piggy" Lambert, led the team to Purdue's only national title in 1932.

Born on October 10, 1910, near Centerville, Indiana, Wooden grew up on a farm that lacked both running water and electricity. Like many farmers of the era, the Wooden family went bankrupt and lost their farm in 1924, after which they moved to Martinsville, Indiana, a town where Wooden became a star high school basketball player. While still in high school he met Nellie Riley, whom he married in 1932.

During his career at Purdue, Wooden played a key role on the squad early on. During his sophomore year, in 1930, he averaged 8.9 points per game and led the Boilermakers to the Big Ten title. The next year, he averaged 8.2 points per game and the

12–5 just missed claiming the 1931 conference title. His senior season, Wooden raked up an unheard-of 12.2 points per game to lead the 17–1 team to the Big Ten title and on to the national championship in a 53–18 win over Chicago. At the end of that season he was named National Player of the Year and received the Big Ten Medal for outstanding merit and proficiency in scholarship and athletics as he graduated with an English degree and excellent grade point average.

Following his time at Purdue, Wooden taught high school students in Kentucky and Indiana, coaching numerous sports and playing professionally with the Indianapolis Kautskys, the Whiting Ciesar All-Americans, and the Hammond Ciesar All-Americans. His multiple careers were interrupted by World War II, when he served as a full lieutenant in the U.S. Navy from 1943 to 1946.

When the war ended, Wooden became the athletics director and coached basketball and baseball at the Indiana State Teachers College (now Indiana State University) in Terre Haute for two years. At the same time he completed a master's degree in education.

From the 1948 season until 1975, Wooden earned a reputation as a legendary coach at UCLA. He became known as the "Wizard of Westwood" and won 620 games in twenty-seven seasons and ten NCAA championships, including an eight-year streak. He was awarded the 1973 *Sports Illustrated* Sportsman of the Year Award. By the time he retired in 1975, Wooden had compiled a collegiate coaching record of 664–162 (.804), including 620–147 (.808) with UCLA.

In 1961, Wooden was inducted into the Basketball Hall of Fame as a player, and in 1973, he was again inducted as a coach. This achievement marked the first time in history a person had been inducted in both roles. He received the nation's highest civilian honor in 2003, the Presidential Medal of Freedom, and was among the first class of the College Basketball Hall of Fame in 2006. Beginning in 1977, the John R. Wooden Award has been the most coveted basketball player of the year award. It has become the basketball equivalent of college football's Heisman Trophy. On September 11, 2010, North University Drive, near the northeast corner of Ross-Ade Stadium, was renamed in Wooden's honor as John R. Wooden Drive. The dedication took place before a home football game against Western Illinois.

John Wooden. *Photo courtesy of Purdue University Athletics Communications.*

John and Nellie raised two children, James Hugh and Nancy Anne, had seven grandchildren, and eleven great-grandchildren. Nellie passed away after a fight with cancer in 1985, and John passed peacefully at the age of ninety-nine on June 4, 2010.

HERE'S TO THE BLACK AND GOLD

KEEPING THE MIND SHARP has always depended on maintaining an active body, and from Purdue's earliest years, athletics was a favorite activity of students. Athletic programs started to become institutionalized in the late nineteenth century, and fans materialized just as quickly. And whether it's a winning season or a bad year, Purdue fans show up to cheer on the teams—the coaches who spur them to excellence, and the young men and women who, in the name of sportsmanship, lead us in school spirit.

Aerial view of athletic facilities, 2001.

ATHLETIC FACILITIES

Purdue has fifteen athletic facilities including Alexander Field, Blake Wrestling Training Center, Boilermaker Aquatic Center, Birck Boilermaker Golf Complex, Holloway Gymnasium, Lambert Fieldhouse, Mackey Arena, Mollenkopf Athletic Center, Rankin Track and Field, Ross-Ade Stadium, Schwartz Tennis Center, Spurgeon Golf Training Center, Varsity Cross Country Course, Varsity Soccer Complex, and the Varsity Softball Complex. Although it is impossible to talk about each of these facilities, we would like to showcase a few of the more historically significant ones.

BIRCK BOILERMAKER GOLF COMPLEX

The Birck Boilermaker Golf Complex includes Ackerman Hills Course and Kampen Course. Formerly known as the Purdue South Course, Ackerman Hills was originally designed by William Diddel and was built in 1934. The course was redesigned by Larry Packard in 1968 and further improved in 1998 with the opening of the Birck Boilermaker Golf Complex. This course is named in recognition of Jim and Lois Ackerman.

The Kampen Course was originally known as the Purdue North Course. It was redesigned in 1998 by Pete Dye, famed golf course architect. Dye's goal was to produce a course that was both challenging for the collegiate golfer and could act as a classroom for Purdue students. The resulting Kampen Course is a unique links-style layout with strategically placed waste bunkers, native grasslands, man-made wetlands, and large greens. It measures over 7,400 yards from the championship tees and 5,300 from the forward tees. It was named in honor of Emerson Kampen.

LAMBERT FIELDHOUSE

Lambert Fieldhouse was built between 1935 and 1938 as the men's gymnasium. Located on the corner of Northwestern and Stadium Avenues, it housed the men's basketball team before the completion of Mackey Arena in 1967. In March 1971, its name was changed to the Ward L. Lambert Fieldhouse and Gymnasium in honor of legendary Purdue basketball Coach Ward "Piggy" Lambert. In 1973, women were allowed to use the facility as well. The building served as the home of the swimming and diving teams before the completion of the Boilermaker Aquatic Center in 2001. Lambert Fieldhouse currently houses the Department of Health and Kinesiology and is used by the track and field teams for practice and competition during the indoor season. It features a tunnel to Mackey Arena as well as a six-lane, 200-meter Rekortan track.

MACKEY ARENA

Renamed in March 1972 in memory of Purdue's late Athletic Director Guy J. "Red" Mackey, the arena was dedicated on December 2, 1967, before a basketball game against UCLA—a close 73–71 loss for the Purdue men. Mackey was built at a cost of $6 million, none of which came from state appropriations. In

Mackey Arena, November 1992.

View of the new Mackey Arena renovations from Northwestern Avenue, 2012.

December 1997, the playing floor was named "Keady Court" after Coach Gene Keady, head men's coach from 1980 to 2005, who is Purdue's all-time winningest coach.

The arena is used primarily for basketball games, but the floor also can be used for non-athletic student and University functions. Among the most notable was April 9, 1987, when President Ronald Reagan gave a speech to the student body in the facility.

Sellouts are the rule in Mackey, where the seating capacity was 14,123 until the 2011 renovation. There are forty-two rows of seats, which form a slight parabolic curve from the bottom row to the top. Among upgrades to Mackey since its initial construction have been new lights, vinyl-wrapped steel bleachers, and a sound system, as well as a four-sided center scoreboard with graphics and statistics boards.

The "floating" effect of the dome is achieved by the use of an indirect lighting system. The lowest intensity is at the center of the dome and increases until the perimeter is at the greatest intensity. All fixtures for the arena are mounted and serviced from the light ring suspended from the dome.

The main scoreboard in Mackey Arena was first used on November 7, 1990 in a Purdue men's basketball game against the Soviet Union. The $750,000, six-ton scoreboard contains 70,000 lights and took six weeks for the South Dakota-based Daktronics Company to manufacture. Hovering above the basketball court, the board is fifteen-feet high and twenty-five-feet-four-inches wide.

A massive $99.5 million renovation and expansion to Mackey Arena was completed and dedicated on November 11, 2011. Included in the renovation were state-of-the-art locker room facilities for men's basketball, women's basketball, men's track and field, women's track and field, baseball, softball, soccer, and wrestling. There are now also three locker rooms for visiting teams. An oversized practice basketball court was constructed on the lower level, allowing both teams to practice at the same time, rather than sharing Keady Court as they previously did. A sports medicine facility, nearly four times larger than the existing one, accessible from most locker rooms and the Intercollegiate Athletics Facility (IAF) via a tunnel, was created on the lower level. A weight training facility, four times the size of the one currently in the IAF, was also part of the project.

Premium seats were added on the east lower side of the bowl, and handicapped-accessible seating was increased by six times its previous capacity. Courtside seats are available in the west pit area, and a second tunnel is to be cut into the bowl to allow for wheelchair accessibility to the floor. There is a new ticket office, replacing the one in the IAF, which features drive-up access via Northwestern Avenue. The concourse was doubled in width, and restrooms and concession stands were drastically increased to accommodate the sellout crowds that usually inhabit Mackey during men's basketball games. Two club spaces were created on the concourse level, one for general fans to the west and a premium club to the east.

NORTHWEST SITE

The Northwest Site houses Alexander Field, Schwartz Tennis Center, and Varsity Soccer Complex. It is located near the intersection of Cherry Lane and McCormick Road on the northwest side of campus.

John and Anna Margaret Ross Alexander Field

John and Anna Margaret Ross Alexander Field replaced the 1,100-seat Lambert Field, which had been the home to Purdue baseball since 1965. Alexander Field was created to honor the late John Alexander and Anna Margaret Ross Alexander, the parents of Dave Alexander, who gave the lead gift for the project. Dave Alexander was Purdue's baseball coach from 1978–91 and an athletics administrator from 1991–94. He holds the record as

An artist rendering of the Northwest Site athletic complex includes the John and Anna Margaret Ross Alexander Field and the Varsity Golf Complex.

Purdue's winningest baseball coach with 407 victories. The $10.3 million baseball stadium seats 1,500 and may be expanded to 2,500 if the need arises. The press box includes media seating, radio and television announcing booths, and a game-day operations area. Television-quality lights allow for night games to be televised.

Dennis J. and Mary Lou Schwartz Tennis Center
The Dennis J. and Mary Lou Schwartz Tennis Center opened on Saturday, December 30, 2006. It is Purdue's first indoor tennis center. The six indoor and twelve outdoor courts are available to the public. Six outdoor courts were added to the original six varsity courts in the fall of 2010 to broaden the facility's ability

Dennis J. and Mary Lou Schwartz Tennis Center.

to hold large tournaments and groups. The 60,000-square-foot facility includes locker rooms for the teams, offices for administrative staff and coaches, an athletic training room, and seating areas for fans on the mezzanine above the courts. A pro shop, located in the lobby, is staffed with knowledgeable people ready to help players with their tennis needs. Schwartz Tennis Center also includes twelve Plexipave-cushioned courts, a layered system to give better support to the athlete's legs during play.

Varsity Soccer Complex

As part of the Northwest Site improvements, the Varsity Soccer Complex received several upgrades. In 2007, a state-of-the-art drainage system and Bermuda grass was added. Additionally, the cement dugouts were removed and replaced by Plexiglas shelters with aluminum benches. In 2012, even more upgrades were made: a centrally located press box and team building that house the home team locker room, lounge, meeting area, and athletic training facility, as well as the visiting team meeting room, concessions, and public restrooms. A new grandstand was also erected on the west side of the primary game field. The second-level press area has room for media, radio and television announcers, and game-day staff. Lights were also installed to allow for night games and potentially even more television coverage.

ROSS-ADE STADIUM

Ross-Ade Stadium is the home field for Purdue football. Originally constructed in 1924, it has been expanded numerous times since, with a maximum seating capacity of 62,500. Unique to the Big Ten Conference, Ross-Ade Stadium is the only stadium that has always featured natural grass on the playing field. The turf used Prescription Athletic Turf (PAT), known as a perfect compromise between Mother

Ross-Ade Stadium construction, July 26, 1924.

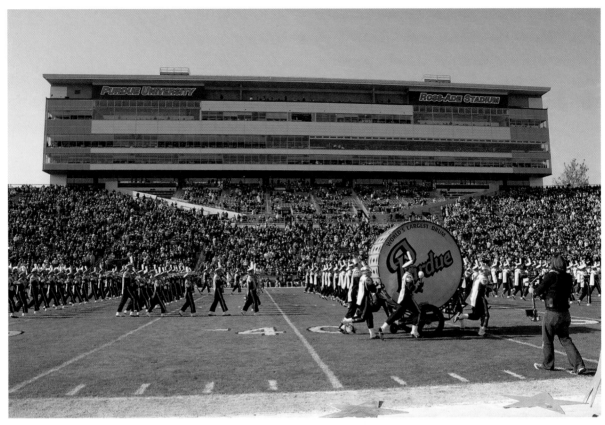

Ross-Ade Stadium, view of the press box, 2007.

Nature's own and artificial turf. It can keep the field playable and virtually divot-proof, even during a storm dumping one inch of rain per hour. A network of pipes connected to pumps capable of extracting water from the turf or watering it makes the system work.

However, after the 2005 season, the field was literally crumbling to pieces due to an aging irrigation system and unusually hot temperatures. After extensive investigation into grass types, the switch was made to Bermuda grass, and when sod was laid in 2006, Ross-Ade became the first Big Ten stadium to play on a Bermuda surface.

Fiberglass seats in the stadium alternate gold and black, with the word "Purdue" spelled out in the north end bleachers. In 2007, the stadium upgraded from a Sony JumboTron television to a new $1.7 million thirty-one-foot by sixty-eight-foot Daktronics videoboard on the south end of the field, providing live television shots and replays.

The stadium was named after its two chief benefactors, Purdue alumni David Ross, industrialist and longtime Purdue trustee, and George Ade, playwright and humorist. Ross conceived the idea for the stadium and selected the site. He and Ade purchased the sixty-five-acre tract of land where the stadium is located and presented it to the University. The stadium was dedicated on November 22, 1924 with a win, 26–7, over arch-rival Indiana University.

THE BIG TEN CONFERENCE

In 1890, Purdue joined the newly organized Intercollegiate Athletic Association of Indiana. The early league included most Indiana public and private colleges. By 1894, Purdue had tallied four consecutive league championships in football.

Concerned about encroaching "professionalism" in the league—professional players on collegiate teams and matches including both college and professional teams—Purdue President James H. Smart began talking with Midwestern university presidents. On January 11, 1895, he organized a meeting in Chicago of seven Midwestern universities to discuss possible regulations and control of athletics. Eligibility rules were discussed, and the presidents' first-known action was made: to restrict "eligibility for athletics to bona fide, full-time students who were not delinquent in their studies." Faculty representatives also established another rule unique for the time: legislation that required eligible athletes to meet entrance requirements and to have completed a full year's work. In addition, they needed to have one year of residence. Freshman and graduate students

Purdue defeats Michigan to win the Big Ten title for the first time since 1909, May 12, 2012.

were not allowed to compete in athletics, and coaches were to be appointed by university bodies "at modest salaries."

On February 8, 1896, a faculty representative of each of the seven universities met at the Palmer House in Chicago to establish standards for the regulations and administration of intercollegiate athletics. The official and original title was the "Intercollegiate Conference of Faculty Representatives," with the league called the Western Conference. The original seven members were Purdue University, University of Chicago, University of Illinois, University of Michigan, University of Minnesota, Northwestern University, and the University of Wisconsin.

The conference became the Big Nine on December 1, 1899, with the addition of Indiana University and the University of Iowa. On January 12, 1908, the University of Michigan withdrew from the conference, but was readmitted in 1917. The Ohio State University was admitted in 1912. The University of Chicago withdrew in 1946, and Michigan State University became the tenth team to join in 1949, when the conference became known as the Big Ten Conference. Penn State became the eleventh team on June 4, 1990. While the name of the conference was not changed, the logo was adapted to include an "11" in the white space between the letters. The conference added a twelfth team to the Big Ten, the University of Nebraska, on July 1, 2011, and began taking part in all sports during the 2011–12 academic year. The conference logo was recreated once again with the number "10" in the word "BIG."

MASCOTS

BOILERMAKER SPECIALS

Late in the spring semester of 1939, sophomore Israel "Izzy" Selkowitz wrote a letter to the editor of *The Purdue Exponent* advocating the construction of a mascot for the University's athletic teams.

Students decided it would take the form of a locomotive to be mounted on an automobile chassis. The Reamer Club inaugurated a campaign to raise the necessary funds to build the mascot. "Look for the silver headgear" was the slogan on 8,000 tags bearing the print of the steaming locomotive. By November 6, 1939, $451 was collected—obviously not enough to create a mobile mascot.

Boilermaker Special I dedication, September 11, 1940. Left to right: President Edward C. Elliott, George Ade, Arch Ward, and Elbert S. Bohlin.

Fundraising efforts continued as three Reamer men journeyed to Chicago for the Purdue–Northwestern football game and a meeting of the Purdue Chicago Club. Paul Hoffman, president of the Studebaker Corporation in South Bend, donated a 1940 Studebaker Champion chassis to the University.

W. H. Winterrowd, president of the Purdue Alumni Association and vice president of the Baldwin Locomotive Works in Philadelphia, offered to build the superstructure for the mascot. Designs were submitted by J. D. Hoffman, a 1940 graduate and former member of the Reamer Club, and modified by another Purdue graduate who was employed by Baldwin. Changes in the chassis were made possible by the generosity of the Ross Gear and Tool Company and the Peter Anderson Motor Company of Lafayette. The chassis arrived in Philadelphia on September 3, 1939. Winterrowd, member of the class of 1907, was a classmate of Clinton "Doc" Anderson, who lent invaluable assistance from his motor company.

Reamer Club members gathered around the Boilermaker Special I for this picture one chilly October evening, year unknown. Left to right, kneeling: John Willsey, Chuck Siler, George Olsen, Clinton "Doc" Anderson, Clarence Myers, Louis Aull, John Post, President Bert Bohlin, Harry Schaefer, Warren Archibald (glasses, no hat), Bill Delmer, and Tom Jelnik. Standing on ground from left to right: Lloyd Richardson, Bill Hudson, Dale Faut, John Emmert, Frank Danowski, Jack Wunderly, and Charlie Rechenbach. In mascot "tender" left to right: Ollie Brachman, Lee Ruffner, Walt Kline, Bob Stecker, Wayne Musser, John McElroy (light coat), Dick Pittenger (behind McElroy), and Greorge Frey. Standing, to right of the mascot cab, left to right: Gordon Griffin, Bob Donahue, Hunter Smith, Bruce Morgan, Bob Payne, (half-hidden by Morgan), Bruce Gibson, Israel Selkowitz, and Bill Knepper.

Boilermaker Special I, September 11, 1940. Left to right: Elbert S. Bohlin (president of the Reamer Club), William F. Taylor (president of the Gimlet Club), and David Rankin (captain of the football team).

The Boilermaker Special, the official Purdue University mascot, was born of a cooperative effort of two members of the class of 1907, the Reamer Club, members of the classes of 1940 and 1941, and the contributions of loyal students and alumni of Purdue. It was presented to the student body September 11, 1940, at a convocation in the Hall of Music.

Until 1953, the Special was used almost exclusively around campus and nearby areas for pep rallies and athletic contests. Wear and tear gradually caused the Special to be used only on a limited basis, and the Boilermaker Special II became both a necessity and a reality in mid-1953.

Almost identical to the original, the second Boilermaker Special used a new International Harvester truck chassis beneath the original superstructure, which was extensively reworked by employees of the Monon Railroad Shops in Lafayette. It was well built, making it possible for travel to out-of-town events. During the next six years, the Special was driven several thousand miles to and from football games, parades, and other Purdue events.

Boilermaker Special II.

Boilermaker Special III.

The Reamer Club, which serves as custodian for the mascot, added a trailer in 1956, which increased passenger capacity. This added burden steadily wore down the old pseudo-locomotive; in 1958, a committee started to plan for Boilermaker Special III.

With the leadership of Don Rosene, E.E. '59 and Phil Anderson, M.E. '59, fund raising and planning began for the new Boilermaker Special. Among the fund-raising efforts was sale of record albums by the Salty Dogs, a Purdue Dixieland jazz band. President Fredrick L. Hovde helped the Reamers get backing from the Fisher Body Division of General Motors.

In September 1960, Boilermaker Special III, weighing nine thousand pounds and measuring twenty-three feet in length, was completed and donated to Purdue by General Motors. It was officially presented to Purdue at halftime during the Purdue-Ohio State football game on October 15, 1960.

By 1992, it became evident to the Reamer Club that the Boilermaker Special III was in a state of disrepair, and that it was necessary to work on replacing the thirty-plus-year-old Special III. A task force of alumni, Reamer Club members, and Lafayette and national business leaders were appointed to start the evolution of the Boilermaker Special V.

Purdue technical graphics students helped the project by using the measurements of the Special III to design a computer model of the superstructure of the vehicle. Wabash National Corporation of Lafayette volunteered its resources to build the new superstructure for Boilermaker Special V. Donations of aluminum from Alcoa in Lafayette, automatic transmission by

Boilermaker Special V before it was painted, 1993.

Boilermaker Special V.

the Allison Division of General Motors, and chassis by Navistar International were key to the construction of the BMS V.

The Boilermaker Special V, which weighed 10,800 pounds, was dedicated at halftime of the Notre Dame football game at Ross-Ade Stadium on September 25, 1993.

For nearly eighteen years the Boilermaker Special V traveled to most away football games as well as other Purdue sporting events in and around Indiana. The BMS V traveled as far east as Richmond, Virginia; as far southeast as Tampa, Florida; as far southwest as El Paso, Texas; and as far west as Pasadena, California. An authentic five-chime freight train horn, as well as three other horns, a bell, and a whistle, aided in the ambiance of the BMS V.

On July 30, 2011, an upgraded version of the Boilermaker Special began serving the Purdue community. Using the same superstructure, the Boilermaker Special VII closely resembles its predecessor. Slightly larger and heavier with a weight of 12,800 pounds, the Boilermaker Special VII was dedicated on September 3, 2011, during halftime of the Middle Tennessee football game. A dedication luncheon was held October 1, 2011 to celebrate the new Boilermaker Special VII.

The reworking of the superstructure was completed by Wabash National Corporation. The new chassis to which it

Boilermaker Special VII.

was fitted was donated by Navistar Corporation of Fort Wayne, Indiana, and built at its Mexico plant. The detail graphics were completed by the Blumling Design Group. In addition to the existing bell, whistle, and horns, an authentic air bell from a Penn-Central Diesel Locomotive was donated. An upgraded diesel engine replaced the well-used engine from the previous version.

The Boilermaker Special participates annually in the Indianapolis 500 Parade, Lafayette Christmas Parade, and area Independence Day festivals. The Special looks to continue the traditions inherent to the mascot and like those before, travel throughout the nation for many more years helping to spread Purdue spirit.

Boilermaker X-tra Special IV.

BOILERMAKER X-TRA SPECIALS

The concept of Boilermaker Special IV, the X-tra Special, was initiated by Robert L. Geiger, a 1978 graduate, through an article in the April 1978 *Purdue Alumnus*

Boilermaker X-tra Special VI.

magazine. In response to that article, Raymond S. Jevitt, a 1950 graduate of Purdue and president of Perkinson Manufacturing in Chicago, offered to donate the materials and labor necessary to make the X-tra Special a reality.

Upon its completion, the X-tra weighed in at 1,343 pounds and measured ten feet long, four and one half feet wide, and seven and one half feet high. It was delivered to the Purdue Reamer Club on October 25, 1979, and was then presented to the University on October 27 at the President's Council Luncheon in the Purdue Memorial Union.

X-tra Special IV was disassembled to make way for X-tra Special VI. Joe Penalza, a Purdue alumnus, designed VI. The X-tra Special VI was dedicated October 19, 1996, at the end of the halftime show of the Homecoming football game against Ohio State. It stands approximately four feet wide, twelve feet long, and seven feet high.

PURDUE PETE

Purdue Pete over the years with Rowdy (back right). Rowdy, a sidekick of Purdue Pete, was a member of the spirit crew from 1997–2007.

In the spring of 1940, "Red" Samuels and "Doc" Epple, founders of University Bookstore, approached Art Evans to develop an advertising logo for the store that would set it apart from other bookstores on campus. Evans came up with a barrel-chested, mallet-wielding boilermaker.

No name was assigned to the character until 1944, when the Purdue *Debris* "borrowed" the image for the pages of the yearbook. The editors called Epple to ask the character's name. On the spur of the moment, he called it "Pete."

Pete was adopted as the University's athletic mascot in 1956. The first person to don Pete's costume was Larry Brumbaugh, an enthusiastic member of the Pep Committee.

Pete's original head and mallet were composed of papier-mâché. Mrs. John Keltner of Union City originally made the head, and Pete's uniform was donated by the Athletic Department.

Over the years since Purdue Pete came to life, he has changed with the times. Theft, disrepair, and new styles have forced out the old Pete heads and ushered in new ideas. The head has evolved from the smallish papier-mâché version to the present huge fiberglass head. His expression has changed as well. The content grin worn by Brumbaugh evolved into a mean look, but again returned to the more pleasant demeanor of today's Pete.

Multiple students now share the role of Purdue Pete, appearing at all home and away football games, home volleyball matches, home men's and women's basketball games, and post-season events. Pete also stops in on Olympic sport events and makes his rounds to alumni and University functions, in addition to local school fund-raisers. He also sometimes visits hospitals and has had several appearances at weddings.

TRAVELING TROPHIES

Annual battles for traveling trophies keep tradition alive and well at Purdue. These trophies maintain rivalries and several are rich with histories of being misplaced, stolen, or originating from unique places.

MONON SPIKE

The Monon Spike volleyball trophy was created in 1981. The traveling trophy was the brainchild of then-Purdue Head Coach Carol Dewey and her senior captain and co-captain at the time, Donna Hardesty and Anne McMenamy.

The trophy is a portion of a railroad tie from the Monon Railroad, with a bronzed spike driven through it. From the spike hang bronze letters of the winning school. As is traditionally done with its sister trophy, the Old Oaken Bucket, a "P" or "I" link is added to the chain annually, signifying the victor of the season's second match between Purdue and Indiana.

When unveiled at the media luncheon in September 1981, the trophy already was adorned with six "P's" and one "I," representing matches dating back to 1975, when the volleyball program at Purdue became a varsity sport. Purdue won twenty-four consecutive matches against Indiana from 1978 to 1985.

The Monon Spike.

THE GOLDEN BOOT

Another representation of the intense rivalry between Purdue and Indiana, the Golden Boot travels between the two schools during the soccer showdown each year. The trophy came into being in 2002 under Coach Robert Klatte, who began the soccer program at Purdue and continues to coach it today.

For each win, the victorious team adds either a "P" or "I" emblem to the trophy. Although the trophy only came into existence in 2002, the links on it date back to the team's first meeting in 1999, which Indiana won. Since then the Hoosiers have been unable to defeat the Purdue team, but were able to tie, 1-1, in 2005 and 2008.

THE CANNON

The Cannon was conceived by Purdue students over 100 years ago, but it was first presented as a trophy by an Illinois alumnus in 1943.

It all started in 1905, when a group of Purdue students took a small Cannon to Champaign, Illinois, in anticipation of firing it to celebrate a Boilermaker victory after the Purdue-Illinois football game. Purdue won the game 29–0, but the students could not fire the Cannon because Illinois supporters Quincy A. Hall and his fellow Delta Upsilon fraternity brothers had discovered it, hidden in a culvert near the Illinois field. They confiscated it before the Purdue students could start their "booming" celebration. The Cannon remained in the fraternity house for a number of years.

Later, Hall moved the Cannon to his farmhouse near Milford, Illinois, where it survived a fire and gathered dust. In 1942, Hall brought it out to be presented as a traveling trophy between the two schools when the rivalry resumed in 1943, following a twelve-year lapse.

At one time, the Cannon was destroyed accidentally and the pieces were given to Purdue. The schools then

Students gathered around the Canon before the Purdue-Illinois game, 1962.

purchased a new and smaller replica of the Cannon. When Purdue is in possession, the Tomahawk Service and Leadership Honorary maintains it; while at Illinois, the Illini Pride shares the maintenance duty.

The Cannon.

OLD OAKEN BUCKET

One of the oldest and most prestigious football trophies in the nation, the Old Oaken Bucket is given annually to the winner of the Purdue-Indiana football game. Chicago alumni from Purdue and Indiana met in 1925 to discuss the adoption of a trophy to symbolize the rivalry between their alma maters.

One Indiana graduate at that meeting told the gathering about the Little Brown Jug trophy between Michigan and Minnesota that dated back to 1909. He believed that it was about time for the Chicagoans to find a suitable trophy for the Purdue-Indiana gridiron clash.

Representatives from each camp were assigned the task of coming up with an idea for a football prize. Russell Gray of Purdue and Clarence Jones of Indiana were given the task of finding that trophy. At a later meeting, they recommended that "an old oaken bucket would be a most typical trophy from this state and should

Purdue defeats IU to win the Old Oaken Bucket, November 26, 2011.

Old Oaken Bucket.

be taken from a well somewhere in Indiana." They also proposed that the chain for the bucket should be made of bronze block "P" and "I" letters.

The first bucket was neither old nor oaken. It was a shiny new model purchased from a Chicago mail-order firm. Clearly, this would not do.

The present bucket was found in disrepair on the old Bruner farm between Kent and Hanover in southern Indiana. Purdue's Fritz Ernst and Wiley J. Huddle of Indiana found the bucket, and it is said that General John Hunt Morgan's command used it during a jaunt through Indiana during the Civil War.

The bucket—rotting and covered with green moss and mold—was taken back to Chicago and refurbished by a carpenter in time for the 1925 game at Bloomington. That year, the Boilermakers and the Hoosiers battled four quarters to a 0–0 tie.

The Old Oaken Bucket has had an exciting history, several times having been kidnapped by partisans from both schools. Twice it was missing so long that it was given up as lost, only to turn up mysteriously just before or after the annual game. Purdue's George Ade and Harry Kurrie, president of the Monon Railroad, presented the bucket as a traveling trophy after the 1925 game. All the letters in the chain are of solid bronze except for the 1929 "P," which is made of gold. After whipping the Hoosiers 32–0 at Bloomington, students contributed "nickels, dimes, and quarters" on the train ride back to Lafayette to purchase the link. Purdue also has a "P" with a diamond in the base representing Purdue's 14-13 victory over Southern California in the 1967 Rose Bowl. Indiana has a gold "I" with a diamond in its base that represents IU's unsuccessful trip to Pasadena in 1968.

SHILLELAGH

In 1957, the late Joe McLaughlin, a merchant seaman and a Notre Dame Irish fan, donated the Shillelagh, which he brought from Ireland to be a traveling trophy between Purdue and Notre Dame. After each football clash between the two schools, a miniature gold football engraved with the winner's initials and the score is attached to the stand of the Shillelagh. The trophy is given to the victor until the next game between the schools.

Shillelagh.

BARN BURNER

Beginning with the 1993–94 season, the Purdue and Indiana
women's basketball teams have played an annual game for the
Barn Burner Trophy. The traveling trophy is similar in concept
to football's Old Oaken Bucket, volleyball's Monon Spike, and
soccer's Golden Boot. It is a wood plaque with a drawing of
a barn and an attached basketball hoop, which best describes
basketball in Indiana. Sara Lee Corporation funded the plaque as
part of its Discover Women's Sports Program.

Purdue has won sixteen of the nineteen Barn Burner Trophy
meetings, including the first three contests and thirteen of the
last fourteen. The Boilermakers won 90–58 in West Lafayette on
February 26, 2012.

In the overall series, Indiana won seventeen of the first
nineteen meetings from 1976 to 1986, but Purdue has turned
the tables by winning forty-seven of the last fifty-five—including
seven in a row, twelve of fourteen, eighteen of twenty-one, and
twenty-seven of thirty-one—to take a 49–25 advantage.

Shillelagh held by Moose
Krause, Notre Dame athletic
director; Joe McLaughlin, trophy
donor; and Guy Mackey, Purdue
athletic director, 1957.

Victory Bell.

VICTORY BELL

The Victory Bell, formerly known as the Purdue Bell, was purchased in 1877 from the Vandusen and Tift Company of Cincinnati. It originally rested on top of the old power plant (called the Boiler and Gas House) and was used as a rising bell and a class bell. It was also rung at ten o'clock each night, at which time the students were supposed to retire.

When the old heating plant was torn down in 1903, the Victory Bell was placed in the locomotive lab. In 1904, when Purdue beat Indiana in football 27–0, the students dragged the Victory Bell out of the museum and took it with them on the traditional victory parade into Lafayette, leaving it on the courthouse steps. After this had occurred several times, the administration grew tired of retrieving the Victory Bell, and President Winthrop Stone ordered it hidden. It was buried in a gravel pit about where Hovde Hall now stands, until the class of 1907 dug it up after a search of three weeks. The Victory Bell was cleaned, and a permanent frame was constructed by students of the University shops.

In April 1906, the Victory Bell was put in the American Railway Museum on campus again. The money to pay for the carriage was donated by the classes of 1906, 1907, 1908, and 1909.

In 1916, the Student Council spearheaded a campaign to provide housing for the historic Victory Bell. Plans were drawn and funds obtained from students, alumni, and faculty. The cornerstone was laid on April 29, 1916, and the building was completed before June commencement of that year. The original Bell House was on the south end of Stuart Field, about 200 feet east of the Armory. In 1939, it was moved to a location between Ross-Ade Stadium and Cary Quadrangle.

The Victory Bell now is brought out by the Gimlet Club for all home football games. Once rung only after every Big Ten home football game victory, the bell now sounds for each Purdue win. It is housed in the stadium garage during the off-season, with care of the Victory Bell being the responsibility of the Gimlet Club.

HALL OF GLORY

The football Hall of Glory, just inside the doors of Mollenkopf Athletic Center, honors past and present Boilermakers, bringing the history of Purdue to life. With information dating from the first football squad in 1887, the Hall of Glory opened in 1998.

Bowl trophies are on display, as is a selection of memorabilia from the 100-plus years of Purdue football. Three "time capsules" show uniforms of the 1930s, 1960s, and the 1990s. Another set of displays and photographs shows a decade-by-decade history of the team. Former and current NFL players are featured in a sports card format in the lobby display. Traveling trophies, such as the Old Oaken Bucket, are also on display.

INTERCOLLEGIATE ATHLETICS HALL OF FAME

Purdue introduced its Intercollegiate Athletics Hall of Fame in August 1994. Thirteen former athletes and coaches were selected for the inaugural class. The Hall of Fame outdoor display, which opened in September 1995, is located northeast of Mackey Arena and features obelisks with the names of Hall of Fame members, flags, and lighting.

Selected by a committee of six former athletes and five administrators from nominations solicited from fans, athletes, and coaches, Hall of Fame members can be former athletes, coaches, or administrators. There is a five-year waiting period from the time a candidate leaves Purdue before he or she is eligible for nomination.

All names and classes of inductees are listed on the Purdue Athletics website.

PURDUE TRAIN WRECK

The crowds were thick and boisterous at the Big Four Railroad Station that cool, gray Saturday morning of October 31, 1903. So many fans wanted to see the Purdue-Indiana football game that two special trains were chartered. Except for the first two cars, which were reserved for the team and the band, the first string of fourteen wooden coaches was filled by 7:30 a.m.

For the first time, Indianapolis was hosting a college game. The 10,000 seats in the new Washington Park Stadium were to be filled by kickoff at 2:15 p.m. Plans called for the specials to arrive shortly after 10 a.m., roughly ten minutes apart. The band and the team would then lead a parade of about 1,000 fans though downtown to the Denison Hotel. There the players would have a snack and get ready for the game. Many planned to stay in town with friends and sweethearts for an exciting weekend.

But plans went awry, and the first train would never arrive. Fifty-nine miles into its journey, the train rounded a curve and crashed into a ten-section group of coal cars that were being switched from a siding. Seventeen people would lose their lives and more than forty were seriously hurt. The dead included thirteen players, the trainer, a coach, a student manager, and a wealthy booster. In addition, twenty-nine players were hospitalized. Purdue's season ended abruptly at 4–2, and the carnage would leave a devastating void through the years.

Purdue train wreck, October 31, 1903.

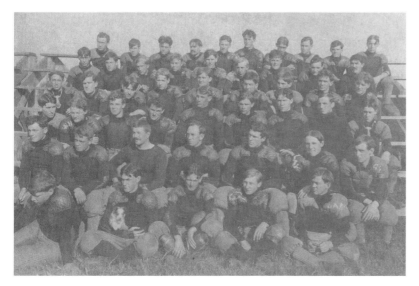

1903 Purdue football team.

The time leading up to the tragedy was filled with anticipation. Many in the Lafayette crowd had been at a bonfire the night before when some zealous freshmen added a few sheds and outhouses to a pyre that bathed the countryside in light for miles around. Several popular ditties had been converted into fight songs with special lyrics, and a half dozen of these appeared on the front page of the morning newspaper. People clustered on the railroad platform, tittering over the words and breaking into snatches of songs.

But there were eerie exceptions to the jubilant mood. I. S. Osborn, the short, wiry Purdue captain, would days later tell of a premonition while on that platform. As he moved toward the train, he sensed the gnawing fear that something was going wrong, but he chalked it up to pregame jitters and climbed aboard.

At about the same time, a former Lafayette postmaster, G. Wilson Smith, rose in his seat in the first coach, where prominent boosters were occasionally invited to join the team. He had a sudden sense of foreboding, a warning, he said later, to move elsewhere in the train. He walked past Osborn and took a seat five cars farther back.

Within two hours, the first four coaches would be on the ground, and the first car, the one with the team, would be reduced to splinters and pieces of human flesh. Both Smith and Osborn, who sustained a broken leg, would survive.

The story of how the wreck happened would unravel over the next several years after the tragedy. Accounts were that when the Purdue Special left Lafayette, a routine message went to the dispatcher in Kankakee, Illinois. The train already had been

BOILER BYTE

PARK IT HERE

During the 1970s, Purdue lovers used to "park" at this wall. Once the residence halls allowed room visitation, the popularity of this hangout diminished. The wall is located on Stadium Avenue west of Slayter Center for the Performing Arts.

granted the right-of-way to Indianapolis, and the dispatcher tapped out the message to stations along the way.

In Indianapolis, a telegraph operator at the Shelby Yard Station signaled in code that he'd heard, and he hastily scribbled the "order" on a flimsy sheet of railroad paper. He turned to give the message to the yardmaster, who would keep the switch engines from using the main line, but the yardmaster had just gone out. The telegraph operator, H. Bishop, figured the yardmaster would be back, and he put the message aside. Soon he was lost in the hypnotic song of the wire, and the flimsy piece of paper became buried under the other messages beside his arm. In two hours, that paper would be in his pocket, and he would have slipped out the door before anyone thought to ask questions. In another week, as a result of the tragedy that ensued, he would be working for another railroad.

Up until the moment of tragedy, it had been a jolly ride. Fullback Harry Leslie, who had played the three previous years and was team manager in 1903, had gone to the second car, where the band and some thirty young women fiddled with those special fight songs. Leslie, who twenty-five years later would become governor of Indiana, could feel the train slowing and see a few low shanties on the edge of the city, and he rose to get his things. As Leslie entered the first car, he saw Osborn sitting quietly in a seat that faced the rear, a preoccupied look on his face. Other players were standing up, reaching for their coats, laughing, and jostling. Some loosened up by stretching in the aisle.

Otis McCormick, a substitute end, started to rise from his seat in the middle of the car but sat down when someone mentioned there were still four miles to go. Assistant Coach

Passenger cars from the 1903 train wreck.

Eddie Robertson plopped onto the armrest beside him and asked if his cold was any better. Robertson then turned to a pair of subs, Gabriel Drollinger and Walter Roush, in the seat ahead.

Someone told a joke, everyone laughed, and then Coach Oliver Cutts, a bulky athlete fresh from Harvard, began to tell a story as he leaned against the door in the back of the coach. Just before the fateful time of 9:45 a.m., Leslie had started to make his way to the middle of the car. He smiled at McCormick. "Hello, Ott," he said, just as the brakes went on and the whistle began to shriek.

R. W. Rusterholz, manager of the student newspaper, felt the cold sweat of the alarm. He had broken a leg in a train wreck in Peoria and knew what it meant when the engineer whistled for emergency brakes. Unaware of what was ahead, he shouted, "Look out, boys!" but by then it was far too late. As Engine 350 came around a bend near Eighteenth Street in Indianapolis, the engineer, W. A. Shumaker, saw that E. J. Smith was backing his ten-car section of steel-constructed, coal-laden cars along the main line. Shumaker applied the air brakes, reversed the engine, and leaped from the cab.

The first four coaches of the train were shattered. The first car, which contained the team, trainers, and managers as well as a few of the most loyal followers, was split in half. The floor was driven beneath a gondola, and the roof fell across the top of another. Bodies were everywhere. All of the casualties were limited to the team's car. All those who had been seated around McCormick now were dead. McCormick somehow had gone through a window and landed on his feet. Players hung from wooden beams and slowly slipped into puddles of blood. Clothing, footballs, padded jerseys, and pennants tied to canes were strewn along the track. Osborn, his legs pinned beneath a beam, waved rescuers away. He knew that only a leg was broken.

In all, there were thirteen players killed in the crash: Thomas Bailey, Joseph Coates, Gabriel Drollinger, Charles Furr, Charles Grube, Jay Hamilton, Walter Hamilton, Russell Powell, Wilburt Price, Walter Roush, George Shaw, Samuel Squibb, and Samuel Truitt. In addition to these, the trainer, Pat McClaire, and a student manager were killed. One Lafayette man, Newton Howard, was a victim, as was Edward C. Robertson, a 1901 grad who had returned to help coach the team in the battle against the Hoosiers. Coach Cutts and manager Leslie were injured.

Debris from the 1903 tragedy.

The second car, which held the Purdue Military Band and a few ladies, tumbled into a gravel pit, the seats were torn loose, and everyone was piled into one end. No one was killed, and all occupants escaped serious injury. It took a few moments for the shaken passengers beyond the fourth car to realize what had happened ahead. But they soon comprehended the severity of the situation and poured out to help.

Women surrounded the injured and tore their petticoats into bandages. In seconds, they were joined by dozens of residents of the shantytown beside the tracks—women and children with buckets of water and men with strong arms to rip through the rubble. Carriages and wagons were commandeered along the nearest street a quarter-mile away, and a procession of bruised and mangled forms hobbled to the hospitals. One young medical student brushed the grime from a vaguely familiar face and stared into the dead eyes of his brother.

Further tragedy was averted when a brakeman had the presence of mind to run back as hard as he could to stop the second special before it could pile into the first. That train was re-routed over the Belt Line into Union Station, arriving shortly after another special from Bloomington laden with Hoosiers. There they all heard the news and together they walked downtown, numbed and shaken. The game was not played, and the money from advance ticket sales was turned over to the Purdue Athletic Association. As a gesture of good faith, IU offered to play a benefit game against Notre Dame to raise additional funds.

W. J. Jones of the U.S. Agricultural Experimental Station at Purdue suggested a gymnasium be built in memory of those who died in the wreck. On November 6, a meeting was held to organize a drive to raise funds. On May 30, 1908, ground was broken. The cost for the new gym was $85,000. The University supplied $25,000. New York Central Railroad donated $15,000, and George Ade gave $2,500. The rest of the money was raised through small contributions. On May 29, 1909, nearly a year later, the Memorial Gym was dedicated. Tradition dictates that everyone bares his or her head when entering the building, which is now known as Felix Haas Hall.

COACHES

BASEBALL

1888–91	No head coach
1892–93	W. M. Phillips
1894–99	No head coach
1900	W. H. Fox
1901–02	Bill Friel
1903–04	J. C. Kelsey
1905	Phil O'Niel
1906–14	Hugh Nicol
1915–16	B. P. Pattison
1917, 1919–35, 1945–46	Ward Lambert
1918	John Pierce
1936–42	Dutch Fehring
1943–44	C. S. "Pop" Doan
1947–50	Mel Taube
1951–55	Hank Stram
1956–59	Paul Hoffman
1960–77	Joe Sexson
1978–91	Dave Alexander
1992–98	Steve Green
1998–Present	Doug Schreiber

Top: Group picture after Purdue defeated Michigan to win the Big Ten title for the first time since 1909, with Coach Doug Schreiber dressed in gold, May 12, 2012.

Bottom: Dave Alexander, Purdue's winningest baseball coach with 407 victories.

Top: 1902 basketball team. Left to right: back row: Coach Freeman, Conroy, Caldwell, Miller, Smith, and Curd (manager); front row: Cook, Peck, Preimann, Lucus, Knapp, and Collier.

Middle: Men's basketball team, 1931–32.

Bottom: Robbie Hummel rips the ball away from Ohio State's Evan Turner, January 12, 2010.

MEN'S BASKETBALL

1897	F. Homer Curtis
1900–01	Alpha P. Jamison
1902	C. M. Besy
1903	C. I. Freeman
1904	No head coach
1905	James L. Nufer
1906–08	C. B. Jamison
1909	E. J. Stewart
1910–12	Ralph Jones
1913–16	R. E. Vaughn
1917, 1919–45	Ward Lambert
1918	J. J. Maloney
1946–50	Mel Taube
1951–65	Ray Eddy
1966–72	George King
1973–78	Fred Schaus
1979–80	Lee Rose
1981–2005	Gene Keady
2005–Present	Matt Painter

WOMEN'S BASKETBALL

1975–76	Deborah Gebhardt
1976–86	Ruth Jones
1986–87	Marsha Reall
1987–96	Lin Dunn
1996–97	Nell Fortner
1997–99	Carolyn Peck
1999–2006	Kristy Curry
2006–Present	Sharon Versyp

MEN'S CROSS COUNTRY

1908	C. H. Wilson
1909–11	Ralph Jones
1912–13	Arbor Clow
1914–15	James Temple
1916–28	Eddie O'Connor
1929–30	Earl Martineau
1931–35	Orval Martin
1936–42	Herman Phillips
1943–45	Homer Allen

1946–51	Dave Rankin
1952–66	No team
1967–72	Roger Kerr
1973–Present	Mike Poehlein

WOMEN'S CROSS COUNTRY

1978–88	Fred Wilt
1989–92	Carol Stevenson
1993–2001	Ben Paolillo
2001–Present	Mike Poehlein

FOOTBALL

1887	Albert Berg
1889	G. A. Reisner
1890	C. L. Hare
1891–92	Knowlton Ames
1893–95, 1901	D. M. Balliet
1896	S. M. Hammond
1897	W. S. Church
1898–1900	Alpha P. Jamison
1902	C. M. Beat
1903–04	Oliver F. Cutts
1905	A. E. Hernstein
1906	M. E. Witbham
1907	L. C. Turner
1908–09	F. Speik
1910–12	M. H. Horr
1913–15	Andrew L. Smith
1916–17	Cleo A. O'Donnell
1918–20	A. G. "Butch" Scanlon
1921	W. H. Dietz
1922–29	James M. Phelan
1930–36	Noble E. Kizer
1937–41	A. H. "Mal" Elward
1942–43	Elmer H. Burnham
1944–46	Cecil Isbell
1947–55	Stuart Holcomb
1956–69	Jack Mollenkopf
1970–72	Bob DeMoss
1973–76	Alex Agase
1977–81	Jim Young

Top: Purdue defeated Duke 62–45 in Coach Carolyn Peck's final game as head coach to win the National Championship, 1999.

Bottom: Women's basketball, Katie Gearlds, 2005.

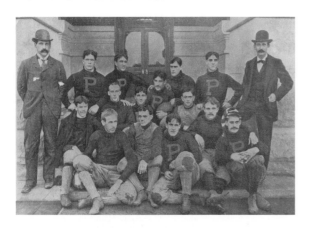

Top left: Football team, 1895.

Top right: 1903 foursome.

Middle: Leroy Keyes gains some yards against the Hoosiers during the November 25, 1967 game in Bloomington.

Bottom: Football quarterback Drew Brees celebrating the November 17, 2000 win over Indiana University at Ross-Ade Stadium which secured a trip to play in the 2001 Rose Bowl.

Purdue football quarterback Caleb TerBush, 2011.

Football coaches, continued

1982–86	Leon Burtnett
1987–90	Fred Akers
1991–96	Jim Colletto
1997–2008	Joe Tiller
2009–Present	Danny Hope

MEN'S GOLF

1921	No coach
1922	G. A. Young
1923–28	Burr Swezey
1929–37	Jack Bixler
1938–44	Harry Allspaw
1945, 1951–74	Sam Voinoff
1946–50	Loomis Heston
1975–93	Joe Campbell
1994–97	Bob Prange
1998–Present	Devon Brouse

Women's golf, Numa
Gulyanamitta, 2010.

WOMEN'S GOLF

1976–90	Paul Snider
1991–93	Susan Stump
1994–97	Bob Prange
1998–Present	Devon Brouse

MEN'S INDOOR TRACK AND FIELD

1911–12	Ralph Jones
1913	Arbor Clow
1914	James Mahan
1915–16	James Temple
1917–29	Eddie O'Connor
1930–31	Earl Martineau
1932–36	Orval Martin
1937–43	Herman Phillips
1947–81	Homer Allen
1982–2001	Mike Poehlein
2001–04	Lissa Olson
2004–Present	Jack Warner

WOMEN'S INDOOR TRACK AND FIELD

1976	JoAnn Grissom
1977	Jim McMillian
1978–89	Fred Wilt
1990–92	Carol Stevenson
1993–2001	Ben Paolillo
2001–04	Lissa Olson
2004–Present	Jack Warner

Men's track team, 1945.

MEN'S OUTDOOR TRACK AND FIELD

1888–99	No coach
1900	F. Homer Curtis
1901	W. J. Hyland
1902–03	Charles Freeman
1904	Ed Wheeler
1905	James Nufer
1906–08	C. B. Jamison
1909	C. H. Wilson
1910–12	Ralph Jones
1913	Arbor Clow
1914	James Mahan
1915–16	James Temple
1917–29	Eddie O'Connor
1930–31	Earl Martineau
1932–36	Orval Martin
1937–43	Herman Phillips
1944–46	Homer Allen
1947–81	Dave Rankin
1982–2001	Mike Poehlein
2001–04	Lissa Olson
2004–Present	Jack Warner

Purdue track, left to right: Ray Marozek, Steve Lutcher, and Al Gaulke, 1939.

Top: Purdue women's track, 2011.

Bottom: Softball, Molly Garst, 2011.

WOMEN'S OUTDOOR TRACK AND FIELD

1976	JoAnn Grissom
1977	Jim McMillian
1978–89	Fred Wilt
1990–92	Carol Stevenson
1993–2001	Ben Paolillo
2001–04	Lissa Olson
2004–Present	Jack Warner

SOFTBALL

1994–2005	Carol Bruggerman
2005–Present	Kim Maher

SOCCER

1997–Present	Robert Klatte

MEN'S SWIMMING AND DIVING

1919–20	M. L. Clevett
1921–22	J. J. Barr
1923	J. J. Merriam
1924	G. H. Aylesworth
1925–38	Larry La Bree
1939–69	Dick Papenguth
1970–85	Fred Kahms
1986–Present	Dan Ross

WOMEN'S SWIMMING AND DIVING

1976	Laura Pfohl
1977–79	Tim Kurtz
1980–81	Sherry Weeks
1982–85	Fred Kahms
1986–87	Kathy Wickstrand–McIntosh
1988–2008	Cathy Wright-Eger
2008–Present	John Klinge

MEN'S TENNIS

1914–16	C. M. James
1917–19	No coach
1920–23	E. R. Sidwell
1924	G. H. Aylesworth
1925–64	Larry La Bree
1965–79	Ed Eicholtz
1980–83	Ron MacVittie
1984–94	Ed Dickson
1995–Present	Tim Madden

WOMEN'S TENNIS

1976–77	Jocelyn Monroe
1978–80	Ann Wilson
1981–82	Nancy Janco
1983–84	Carrie Meyer
1985–86	Ed Dickson
1987–91	Helyn Edwards
1992–2007	Matt Iandolo
2007–Present	Laura Glitz

Top: Soccer, Jessica Okoroafo, 2005.

Middle: Men's swimming and diving, David Boudia, 2008. Boudia was a member of the 2008 and 2012 U.S. Olympic Team. He won a bronze and gold medal at the London 2012 Olympics.

Bottom: Women's swimming and diving, 2011.

195

Top: Men's tennis, P.J. Jones, 2010.

Bottom: Volleyball, Rachel Davis, 2010.

VOLLEYBALL

1975–94	Carol Dewey
1995–99	Joey Vrazel
1999–2002	Jeff Hulsmeyer
2002–Present	Dave Shondell

WRESTLING

1913–14	N. Embleton
1915–22	Fred Paulsen
1923–24	W. S. Von Bermuth
1925–29	Herb Miller
1930–31	Leslie Beers
1932–33	Guy Mackey
1934–37	Program discontinued
1938–69	Claude Reeck
1970–75	Don Corrigan
1976–80	Mark Sothmann
1981–88	Bill Trujillo
1989–92	Mitch Hull
1993–2007	Jessie Reyes
2007–Present	Scott Hinkel

ATHLETIC DIRECTORS

1904–05	O. F Cutts
1906–14	Hugh Nicol
1915–18	O. F. Cutts
1919–30	N. A. Kellog
1931–36	Noble E. Kizer
1937	R. C. Woodworth (interim)
1938–39	Noble E. Kizer
1940	Edward C. Elliott (interim)
1941	A. H. Edward
1942–71	Guy "Red" Mackey
1971–92	George S. King, Jr.
1992	John W. Hicks (interim)
1993–Present	Morgan J. Burke

Top: Men's basketball, E'Twaun Moore dunking the ball, 2011.

Bottom: Women's swimming and diving, 2010.

MENTIONING THE HONORABLE

PURDUE HAS A LONG TRADITION of honoring distinguished people who have contributed to the University. Whether student or alumnus, faculty or administrator, brain or jock, or just a loyal supporter of the University, recipients of these various awards have helped to bring national recognition to Purdue. Some of these awards are memorialized with plaques that remind us of our forebears' standards of service; some of them are established in the name of an outstanding individual; some include modest cash awards. They all promote and pay tribute to excellence.

MEMORIAL AWARDS

FLORA ROBERTS AWARD

The Flora Roberts Award for the outstanding senior woman was provided for in her will. Roberts, a graduate of the Purdue class of 1887 and former librarian, died in 1925. Awarded to the best all-around female member of the graduating class, the Flora Roberts Award is designed to commemorate "the ideal Purdue woman," who is outstanding in "character, citizenship, leadership, and scholarship."

The Flora Roberts Award was first given in 1927. During the World War II years, the award was discontinued.

In March 1958, the Reamer Club presented to Vice President R. B. Stewart a plan to honor the outstanding senior woman. It was found that this proposed award somewhat paralleled the Flora Roberts Award. A joint student-faculty committee recommended to the Board of Trustees the two awards be combined and that the Flora Roberts Award be re-instituted. Awards have been presented each year since 1958.

The names of the winners of the Flora Roberts Award are inscribed on an obelisk at the northeast corner of the Purdue Mall. The awards are presented during the University Honors Convocation in April. In earlier years, the awards had been on plaques along the Hello Walk.

G. A. ROSS AWARD

George A. Ross of Lafayette, a 1916 graduate of Purdue University and the first full-time executive secretary of the Purdue Alumni Association, presented the University with an endowment to establish an award for the outstanding student in each graduating class. The G. A. Ross Award was first given in 1959.

The award is presented annually to a senior male who has demonstrated "high standards of academic achievement, evidence of outstanding leadership, strength of character, and overall contributions to the University." The recipient of the award receives the G. A. Ross medal, a certificate, and a cash prize. The names of the winners are inscribed on an obelisk at the northeast corner of the Purdue Mall.

During his undergraduate years at Purdue, Ross was quite active in student affairs. He served as editor of *The Purdue*

BOILER BYTE

POT AND DERBY WEEK

Pot and Derby Week was the week before the first football game, when the seniors would try to steal freshmen's caps and the freshmen would try to steal the seniors' cords, canes, and derbies. "Stolen" items had to be returned the Saturday of the first home football game.

President Hovde presents the
G. A. Ross Award to Robert
Sidney Sorensen. George Ross
is shown at right, 1963.

Exponent for almost two years and was a member of Alpha
Tau Omega social fraternity, Sigma Delta Chi professional
journalistic society, Iron Key, Purdue Union building committee,
and Tau Kappa Alpha debating honorary, of which he was one of
the founders.

DISTINGUISHED ALUMNI AWARD

This award recognizes meritorious service to Purdue University
and the Purdue Alumni Association. Established in 1945, this
is the Alumni Association's highest award and can only be given
with the approval of the Alumni Association Board.

The Special Boilermaker Award,
presented by the Purdue Alumni
Association.

Special Boilermaker Awards presented to, from left, David Downey, Betsy Marti, and Gene Keady at the Old Oaken Bucket football game against Indiana University, Saturday, November 20, 2004.

SPECIAL BOILERMAKER AWARD

This award recognizes a person or group of persons who have contributed significantly to the improvements of campus life for a substantial number of Purdue students. Established in 1981, a special memento is presented to the recipient and a nameplate is added to a plaque in the Alumni Association office, as well as a kiosk located in the Purdue Mall.

ATHLETIC AWARDS

GUY J. "RED" MACKEY AWARD

The Mackey Award recognizes athletes who exemplify the overall success of the University's intercollegiate athletic program. At the close of its season, each varsity squad selects by secret ballot the senior nominee for this award. The criteria for the nomination include competitive spirit, positive attitude, loyalty, self-discipline, hard work for the best of the team, and a willingness to help others.

The award is named for the late Guy J. "Red" Mackey, athletic director from 1942 to 1971.

NOBLE E. KIZER SCHOLARSHIP AWARD

Noble E. Kizer was the Purdue football assistant coach from 1925 to 1929. Kizer served as head coach for seven Purdue football teams from 1930–37, as well as athletic director from 1931–36 and 1938–39, and compiled one of the most successful records in school history. His record of 42–13–3 converted to a .750 winning percentage, the best of any Purdue head coach of more than two seasons tenure. Included among his achievements were two Big Ten Conference co-championships in 1931 and 1932. Kizer's teams went 9–1 and 7–0–1, respectively, during those campaigns.

Ill health forced Kizer's retirement from coaching and the position of athletic director in 1937. After a one-year leave of absence, he returned to the athletic director's post in 1938 until his untimely death in 1940. This award, offered in his name, goes to the junior or senior football letter winner with the highest grade point index for the two semesters preceding the award.

Noble E. Kizer Scholarship Award.

STANLEY COULTER CUP

Stanley Coulter, first dean of the School of Science, established an award for track athletes to encourage excellence in the sport he loved. He often served as an official.

In 1900, Coulter offered a handsome gold medal to any Purdue student who would run the 100-yard dash in ten seconds or better while competing in a contest with some other school. The same offer was made to anyone equaling or lowering the conference record of 21.6 seconds for the 220-yard dash. No man could win the medal twice. In 1902, Victor Rice clipped the 100 in ten seconds flat and won the medal. Not until 1909 was the award given again. At that time H. B. Hench, class of 1910, carried away the honor. He chose a cup instead of a gold medal as his award.

HELEN B. SCHLEMAN AWARD

The Reamer Club annually sponsors a scholastic award for women's volleyball. The award goes to the junior or senior major letter-winner on the basis of that individual's academic achievement for the two preceding semesters. The award is named for Helen B. Schleman, dean of women at Purdue from 1947 to 1968.

Schleman joined the Purdue staff in 1934 as director of the first women's residence hall. She was named dean of women in

J. W. Marriott III accepts the Distinguished Pinnacle Award from President Martin C. Jischke at the President's Council annual dinner. The J. Willard and Alice S. Marriott Foundation that made the $4 million lead gift created the $12 million building named Marriott Hall, which now houses the Department of Hospitality and Tourism Management, Friday, October 27, 2006.

1947, served as president of the National Association for Women Deans, and founded the Span Plan program for adult students. After retirement, she continued to be active, directing her attention to rights and opportunities for retired personnel and women. She also helped gain national recognition for female athletes through her work on the Executive Council of the Purdue Sportswomen Society. Schleman passed away in 1992.

VARSITY WALK AWARD

Bob Verplank, class of 1957, originated the idea of Varsity Walk as a project of the Purdue Reamer Club spring pledge class of 1956. The walk was located on the Purdue Mall with the Electrical Engineering and Mechanical Engineering buildings to the south and the Physics and Chemical Engineering buildings to the north. In the spring of each year, the Reamer Club selects the outstanding senior who has participated in varsity sports and has "brought the greatest national recognition to the University" as the Varsity Walk Award winner. The Varsity Walk Award recipients are listed on the obelisk at the northeast corner of the Purdue Mall.

When the walk was originally constructed, several items were placed in the concrete: fourteen pennies, one for each member of the spring 1956 pledge class; one 1956 class button donated by Artie Parikh of India, showing the honor is international; one Chesterfield cigarette butt; and one stick of Doublemint gum. The small award block was chained to a much larger block of concrete several feet below the surface.

PRESIDENTIAL AWARDS

DISTINGUISHED PINNACLE AWARD

The Distinguished Pinnacle Award is presented to alumni in recognition of leadership gifts and philanthropic contributions to the University. The award is considered the University's highest honor for donors, and recipients are selected by the Purdue President's Council. The Council was established in 1972 and is comprised of approximately 5,400 families that give at least $1,000 annually and about 650 corporations that have made cumulative gifts of more than $100,000 to the University.

ORDER OF THE GRIFFIN

The Order of the Griffin ranks among the highest honors given by the University. Presented by the president, it is given to individuals whose commitment and service to the University go above and beyond the call of duty and whose service has greatly benefited the University. Recipients have been diverse in their roles at Purdue, from Nobel Prize winner Herbert Brown, to astronauts Neil Armstrong and Eugene Cernan, to former Purdue football coach Joe Tiller.

Rabindra Mukerjea, Purdue executive director of strategic planning and assessment, receiving the Order of the Griffin from President France A. Córdova at the President's Forum in Purdue Memorial Union, Tuesday, September 28, 2010.

WORLD'S LARGEST DRUM

Purdue

BANG THE DRUM

THE CRISP AUTUMN AIR, the roar of the crowd as the receiver scores another touchdown for Purdue. But what would a Purdue football game be like without the Purdue "All-American" Marching Band? It rouses spectators' spirits and affords valuable experience for talented individuals. From modest beginnings in the Purdue Student Army Training Corps, the band has attracted innovative administrators and talented individuals, and has come to be one of the premier marching bands in the world. As the band leads spectators in a rousing rendition of "Hail Purdue," fans admire the precision of their intricate movements and join in the team spirit.

DEPARTMENT OF BANDS

The Purdue Band was first formed as a drum and bugle corps for the Purdue Student Army Training Corps, a predecessor of ROTC. In October 1886, the student newspaper noted that the band "as thus far organized consists of Floyd and Lutz, cornets; Hicks, baritone; Remster, alto; Butterworth, tuba." From those five musicians attached to military training came the Purdue University Bands.

Purdue Band, 1896.

The drum and bugle corps played sporadically during the early years, depending upon whether anyone qualified to drill the group happened to be on the University staff. There was little or no musical training available. The members of the band were required to furnish their own uniforms, instruments, music, and maintenance funds.

When football was introduced at Purdue in 1887, students soon noticed the natural affinity between the sport and bands. Band reorganization was a frequent activity during the early years because there was no permanent director. Band directors, who were professors and students, came and went and were elected by the bandsmen. Gradually, the band grew in both size and quality, with the 1900 *Debris* claiming, "It can now be classed foremost among the best college bands in the country."

By 1902, the band had grown to fifty members. Its main role still was to perform for military drilling, inspections, and ceremonies. It was this situation that Paul Spotts Emrick encountered in the fall of 1904 when he joined the band as a

> *It [the band] can now be classed foremost among the best college bands in the country.*
>
> *—1900 Debris*

freshman. Emrick, from Rochester, Indiana, came from a family of band directors and already had experience conducting musical groups for dance and dramatic productions. In addition to his favored clarinet, he could also play the violin, the cornet, and several other instruments.

With his musical background, it was not surprising that Emrick was elected president and director of the band as a sophomore. He was re-elected his junior and senior years, and went on to serve in that capacity until his retirement in 1954. It was during his senior year in 1907 that he had the band break ranks and form the letter "P" on the football field, the first letter ever formed by a band on the gridiron.

Since its inception, the Purdue Bands have come a long way from drum and bugle corps to the present Department of Bands, which consists of fifteen musical ensembles that have performed to audiences all over the world.

Purdue Band, 1903.

The groups include the "All-American" Marching Band, made up of approximately 400 members; the Concert, Collegiate, and Variety Bands, open through audition to any student enrolled in the band program; the Jazz Bands, featured in many music educators' conferences and clinics; the Symphonic Band, with about ninety of the most select players in the Department of Bands; the University Symphony Orchestra, with all the instruments of a large professional symphony orchestra, including more than sixty strings; and the various wind and percussion ensembles.

Emrick served as band director for forty-nine years.

Purdue Military Band in front of Eliza Fowler Hall, 1924.

While directing the marching band and creating its many innovations, he also served on the engineering faculty.

Following Emrick as the director of bands was Al G. Wright. Born in London, England, he received his bachelor's and master's degrees from the University of Miami, where he served as the coordinator of the Orange Bowl halftime committee. He came to Purdue in 1954 from a position as director of the Miami Senior High School Band and Orchestra. Among his innovations were the introduction of the "Boilermaker Strut," which features a high knee lift, hand flash, swagger, and instrument "chop," and the Golden Girl, Girl in Black, and Silver Twins. Recognized as one of the nation's foremost authorities on marching and symphonic bands, he retired in 1981 and was named director emeritus.

Purdue Band showing their new uniforms, 1958.

Purdue Military Band in the Armistice Day celebration, November 11, 1929.

Serving as director following Wright was William C. Moffit, a former director at the University of Houston. He was known throughout the country for his marching band music arrangements and his Patterns of Motion marching techniques. He served until August 1988.

Following in the footsteps of great directors before him, David Leppla joined the staff in 1989. He received his bachelor's degree from University of Dayton and his master's and doctorate from The Ohio State University. He also served as a staff arranger for Band Music Press, Inc. Leppla retired in spring 2006.

The present director is Jay Gephart, who earned a bachelor's and a master's degree from Indiana University. He joined the faculty of Purdue University in the fall of 1995 after having completed twelve years as a public school band director. He was elevated to director in 2006 after Leppla's retirement. In 2010, his band became the first of all Big Ten schools to march in the Macy's Thanksgiving Day Parade, with the Boilermakers leading the entire procession.

Purdue "All-American" Marching Band entering the stadium, Homecoming 2010.

Block "P" formation, 2010.

The many achievements of the Purdue "All-American" Marching Band include these firsts:

1907	Broke ranks and formed a letter—Block "P"
1919	Carried all the Big Ten colors on the field, and first appearance at the Indianapolis Motor Speedway
1920	First to play opponent's school song
1921	Introduced "World's Largest Drum"
1930	Used fanfare trumpets on the field
1935	Used lighted night formations and gained nickname "All-American," thanks to a Chicago sportscaster
1954	Used a dance line of majorettes
1963	First college band to play at Radio City Music Hall
1969	First bandsman on the Moon, Neil Armstrong, who played baritone in the Purdue Bands in 1952
1992	First college marching band to appear in the Singapore Chingay Procession
2008	First college band invited by China to perform
2010	First Big Ten band to perform in the Macy's Thanksgiving Day Parade

Boilermaker Special formation, 2010.

GOLDEN GIRL

The tradition of the Golden Girl began in 1954. It was the era of quarterback Len Dawson, whose prowess on the field prompted the press to dub him Purdue's "Golden Boy." At the same time, Al G. Wright, now director of bands emeritus, brought his first twirling protégée, Juanita Carpenter, to the field. Dawson soon graduated, leaving Purdue without a "Golden Boy." Carpenter also graduated, but the Golden Girl title remained, becoming a movable crown passed down through the generations.

GIRL IN BLACK

In 1962, another solo twirler position was created as a backup for the Golden Girl. June Ciampa, who served as the fifth Golden Girl, was the first to perform as the Girl in Black, which was originally called the "International Twirler."

SILVER TWINS

The Silver Twins were added to the "All-American" Marching Band in 1960. Although the original Silver Twins were identical twin sisters, there have been many featured twirlers who were look-alike "twins." These two twirlers always appear together in performances and photographs.

Top: Golden Girl Merrie Beth Cox performs at the Indiana State Fair, 2010.

Middle: Girl in Black Meg Merdian performs at the Indiana State Fair, 2010.

Bottom: Purdue Silver Twins, Sara and Chellie Zou, make time for a young fan following their performance on the Family Arts Main Stage at the Indiana State Fair, 2011.

Big Bass Drum, 1958.

BOILER BYTE

REROUTED FOOT TRAFFIC

Underground pedestrian corridors connect the graduate houses, Krannert Building, and the Purdue Memorial Union. These corridors serve to reduce pedestrian traffic across State and Grant streets. One corridor extends from the graduate houses to the southeast corner of the Union. Also connected to this tunnel are the Grant Street, Wood Street, and Marsteller parking garages and the Krannert Center for Executive Education and Research.

BIG BASS DRUM

Purdue's famous Big Bass Drum, "The World's Largest Drum," debuted in 1921, introduced by Director Paul Spotts Emrick. Standing more than ten feet high when mounted on its field carriage, the "Monster," as it is affectionately called by its manufacturer, measures eight feet in diameter and is nearly four feet between its two huge heads. Although its heads have been replaced, the drum is still the original built by the Leedy Company of Indianapolis in 1921.

Since its debut, the Big Bass Drum has become the world's most famous percussion instrument. As Professor Al G. Wright has said, "There may be large drums in Burma, Red China, and other exotic places. However, as far as we know, the Purdue drum is the largest drum in actual daily use." Too large to pass through the door of a railroad baggage car, the drum originally required its own special truck.

Purdue's giant almost had competition for the title of largest bass drum in the world at one time. Members of Kappa Kappa Psi took it to their national convention in Wichita, Kansas, in August 1961. The University of Texas was challenged to a big bass drum push. Members of the band fraternity pushed the Big Bass Drum through all the large cities between Lafayette and Wichita, including Indianapolis, St. Louis, Kansas City, and Topeka. The Texas drum did not show up, so Purdue's drum was officially declared the world's largest drum by the convention.

Big Bass Drum, 2007.

In years past, the drum's heads were made of animal hides and were signed by mayors of cities and governors of states that the drum passed through in its travels. The signature of President Harry Truman, along with those of Purdue astronauts Virgil "Gus" Grissom and Neil Armstrong, adds color to the story of the Big Bass Drum. The drum's heads are now synthetic.

Each senior in the "All-American" Marching Band gets to strike the Big Bass Drum during the last home football game of the year. This has become an important tradition of the band, and is considered to be a great honor.

Digger Phelps, ESPN analyst, hits the Big Bass Drum (which has the Macy's Thanksgiving Day Parade head on it) at ESPN College GameDay, Purdue verses Michigan State, January 22, 2011.

I AM AN AMERICAN

"I am an American. That's the way most of people put it, just matter of factly. They are plain words, those four. You could write them on your thumbnail, or you could sweep them clear across a bright autumn sky. But remember, too, that they are more than words. They are a way of life. So whenever you speak them, speak them firmly; speak them proudly; speak them gratefully. I AM AN AMERICAN!"

Before the flag raising and the singing of the "Star Spangled Banner" at the beginning of each football game played at Purdue's Ross-Ade Stadium, this statement is read aloud by the band announcer.

I am an American. That's the way most of people put it, just matter of factly. They are plain words, those four. You could write them on your thumbnail, or you could sweep them clear across a bright autumn sky. But remember, too, that they are more than words. They are a way of life. So whenever you speak them, speak them firmly; speak them proudly; speak them gratefully. I AM AN AMERICAN!

—Al G. Wright

Al G. Wright wrote "I Am an American" around 1967, when he was director of bands at Purdue, in response to a column by Lafayette *Journal and Courier* publisher Jack Scott. In the column, Scott made the comment calling for more patriotism. Wright had read a poem similar to "I Am an American" and became inspired to write his own version. It was intended to be used for only one pregame show because Wright liked to have a different show each week. However, everyone liked it so much, they wanted the show to be repeated. Wright, though, did not repeat it until he received several letters requesting him to put it back in the show. The tradition has continued since the 1964 football season.

The ceremony has been performed at the Rose Bowl, the Peach Bowl, the Bluebonnet Bowl, the Alamo Bowl, and the Outback Bowl. It was not performed at the Liberty Bowl because they have their own similar ceremony, and it was not performed at the Capital One Bowl due to strict time constraints for the pregame show.

PURDUE MUSICAL ORGANIZATIONS

Founded in 1930, Purdue Musical Organizations has a history that dates to the early years of the University. In 1893, the first Glee Club was organized with eleven students under the direction of Lafayette organist Cyrus Dadswell.

Important in the history of the Glee Club was E. J. Wotawa, who directed the group in 1910 and later composed "Hail Purdue."

It was not until 1933 that the Glee Club had its first full-time director, Albert P. Stewart. He began his association with Purdue in 1930 when the Women's Glee Club sought his leadership. Carolyn Shoemaker, dean of women, convinced Stewart, a local music teacher and dance bandleader, to lead the group.

With the success of the women's choral group, Stewart approached President Edward C. Elliott for money to start another musical group. Though Elliott declined, Stewart persevered, developing singing groups without the backing of the president. After Elliott began seeing the good reviews concerning the singers and their young director, he decided that there was great value in Purdue's singing student ambassadors. As a result, money for robes for the University Choir came from the president.

Eight years later, in 1938, Elliott sought and obtained $2.2 million in federal and state funding to build a huge, acoustically perfect home for music at Purdue. The Hall of Music was later renamed for the president as the Edward C. Elliott Hall of Music. With a long history of prominence, the Purdue Musical

Purdue Varsity Glee Club, 2006.

A member of the PMO Specialties Group serenades Purdue Vice President for Student Affairs Melissa Exum at the Indiana State Fair, 2011.

Organizations have conveyed music from the University around the world. PMO works to make music that fosters a spirit of camaraderie among students. Although Purdue offers no degree program in music, PMO is recognized internationally for the quality of its programs and performers.

PMO fulfills their mission of "rich in tradition and musical excellence, we will develop leadership skills in our students through service, dedication, discovery, and a commitment to the future while inspiring audiences everywhere" through their six choral ensembles and one handbell choir. Currently, these ensembles include the Purdue Varsity Glee Club, Purduettes, Purdue Bells, University Choir, Heart & Soul, All Campus & Community Chorale, PMO Specialties, and the PMO Kids Choir.

Stewart retired in 1974 and was succeeded by one of his assistants, Bill Luhman. William Griffel is the present director of PMO, which celebrated its seventy-fifth anniversary in 2008.

PURDUE CHRISTMAS SHOW

Since its humble beginnings in 1933, the Purdue Christmas Show has embodied the true spirit of the holiday season. Featuring specially tailored vocal arrangements, a myriad of musical styles, and the immeasurable talents of dedicated students from a variety of academic disciplines, this annual production continues to delight audiences of all ages. Originally conceived as a Christmas Convocation for Purdue students by Albert P. Stewart, the founding director of Purdue Musical Organizations, the Purdue Christmas Show quickly gained momentum through the use of innovative sets and staging, unique and dynamic choral masterpieces, and by capitalizing on the ever-changing sounds of popular and classical literature.

As student membership in Purdue Musical Organizations continued to grow and the professional qualities of the show became the standard tradition, the Purdue Christmas Show continued to establish itself as a treasured holiday tradition that grew to attract live audiences of more than 35,000 people during five separate performances each year. In addition, the Purdue Christmas Show soon became an important entity in the life of the Greater Lafayette community and surrounding areas, enhancing the already-teeming calendar of holiday happenings

The PMO Christmas Show annually fills up Elliott Hall of Music for six performances in one weekend every December, 2010.

The Purdue Bells performing at the PMO Christmas Show, 2009.

and providing heartfelt motivation for Purdue alumni to return to campus each year to relive this special event. Exciting and memorable presentations by individual vocal and instrumental ensembles and small specialty groups were often enhanced by dramatic and comedic material that led the audience through a series of themes and vignettes in each season's production. This annual celebration of Christmas became a perfect vehicle to share the talents found within the ensembles of the Purdue Musical Organizations.

Although the Purdue Christmas Show is firmly anchored in a rich tradition, the staff and students have always been forward-thinking and gear up for the future when planning and executing each season's performances. Traditional and recognizable sacred and secular holiday melodies and choral works are carefully intertwined with music representing nearly every style from pop to jazz to country to swing to gospel to musical theatre. The Purdue Christmas Show will continue to enthrall, inspire, and entertain audiences by showcasing the brightest and best that Purdue has to offer as it has done for over seventy-five years.

SONGS AND CHEERS

Fight songs and cheers are the lifeblood of tradition at Purdue. They give students and alumni a way to come together in support of the school they love the best, expressing pride and appreciation for the University. Many have been around almost since the school's beginning. It all started with the fight song, "Hail Purdue."

Two Purdue men, Edward Wotowa, class of 1912, and James Morrison, class of 1915, were responsible for "Hail Purdue." Morrison wrote the words in 1912 and sent them to Wotowa, suggesting that he set them to music. The song was presented at a convocation by the Glee Club, of which Wotowa was a member. It was a big hit, and it has been sung and played at Purdue ever since. The song originally carried the title "Purdue War Song" and was dedicated to the Glee Club. "Hail Purdue" was copyrighted in 1913.

HAIL PURDUE

To your call once more we rally
Alma Mater, hear our praise;
Where the Wabash spreads its valley
Filled with joy our voices raise.
From the skies in swelling echoes
Come the cheers that tell our tale
Of your vict'ries and your heroes
Hail Purdue! We sing all hail!

Chorus:
Hail, Hail to Old Purdue!
All hail to our old gold and black!
Hail, Hail to Old Purdue!
Our friendship may she never lack,
Ever grateful, ever true,
Thus we raise our song anew,
Of the days we've spent with you
All hail, our own Purdue.

When in after years we're turning
Alma Mater, back to you,
May our hearts with love be yearning
For the scenes of old Purdue.
Back among your pathways winding
Let us seek what lies before,
Fondest hopes and aims e'er finding
While we sing of days of yore.
(Repeat Chorus)

Purdue Drumline, 2010.

Top: The refurbished Big Bass Drum and new truck to haul it, May 1937.

Bottom: The Big Bass Drum at the Purdue versus Southeast Missouri football game, 2011.

PURDUE HYMN

Close by the Wabash
In famed Hoosier Land
Stands old Purdue,
Serene and grand,
Cherished in mem'ry
By all her sons and daughters true
Fair Alma Mater, all hail Purdue!
Fairest in all the land,
Our own Purdue!
Fairest in all the land,
Our own Purdue!

BACK HOME AGAIN IN INDIANA

Back home again in Indiana
And it seems that I can see
The gleaming candle-light,
still burning bright
Through the sycamores for me
The new mown hay sends all its fragrance
Through the fields I used to roam
When I dream about the moonlight on
the Wabash
And I long for my Indiana home.

FIGHTING VARSITY

Here's the fighting Varsity
That wears the Black and the Gold,
They fear no foe, as they hit them low
Let's give them all

Three mighty cheers
Rah! Rah! Rah!
Here's the fighting team, Boys,
That fight for Old Purdue,
And with loyal hearts
We will play our parts
As we yell for Old Purdue.

Purdue! Purdue! Rah! Rah!
Purdue! Purdue! Rah! Rah!

Hoo Rah! Hoo Rah!
Bully for Old Purdue!

(Repeat first verse)

FOR THE HONOR

Come along, let us join in a song,
Hail to Old Purdue!
On the Wabash she stands
With her welcoming hands
As an Alma Mater true.
Far and Wide, she's our
Own Hoosier pride,
Ever we loyal will be,
So we'll sing it out
And we'll raise a shout
For our University.

Chorus:
Then hail, all hail to Old Purdue!
The pride of all the West,
We'll sing out the story
And we'll tell of the glory
Of the school we love the best.
Then hail, all hail, to Old Purdue!
Our Alma Mater true,
And we'll ever stand
Ev'ry heart and hand
For the honor of Old Purdue.

Fight on Purdue,
We're all for you,
Fight Purdue! Fight Purdue!
Fight! Fight! Fight
Once again in a mighty refrain
Hail to Old Purdue!
From the ends of the Earth
Men have heard of her worth
And have found her to be true.
She's so grand, she's the
Best in the land,

Drum Major Cherrie Lemon leads warm-ups before the Homecoming game, 2010.

Top: Little Caesars Pizza Bowl pregame show, 2011.

Bottom: Performing in South America, date unknown.

For the Honor Continued...

Ne'er may her full worth be told,
Tho' both loud and long
Her alumni strong
Will sing of the Black and Gold.

(Repeat Chorus)

OH PURDUE

Oh Purdue, Oh Purdue
How you make me shiver
With your old Sweet Shop
And your Wabash River
Oh, I love you with my heart
And I love you with my liver
Oh, Purdue *stomp, stomp*
By the river *stomp*

Oh Purdue, Oh Purdue
You're my chosen school
With your parking lots
And reflection pool
Oh your men are so many
And your women are so few
Oh so few *stomp stomp*
At Purdue
Whoo!

HELL YES

Hell yes!
Hell no!
Come on Purdue!
Let's go!!!

HELL NO

Hell no!
Hell Yes!
Come on Purdue!
You're the best!!

BLACK AND GOLD

Come on, Black!

Come on, Gold!

Come on, Purdue!

Give 'em hell, Yeah!

PURDUE YELL

Purdue! Purdue! Rah! Rah!

Purdue! Purdue! Rah! Rah!

Hoo Rah! Hoo Rah!

Bully for Old Purdue!

Humpty Dumpty, woopdee do

What's the matter with Old Purdue?

Rickety, rackety, rickety, right!

Old Purdue is out of sight!

Saaaaay what? That's what,

What's what?

That's what they all say!

What do they all say?

Purdue! Sis boom bah!

Purdue, yeah!

Fight Purdue Fight

Fight Purdue Fight!

Fight Purdue Fight!

Fight Purdue!!

Fight Purdue!!

Fight, Fight, Fight!!!

Yeah!!!

Aye!!!

Thgif, Thgif, Thgif!!

Eudrup Thgif!!

Eudrup Thgif!!

Thgif Eudrup Thgif!

Thgif Eudrup Thgif!

Eerht-owt-eno

Top: The Big Bass Drum, 2005.

Bottom: Miss Boilerette Rachael Bazzell performing at the Indiana State Fair, 2010.

225

AG CHEER

Hogs, corn, cattle, hay,
Liquid ammonia, NPK,
Protein concentrate, supplement A,
Lambs, rams, withers, ewes,
Pitchforks, scoop shovels,
Yeah Purdue!

ENGINEER'S YELL

E to the X, DY, DX
E to the X, DX!
Cosine, secant, tangent,
Sine, 3.14159!
Square root, cube root, BTU,
Slipstick, slide rule,
Yeah Purdue!

HOME EC YELL

CDFL, E, and FH, Fashion Retailing,
Dietetics, Pots and Pans,
Needles and Thread, Home Ec
A field that will never be dead!
Food Research, Home
Management, too,
Homemakers are a
Credit to Old Purdue.

MATH YELL

Algebra, geometry.
Linear graphs,
Calculus, derivatives,
We love math!
Finite, trig, and
Modern, too!
They're all found at
Old Purdue!

PHARMACY CHEER

Pharmacy, Pharmacy,
That's our art!
F A for Pharmacy
R T for Art!
F A R T Pharmacy, Yeah!

PHARMACY YELL II

Pharmacy, Pharmacy
That's our kicks!
We're here for five years,
Maybe six!
Tablets, capsules, "The Pill" too,
That's pharmacy at Old Purdue!

POLY SCI

(sigh)
(sigh)
(sigh)

C. S. YELL

Two bits
Four bits
Eight Bits a byte
All for C. S.
Stand up and,
PUCC Purdue PUCC
PUCC Purdue PUCC
PUCC Purdue PUCC Purdue
PUCC! PUCC! PUCC!

Two nights
Four nights
Eight nights at PUCC
All for C. S.
Lay down and,
PUCC Purdue PUCC
PUCC Purdue PUCC
PUCC Purdue PUCC Purdue
PUCC! PUCC! PUCC!

Top: Silver Twins performing during the halftime show of the Purdue versus Toledo game, 2010.

Bottom: Pregame show, Purdue versus Middle Tennessee, 2011.

JOIN THE CLUB

THERE ARE HUNDREDS OF THEM, some dating from Purdue's earliest years, and there is a place for all in Purdue's student organizations. Some are unique to Purdue, while others are chapters of national organizations. They all share a commitment to excellence, be it in academics, service to the University and community, or the development of a particular skill. These organizations bind students together, provide a home away from home, and afford opportunities for study breaks. Many years after graduation, former members of student organizations remain immersed in the life of Purdue, sometimes acting as advisors to the same organizations that nurtured them.

ALPHA PHI OMEGA (APO)

Alpha Phi Omega is a national co-ed service fraternity that has active chapters on more than 350 college campuses nationwide. The Alpha Gamma chapter of Alpha Phi Omega was founded at Purdue University on November 17, 1931 by sixteen students and five advisors. It became a national chapter of Alpha Phi Omega on May 20, 1932, and it has since participated in many services activities.

Members live by the cardinal principles of leadership, friendship, and service. The four areas of service that it focuses on are service to the community, campus, nation, and to the members in the chapter. Campus projects include swim meet timing, ushering for performances in Loeb Playhouse, and helping with dance marathon events and food drives. In the community, one of APO's regular projects is helping the Lafayette Christian School make apple pies for its fundraiser over fall break.

The APO pledge program is designed to give potential members an insight into the service the organization does, the companionship it offers, and the abundance of leadership positions available.

BOILER GOLD RUSH

Students at Boiler Gold Rush participating in various activities outside the Recreational Sports Center, 2009.

Boiler Gold Rush, Purdue's freshman orientation program, was founded by Roger Sharritt, former manager of Cary Quadrangle, in 1993. The idea behind the program is that it is imperative for

Purdue freshmen participating in Boiler Gold Rush gather on Slayter Hill for a pep rally, 2011.

freshmen to have help in making the personal, academic, and social transitions from high school to college. Meeting in small groups with current students as mentors helps the freshmen become comfortable with Purdue, making it feel more like home.

Originally run through the residence halls, the first program was hosted in Shreve Hall during June 1993 in conjunction with Day on Campus. Initially called Corn Camp, the first program involved 100 freshmen and fifteen staff members. In 1994, Corn Camp moved to Cary Quadrangle, changed formats, and attracted larger numbers. The two one-week sessions involved 400 incoming freshmen and about fifty staff members. The 1995 Corn Camp program saw more changes. It was renamed Boiler Gold Rush (BGR) and moved to August, incorporating all residence halls. This change allowed students to move directly into the room they would be living in for the entire year.

In 1997, responsibility for planning BGR shifted to the Office of Admissions, and the program was opened to all incoming freshmen. Today, Boiler Gold Rush is a six-day, student-run orientation supervised by four professional staff members. Now, more than 5,500 freshmen and 500 student volunteers take part in BGR each year. In addition, numerous student organizations, faculty, and staff contribute their time, effort, and resources to the success of BGR.

In addition to BGR, the student staff is involved in yearlong recruitment and orientation efforts through the Office of Admissions. These include Preview Days, Golden Honors Day, Purdue's for Me, out-of-town receptions for admitted students, Minority Students Weekend, and Winter Welcome for transfer students.

COOPERATIVE HOUSING

The idea of cooperative housing at Purdue was made a reality in 1933 by a group of women in the School of Home Economics who banded together in the face of financial hardship. At that time they formed the Women's Cooperative House. Two years later, in 1935, men followed suit, founding Wesleys Boys' House. Since the early 1930s houses have come and gone, but cooperatives live on at Purdue, and today there are twelve houses—five for men and seven for women.

In Cooperative houses, students live and work together to promote friendship, leadership, and life skills. They contain anywhere from fourteen to sixty members who share house maintenance responsibilities, as well as meal preparation. Their work, which typically consists of two to four hours of house duties a week, replaces the need for hired help, which creates comfortable and affordable living for students.

The sharing of experiences in co-ops is one of the system's strongest assets. In the 1940s, a variety of such activities developed: trade dinners, camp-outs, hog roasts, caroling, and picnics. In 1940, the Student Cooperative Association sponsored its first dance in the Purdue Memorial Union.

The oldest house on campus is Marwood, a men's cooperative that was founded in 1936. Ann Tweedale, established in 1937, is the oldest women's house in operation, created when members of the original Women's Cooperative House divided. It is named after the woman who started the first cooperative store in Rochdale, England.

All cooperatives belong to the Purdue Cooperative Housing Association, the student organization that Purdue University officially recognizes. The PCHA board is composed of one student representative from each house and four faculty/staff advisors from Purdue Research Foundation, the Office of the Dean of Students, and Physical Facilities. This board helps advise the houses on decisions concerning their finances, maintenance, and membership.

THE DEBRIS

Continuously published from 1889 through 2007, the Purdue *Debris* yearbook debuted the same year as Purdue's student newspaper, *The Purdue Exponent*. Four *Debris* editors, including John McCutcheon, had once written for *The*

BOILER BYTE

THE BIRDS AND THE BEES

The Department of Entomology, part of the College of Agriculture, hosts the annual Bug Bowl (a tradition since 1991), which features such delights as cockroach racing, an insect petting zoo, and—oh, yum—chocolate-covered crickets. Purdue began offering entomology courses in 1875, but there were no students enrolled in the School of Agriculture and Horticulture (as it was called) until 1880. The department houses an insect collection of 1.6–1.8 million specimen.

Purdue, the student newspaper predecessor of *The Purdue Exponent.* President James Smart dismissed the editors of *The Purdue* after they ignored warnings not to publish a special edition at the end of the 1887–88 academic year. McCutcheon, later a Pulitzer Prize-winning cartoonist who enjoyed a long career with Chicago newspapers, and his cohorts then turned their efforts toward creating a yearbook.

The name *Debris* was chosen because of its relevant meaning: "a collection of works." Over the years, the *Debris* has reflected the life and mood of the Purdue campus, highlighting student activities and events; athletics; faculty; and, of course, formal pictures of students. Among noted staff was the late alumnus "Popcorn King" Orville Redenbacher, a 1928 graduate in agriculture.

For several years, the *Debris* sponsored a beauty pageant, and many young women dreamed of being "Debris Queen." The *Debris* staff was comprised of student workers who were responsible for all aspects of the book, ranging from content to layout and design. Sadly, the *Debris* ceased publication after the 120th volume due to steady decline in sales over a period of many years—something not unusual for college yearbooks during this time. Today, every *Debris* is available in the Purdue University Libraries Archives and Special Collections Division as physical copies and also as scans available online.

THE PURDUE EXPONENT

The Purdue Exponent, founded in 1889, was an official student organization until 1969. The first editor of *The Purdue Exponent* was E. Eugenie Vater, a student and daughter of Lafayette newspaper-man and banker Septimus Vater. The first issue outlines a vision for the paper, that "it would contain chunks of wisdom and ladles of wit . . . combined with all the little newslets of our busy community within these gates." *The Purdue Exponent* followed an earlier paper, *The Purdue,* once edited by John T. McCutcheon.

Until the late 1960s, *The Purdue Exponent* focused on campus news. During the turmoil that was taking place in the country and on college campuses, *The Purdue Exponent* replaced social and local news on the front page with national news. Editorials contained graphic language, and in 1968, the Board of Trustees authorized the firing of the editor. The resulting controversy

The Purdue Exponent office in March 1933.

led to the formation of a commission to investigate. The group determined that the University remain the editor of *The Purdue Exponent* but recommended that an independent corporation be formed to become the new publisher. The result was the establishment of the Purdue Student Publishing Foundation.

In the following years, *The Purdue Exponent* overcame financial problems and restored credibility. In fall 1975, *The Purdue Exponent* began free distribution of the daily paper and became one of the twenty best college newspapers in the country. In 1989—100 years after its modest beginning—*The Purdue Exponent* moved to its own building on Northwestern Avenue across from campus. Today, *The Purdue Exponent* employs more than 150 students on its staff, which sells ads, writes and edits stories, and develops video for its print and web editions.

GIMLET LEADERSHIP HONORARY

The Gimlets were established at Purdue in 1922 as a means for students to support Boilermaker athletics. At its origin, 150 men "pledged to improve university athletics, create a heightened sense of spirit of loyalty and be of general service to Purdue at all times." One of its first projects was providing meals for the football team after practices. The Gimlets would gather an audience to go watch the team's practices and scrimmages, and then feed the team. In the early 1930s, the Gimlets raised money for minor sports, when the University was unable to do so.

In 1976, the club reorganized to become a leadership honorary composed of leaders among fraternities. Members of the Gimlet Leadership Honorary are junior and senior Greek students, belonging to a social fraternity or sorority, who have demonstrated leadership, either in their houses or in the Purdue community. While the Honorary began as a male-only organization, in the spring of 2005 it changed its constitution to permit female members.

Gimlet's most visible role on campus, since its formation, has been its role as caretaker of the Victory Bell. After the Victory Bell was drug out by students for football victories in the early 1900s, buried, then placed in a museum, the University placed its care in the hand of the Gimlets. The Victory Bell is rung at the conclusion of home football victories. Members can be seen on the sidelines wearing traditional black wool sweaters with gold "G's."

The Gimlets, who have proven to be campus leaders in spirit and spirit-boosting projects, participate in community service projects throughout the year, as well as making appearances at various athletic events when available.

GOLD PEPPERS

The Gold Peppers, a women's organization, was founded in 1925. Both sorority and independent women were eligible for membership. Mortar Board decided to sponsor Gold Peppers at the suggestion of the Gimlet Leadership Honorary. The purpose of the Gold Peppers was to arouse interest among co-eds in athletics. Gold Peppers encouraged the members of their groups to attend the pep sessions and athletic contests to aid in cheering Boilermaker teams. Members were chosen on the basis of campus activities and interest in athletics. The organization thrived through the 1960s but died out in the early 1970s.

GRAND PRIX

A tradition was born amid the roar of lawn mower engines at Purdue on May 17, 1958. The Purdue Grand Prix was the result of a dream of a few passionate students who wanted a

"The Greatest Spectacle in College Racing," the Purdue Grand Prix, was first seen on campus in 1958.

way for engineering students at Purdue to exercise their skills, knowledge, and enthusiasm.

The first kart race was run on a field and adjacent parking lot near the Recreational Gymnasium. Each kart was built from scratch, had a lawn mower engine, and could barely exceed thirty miles per hour. After 144 laps, or sixty miles, at an average speed of 22.6 miles per hour, James Moneyhun of Gable Courts won the first Purdue Grand Prix.

In 1969, the race was moved to a new location, a track carefully modeled after a kart championship track in Japan, located northeast of Ross-Ade Stadium. In what has become known as "The Greatest Spectacle in College Racing," the Grand Prix Foundation's purpose is actually to raise money for student scholarships. The race was originally run by the Purdue Auto Club, with the Grand Prix Foundation taking over in 1966.

In 2009, the track was relocated again, just in time for the fifty-second annual race. Located at the corner of McCormick Road and Cherry Lane, the $1 million track resembles its predecessor but is wider and safer for drivers and pit crews. The project also included a highly sophisticated scoring system, which allows kart crews, spectators, and media to receive up-to-date information.

Grand Prix history was made in 1968, when Al Brittingham won the race for the second year in a row. Dough Hodgton did the same in 1991, but then Ian Smith set a new record by winning the race three consecutive years, from 1993 to 1995. The Smith family has maintained a history of winners, with Ian's Uncle Tom starting the trend in 1989, and brother Dustin (1996), cousin Kyle (1998), and youngest brother Clayton (2004 and 2006) continuing it.

Over the years, the foundation has expanded the race weekend to include a variety of activities, ranging from the Grand Prix Bed Races to a parade and carnival, as well as the Grand Prix Student Ambassadors Program, which replaced the long-standing tradition of the Grand Prix Queen.

THE GREEK SYSTEM

In 1875, the University's first fraternity, the Delta Delta chapter of Sigma Chi, was founded. In 1877, though, the University adopted a rule requiring every student to make a pledge not to join a college secret society. They agreed to not disturb those who were already members of the fraternity chapter, but all incoming freshmen had to take this oath. In June 1879, it was changed to an annual pledge to make students more aware of the regulations. In the spring of 1881, a petition was circulated to rescind the rule. It was referred to the faculty, where the rule was modified so that students were to choose either an annual or duration pledge. The faculty believed that Greek and secret societies were elements from elitist, classical education. Such societies, they reasoned, were inappropriate in a democratic institution dedicated to a technical education.

The issue reached a crisis point in the fall of 1881 when Sigma Chi member Thomas P. Hawley was refused admission to the University because of his refusal to sign the anti-fraternity pledge. His guardian, Samuel T. Stallard, sued the faculty in circuit court. Judge David P. Vinton ruled that the required pledge was reasonable and valid.

The case then was appealed to the Indiana Supreme Court. During the trial, the administration placed surveillance on students for illegal fraternity activities. Five students were expelled, leaving only one member of Sigma Chi on campus.

On June 21, 1882, the Supreme Court ruled that "there was no impropriety in either becoming a member of or being otherwise connected with the Sigma Chi fraternity . . . and that the objection seemingly entertained by the faculty against other fraternities of the same class was unfounded." This ruling so upset President Emerson E. White that he published a new set of rules that allowed fraternity membership, but kept fraternity

BOILER BYTE

FRESHMAN CAPS

Freshman caps were introduced in the fall of 1907 by the freshman class. Worn at all times on the back of the head, the caps, nicknamed postage stamps, were green with different colored buttons adorning the top. Orange buttons stood for agriculture, red for civil engineering, purple for chemistry, white for electrical engineering, blue for mechanics, and black for science. The class of 1915 introduced green tuques that could be worn in the winter when the weather turned cold.

In 1916, the class of 1919 introduced the custom of cap burning. Freshmen would parade down State Street, across the Levee, and down Main Street to the Lafayette Theatre. On their marches they were showered with eggs thrown by upperclassmen who were hiding along the route. Upperclassmen attempted to steal the sacred caps from the freshmen. After rushing to the theatre, the freshmen returned to Stuart Field, where songs and cheers were sung. Then the caps were burned. Before 1920, only men wore the caps, but after that year women also wore the green caps.

Green freshman caps, or "pots," continued to be a campus tradition through the 1960s.

Members of the Iron Key gathered around the flag pole at the dedication of Freedom Square on the south lawn of the Purdue Armory. The event was held on Sunday, September 11, 2011, just prior to the Purdue 9/11 Tenth Anniversary Commemorative Ceremony.

members from receiving honors and enjoying other opportunities given to non-fraternity students.

The Indiana General Assembly in 1883 attached a rider to Purdue's annual appropriations bill that forced the faculty to repeal all anti-fraternity legislation before any funds would be released to the University by the state. President White soon resigned and was succeeded by James H. Smart, who was more sympathetic to the fraternity system. From that point, the Greek system has grown to be one of the largest in the country.

IRON KEY

Founded at Purdue May 14, 1910, Iron Key is a senior leadership honor society. Membership is limited to ten seniors. Originally for men exclusively, Iron Key was made co-ed in the 1970s.

New members are chosen by current members based on scholarship, positions held in student organizations, high ethical character, and the desire to lead on the Purdue campus anonymously. Iron Key members work on a project during their senior year that will benefit the University. Funding comes from donations by the Purdue Alumni Association, Iron Key alumni, and other sources in the University and local community. Strictly nonpolitical in policy, Iron Key aims to be representative of the class and student body.

The mission of the club and the point of each year's project are to do good for the sake of goodness alone. Members do not ask for attention for the good they do, and they expect never to receive it. Therefore, part of the challenge for current members is to remain anonymous about their membership in the society.

It is the policy of the society to be secret so that no public announcement of membership is made until the close of the academic year.

MORTAR BOARD

Founded at Syracuse University in 1918, Mortar Board was the first national organization honoring senior college women. The Purdue chapter of Mortar Board was founded in the fall of 1926.

Mortar Board remained a society strictly for senior women until 1975, when men were first included. Mortar Board members are selected on the basis of superior scholarship, dedicated service to the University community, and outstanding leadership.

Mortar Board has awarded more than $851,000 in fellowships and awards to Purdue students, student organizations, and staff since 1945. The money for these donations comes largely from the annual sales of a popular calendar, appropriately named the Mortar Board. First published in 1945 as the "Reminder Calendar," the Mortar Board contains callout schedules, important school dates, lists of organizations, and, of course, the words to "Hail Purdue."

The Purdue chapter of Mortar Board is named to honor Dean of Students Emerita Barbara Cook, who advised the University's Mortar Board chapter from 1956–86. To honor Dean Cook, Mortar Board, along with friends and former students and Mortar Board members, donated a University marker near the corner of Stadium and Northwestern avenues.

OLD MASTERS

The Old Masters Program was created in 1950 after student leaders, business representatives, and University officials met and defined success as "honesty, personal integrity, and a good philosophy." This sparked the idea to invite a group of successful and outstanding individuals to campus to share ideas and experiences with the student body.

Members of Mortar Board, in green, pose for a picture with the women's volleyball team after the twenty-second annual Mortar Board Premier, a four team, round robin tournament, August 25, 2012. The Mortar Board Premier has been played every year since 1990 with the exception of the 2001 season, when the tournament was cancelled following the 9/11 tragedy. Fifty-four different teams have participated in the tournament over the years.

Top: Each fall during the Purdue Alumni Association's annual Alumni Weekend, PASE hosts a Networking Dinner for students and alumni to meet and greet. *Photo courtesy of the Purdue Alumni Association.*

Bottom: Since 2008, the week after Spring Break is PASE's annual Nearly Naked Mile, a community service activity that benefits Lafayette Transitional Housing. Students bring clothing and household items to donate, then participate in a mile-long run/walk. There are costume contests that bring out the creative side of students and trivia contests that test the students' Purdue knowledge. Participation continues to rise each year, as does the amount of goods donated toward the community service project. *Photo courtesy of the Purdue Alumni Association.*

The first group of nine Old Masters in 1950 has been followed by more than 500 prominent personalities visiting campus to inspire students. Those selected as Old Masters are exceptional people who have made significant contributions to their fields. Although not all Old Masters are Purdue alumni, each possesses the same desire to share philosophies and experiences with Purdue students.

The Old Masters Central Committee, consisting of twelve students and a faculty advisor, is responsible for planning the annual program. During their stay on campus, Old Masters are escorted by a group of hosts and hostesses, called Ho-Ho's.

Old Masters visit classrooms and residence units and attend informal breakfasts, luncheons, and dinners. In these informal settings, Purdue students are encouraged to engage in open discussion with the Old Masters.

Through the Old Masters Program, Purdue students honor those who have given of themselves and achieved success. The ideas and inspirations of the Old Masters continue to resonate in the hearts and minds of the student long after the guests have become a part of Purdue history.

PURDUE ALUMNI STUDENT EXPERIENCE (PASE)

The Purdue Alumni Student Experience, or PASE, is the student membership of the Purdue Alumni Association. PASE provides opportunities to promote Purdue and tradition on campus, cultivates relationships between students and alumni through networking opportunities, and enhances the college experience through fun, memorable events. PASE sponsors events such as a Networking Dinner, Fun Football Fridays, Nearly Naked Mile, Behind the Scene Tours, Senior Send Off, and many other events. The organization's catchphrase, "Loyalty begins here," illustrates its mission to encourage students to begin making connections with alumni and classmates.

Each semester PASE offers members a prime networking opportunity. In the fall, a networking dinner lets students share conversation with notable Purdue alums in their chosen field, creating opportunities to talk about starting a career path. During the spring semester, PASE hosts a series of networking connection events for individual schools for students to improve their networking skills with alums from their school. Afterward, there is a reception filled with successful alums, eager to help the students practice their newly learned skills.

PURDUE DRILL TEAM

Organized in 1947 by a group of seven ex-marines, the Purdue Drill Team was unique in its success and its makeup. The Drill Team drew participants from all branches of the Reserve Officers' Training Corps (ROTC), including U.S. Army, Navy, and Air Force (beginning in 1949), as well as civilian participants who had drill experience.

The Purdue Drill Team won national collegiate titles in 1955, 1956, 1958, 1959, 1960, and 1962, and was a runner-up in 1957, 1961, and 1963. The team also marched in the Cherry Blossom Festival in Washington, DC, winning first place honors five times, and the Indianapolis 500 Parade Drill Competition, where the team was the champion from 1957 to 1959.

Drill team members completed a one-year pledgeship, which challenged members physically and mentally. Pledge classes designed new drill routines for the team, providing an influx of new ideas that kept the team on the leading edge of competition.

Considered the best in the nation for many years, the Purdue Drill Team was invited to the White House and performed for President John F. Kennedy. The team also was slated to appear on Ed Sullivan's *Toast of the Town* television program, but the stage was too small to accommodate the drill team routine.

When compulsory military training for male Purdue students ended in 1965, participation in ROTC and the Purdue Drill Team dropped. Numbers continued downward as students turned their attention to civil rights, outer space, Vietnam, and other concerns. By 1970, only fifteen members were on the team and it was disbanded. Although there is no longer a unified Purdue Drill Team, individual teams from each of the ROTC branches are active and continue to compete at the national level.

In April 2001, Purdue Drill Team alumni reconvened at the University to present the first Purdue Drill Team Annual

BOILER BYTE

WBAA

WBAA is the oldest continually-operating radio station in Indiana, celebrating ninety years at Purdue in 2012. WBAA received its license on April 4, 1922, and made its first official broadcast on April 21.

Joining the 920 AM station in 1992 was WBAA 101.3 FM. Both stations broadcast twenty-four hours a day. The AM station features international, national, and regional news information along with National Public Radio programs. On the FM side, the focus is on classical music and other arts programs. WBAA also broadcasts online.

First located in the original Electrical Engineering Building, WBAA moved to the newly completed Electrical Engineering Building in 1926, then to its present home, Elliott Hall of Music, in 1940.

Among student announcers trained at WBAA is the former ABC sportscaster Chris Schenkel.

ROTC Award. The award goes to the outstanding cadet, in any of the ROTC branches, who makes the most significant contribution to his or her respective drill team. The award hangs on the south wall of the Armory drill floor.

PURDUE RAILROAD CLUB

The Purdue Railroad Club was founded in 1935 by A. V. Johansson, EE '39, and Frank G. Willey, EE '37. Early club members shared an interest in model railroading and built a model railroad layout in the "attic" of the Mechanical Engineering Building. In 1947, the club relocated to its present quarters in the basement of the Purdue Memorial Union.

The club honors the history of railroading with two signals, a Monon semaphore and a Pennsylvania Railroad position light. Both artifacts are original and on display in working condition. The Monon semaphore was a donation from Monon in 1953, while the Pennsylvania Railroad signal was donated by Conrail in 1993.

Building, maintaining, and operating the club's model railroad layout is by far the favorite activity of club members. The layout is built to HO scale, which is about 1/87 real size and covers more than 600 square feet. The layout created in 1960 served the Club for many years with a major modification in 1988, which removed all remaining true-scale track, and a second one in 1992, which provided double mainline operation. In 2008 construction began on a completely new modern layout using digital command control, the most up-to-date operating method. Although the model railroad layout is not patterned after any specific locale or era, sharp observers will notice it has a modern flavor. Members run their own model trains on the layout as well as club-owned equipment.

The general track arrangement includes two large railroad yards, an industrial area, and a sizable staging area, all connected by a mainline that loops around both rooms. Several sidings are located along the mainline to allow trains to meet and pass each other. In addition, various track spurs serve the industries that generate traffic for the railroad.

Club members hold formal operating sessions several times each semester. Each

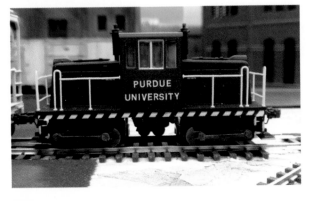

Scale model of the Purdue engine which used to shuttle coal to the North Power Plant. *Photo courtesy of John Feister.*

session brings to life the operations of an actual railroad in a specific era. Yardmasters use switch lists to build trains in predetermined combinations, and engineers then run the trains over the line following timetables and special train orders. The dispatcher oversees all train movements and communication with other operators using radio headsets.

Club members share an interest in railroading, either model or prototype, and some have an interest in railroading as a career. Many alumni of the Purdue Railroad Club have distinguished themselves both in the railroad industry and in model railroading.

Roundhouse building in the Purdue Railroad Club layout housing a mixture of club-owned and member-owned model engines. *Photo courtesy of John Feister.*

PURDUE STUDENT GOVERNMENT

Student government in one form or another has a long history at Purdue. Early on, dating from 1919, student government at the University operated through a Student Council of thirteen members. In 1933, the council approved a constitution for the Purdue Student Federation, which included a representative Student Senate and an executive branch. Also included within the Student Federation were the Student Union and Activities Council.

The Student Senate—like the present body—had power to pass legislation concerning student affairs and make recommendations on matters concerning students and the University. Among its early accomplishments were a licensing system for student cars, an investigation of the nature and purpose of honorary fraternities, enforcement of campus traditions, and registration of student organizations.

By 1942, the Student Senate became a separate organization from the Student Union and Activities Council. In 1947, the Student Senate reorganized into the Student Council, with executive, assembly, and court branches. Further reorganization in 1953 brought about three modified branches: Student Senate, administrative, and court. The Student Senate included elected representatives as well as presidents of campus housing units and several student organizations. Student government at that time was oriented more toward student organizations than toward the student body as a whole.

In the late 1950s, some suggested that the Student Senate be more representative of the entire student population. A massive reorganization in 1961 and adoption of a new constitution in 1965 led to the organizational structure that continues today.

The constitution, modeled on the U.S. governmental structure, contains three branches, each with distinct responsibilities and each with some checks on the other two: executive, legislative, and judicial. Importantly, the new structure allowed for a representative structure based on housing units.

The 1960s and early 1970s saw many changes that affected the way Purdue Student Government operated. For example, the University Senate opened some of its committees to student representatives and granted a speaking seat to the student body president. In 1970, the Board of Trustees agreed to grant a speaking seat to an elected student body representative. In the controversial days of the late 1960s, the Student Senate became a lively forum for student opinion, and student government moved increasingly into the political arena. At the same time, many of the executive departments of student government, perhaps considered too mundane, ceased to exist as efforts turned to addressing the issues of the day.

A reshaping of student government began in 1973, as leaders worked to define modern priorities; to work effectively within existing University structures and student organizations; to keep the student body informed on issues; to receive input from the student body about issues; to act as an advocate and facilitator for students; to greatly increase direct student services; and to provide for a firmer financial base.

In 1976, a new constitution was approved and a new name—Purdue Student Association—adopted. The executive, legislative, and judicial branches were retained. The purposes of PSA outlined in the constitution include providing services in the interest of students; providing opportunities for students to participate in activities that develop their potentialities; and encouraging student concern and involvement in University, local, and national issues and questions.

In 1988, the group reverted back to the 1961 name, which reflected the purpose of the organization: Purdue Student Government. The reasoning behind the reversion was that as the Purdue Student Association, its responsibilities were not overt, and for the sake of clarification the name change was necessary.

BOILER BYTE

WOMEN IN THE AIR

In 1939, the first two Purdue women, Jeanett Morris and Joan Geer, were accepted for the Civil Aeronautics Authority flight-training program. Geer, from Lowell, Indiana, was the first coed in the country to pass the CAA flight tests. Since then, Purdue alumnae have been flying high in the space program: Mary Ellen Weber (BS '84, Chemical Engineering) has flown on two space shuttle missions, and Janice E. Voss (BS '75, Engineering Science) logged an incredible 18.8 million miles in five missions.

Today, the Purdue Student Government continues to be the voice of the student body, linking students to faculty and administrators. It strives to enhance the student experience at Purdue through programming and acting on the behalf of students' needs.

PURDUE STUDENT UNION BOARD

Even before the Purdue Memorial Union was opened in 1924, the Purdue Student Union Board was an active organization dedicated to serving the student body. In 1920, the board consisted of five students; now there are more than 100 active members and a twelve-member board of directors for the organization.

The PSUB student organization, a part of the Purdue Memorial Union, provides students with a voice in the cooperative management of the Union. The group provides students, faculty, staff, and the community with a variety of programs that enrich and entertain while recognizing Purdue's diversity of interests and experiences.

PSUB sponsors concerts, films, the annual Homecoming parade, and numerous other activities. PSUB happily contributed to some of the Union's growth as well, sitting alongside Union faculty and staff as it went from the blueprints to the grand opening of the many new food service operations, including the latest renovations to the Union Commons area and Pappy's Sweet Shop that brought new design and new life to the building.

One of PSUB's long-standing events was University Sing, which evolved from the yearly celebrations surrounding May Day. In 1925, students and townspeople met in Ross-Ade Stadium to hold a U Sing. On May 10, 1930, the first official University Sing was held on the steps of Fowler Hall following the traditional May Day celebration.

The annual competition, which put housing units against others in a singing contest, was suspended after 1998.

While PSUB's programs and student leadership change every year, its mission and purpose on campus has remained the same for almost 100 years: to provide a variety of programs and services to the campus and community that both enrich and entertain. It strives every year to cultivate a dedication to leadership and a drive for success in every member of PSUB so that with every "new board," PSUB brings more life and spirit to the Union and to the campus as a whole.

Paint Crew on ESPN College GameDay, Purdue verses Michigan State, January 22, 2011.

STUDENT FAN SECTIONS

GOLD MINE

The Gold Mine Women's Basketball Student Section is comprised of Purdue University students dedicated to supporting the team. As of the end of the 2011–12 NCAA season, Purdue Women's Basketball has competed in three NCAA Final Fours and seven conference championships, and Purdue holds the titles for eight Big Ten Tournament championships, as well as the 1999 NCAA championship title.

Any undergraduate or graduate student may join the Gold Mine by simply signing up at the Athletic Ticket Office. Becoming a Gold Mine member has many benefits, including reserved seating, special events with the team, premium Big Ten Tournament tickets, road trips to away games, a T-shirt, and a post-season party with the team.

PAINT CREW

The Paint Crew is a student organization that supports Purdue Men's Basketball. The organization was originally founded in the early 2000s and was named the Gene Pool after then Head Coach Gene Keady. In 2005, when Matt Painter took over as head coach, the club took on the name "the Paint Crew." The Paint Crew became well known for wearing all black and sitting in a large group directly across from the entrance to the playing floor in Mackey Arena, creating an intimidating sea of black that is the first thing seen by opposing players as they run out onto the floor. With help from the acoustics of Mackey Arena, the Paint Crew has made Mackey one of the loudest venues in the nation. The Paint Crew currently has around 2,500 paying members, making it one of the largest student organizations in school history.

The Paint Crew is known to go to great lengths to support the Boilermakers. The Paint Crew has made trips as far west as central Missouri, as far east as eastern Pennsylvania, as far south as central Alabama, and as far north as central Michigan. Road trips are one of many benefits that come with the membership. Paint Crew members also enjoy T-Shirts, pregame scouting reports, priority seating, and local discounts with their membership.

ROSS-ADE BRIGADE

The Ross-Ade Brigade is the football student section and made its debut during the 2011 season. During the season, membership of the group increased from 500 to more than 1,700 students. Members of the Ross-Ade Brigade fill the general seating section of Ross-Ade Stadium, uniting to cheer on and support the Boilermakers on the football field below.

Paint Crew cheering at senior day, Purdue versus Illinois, for JaJuan Johnson and E'Twaun Moore, capping the end of an undefeated home schedule for the season, 2011.

THE SPIRIT OF PURDUE

WHEN IT COMES TO SCHOOL SPIRIT, one organization stands out among all others at Purdue: the Reamer Club. Many of the characteristics that exemplify student excellence are embodied in its members. Originally formed as a group of off-campus students, today's Reamers lovingly hand down Purdue University's traditions from one generation to another. United in school spirit, they engage in fund-raising activities for Purdue athletics and cheer on Purdue's teams, whether they be at home or on the road.

Reamers at the Lions Fountain, 1942.

HISTORY OF THE PURDUE REAMER CLUB

The exact circumstances that led to the organization of the Purdue Reamer Club are not fully known. Several stories though—rumors at best—tell about the beginning of the organization.

In the early part of the twentieth century, University housing for male students was at a premium. Purdue Hall, built to house those lucky few who were nominated by their home counties to go to Purdue tuition-free, was unavailable to regular students. Ladies Hall, built in 1874, was only for the few female students enrolled at the time.

Men had only two choices for housing: join a fraternity or live off campus. Many men considered fraternities, a relatively new idea on campus, to be childish because of the secret ceremonies, handshakes, and so on. Those men opted for living off campus. As most vacancies for students were across the Wabash in Lafayette, transportation could be a problem—as was the potential for meeting new friends.

Because the Greeks were more organized and knew more people, they easily controlled the extracurricular activities. They were the major leaders in larger activities at the time, such as the *Debris*, *The Purdue Exponent*, prom, and the Military Ball. Even though officers for these organizations were decided by the student body, the independents offered only token opposition.

In the spring of 1922, the Greeks were becoming more divided among themselves in the quest to get their respective candidates slated on an election ticket. C. C. Reeder, an independent student, saw the potential of getting non-Greeks elected because of this division. He formed a group of off-campus students, the "Unorganized Student Association." Unfortunately, the group lived up to its name.

Reeder returned in the fall with a new approach: forming the Purdue Independent Association. PIA fared better than its predecessor, remaining active until the mid-1950s. PIA members' interests were diversified in the quest to find new ways to help their fellow students and the University. The Greeks had formed the Gimlet Club to increase school spirit among fraternity men. In September 1922, a group of sports-minded PIA members met to consider the possibility of furthering the interest of the non-fraternity men in both varsity and intramural sports. They concluded that an organization similar to the Gimlets would be best.

The group's first constitution called for the formation of the Reamer Club. The name "Reamer" was selected because

Group of Reamers on Boilermaker Special III singing at the Lions Fountain, 1967.

A group of Reamers posing for a group photo before the Tupperbowl, a game of flag football played each semester between the Reamer Club and the Tomahawks, Spring 2011.

PIA believed the "Reamers would smooth out the holes the Gimlets made." In other words, they would finish the tasks that the Gimlets undertook. The dean of men refused to recognize the club for two reasons: it was an organization within an organization, the PIA, and he feared the primary purpose was to rival the Gimlets. He concluded that the dean's office needed more control over the proposed club.

The constitution of the club was finally approved in October 1923, thus establishing the Purdue Reamer Club. The constitution called for a group that was separate from PIA and that the group was to obtain the "good will and cooperation of all groups." Drawn up under rather difficult circumstances, the constitution, even with revisions, was sketchy at best as to the purpose of the club.

Some other highlights from Reamer Club historical records include:

- It is interesting to note that in 1924, eight Reamers, with C. C. Reeder at their head, were directly responsible for casting the votes that determined whether West Lafayette would become a city.

- A banquet was held in October 1924 at the Elks Club in Lafayette. Football Coach Jimmy Phelan was the guest speaker for the program, which paid tribute to the Purdue athletic team and to the student body for its support. At the same time the banquet was held, the names for the pledges for the semester were announced.

- A new constitution was adopted on June 2, 1926. Dean M. L. Fisher spoke at the first initiation, conducted after the adoption of the new constitution, which addressed a purpose for the outstanding group of men instead of "just another honorary."

- In the fall of 1927, according to *The Purdue Exponent*, the Reamer Club acted as official escorts for the football parade, which gave the team a send-off to the Harvard game that year. During this period, the club pledged outstanding sophomore men. It was not until 1932 that this practice was changed to pledging only juniors and seniors. Sophomores were not eligible again until the fall of 1973, and second-semester freshmen were not allowed to pledge until the spring of 1990.

- The 1927 *Debris* points out that the Reamer Club was active in organizing pep rallies and whitewashing sidewalks and windows with the usual Purdue-Indiana battle cries before the annual event.

- The club also promoted the traditional freshman-sophomore battle for 1929. The University administration strongly disapproved of this event; it is said to have been discontinued after one student died from accidental injuries sustained in the fracas. No further mention of the battle is made in club records.

- If publicity is an accurate gauge of activity, the club was comparatively dormant during the years 1929 and 1930. One noteworthy task was undertaken as the club organized sightseeing tours for independent alumni at Homecoming so they could see how the University had changed since their graduation.

- In 1930, the Reamer Club, in cooperation with the Gimlets, sponsored a Freshman Smoker and a general get-together for the fall semester of that year. One of the first meetings of its type, the Smoker did much to help orient new students to Purdue and campus life. In the same semester, the club sponsored a dinner-dance called the "Bucket Brawl," held November 21, the night before the Purdue-IU football game.

- At the first meeting of the fall 1931 semester, it was suggested that the club sponsor a glove sale before the Iowa football game. Two thousand pairs of gloves were ordered

Reamer Little Caesars Pizza Bowl crew getting ready to help with flags for the pregame show, 2011.

The Reamer Club participates in a number of philanthropic activities each semester. This photo shows the Reamers who stayed the entire night for Purdue Relay For Life, holding the Cup of Hope which the club was awarded for having the most overall participation in the Relay For Life activities, 2012.

and sold at the game for twenty-five cents a pair. The gloves were a distinctive gold and black color and were worn by the rooters at the game. The group was organized to carry out a series of drills similar to the ones once executed by Block P. It was during the fall semester that the Reamer Pot (the hat traditionally worn by Reamers) was adopted, and on April 4, 1932, it was decided to permit pledges to wear pots without the fold felt "R." Following initiation, the "R" was added to signify that the pledges had become active members.

- During the Depression years from 1929 to 1933, the club assisted the athletic department in raising funds for team expenses. In April of 1933, for example, the club sponsored a show at the Mars and Luna theaters in Lafayette, with half of the proceeds going to minor sports. Carnivals, boxing matches, and lotteries were organized to help defray the expenses of the swimming team and, in general, to lighten the financial burden of the athletic department.

- In the late 1930s, the Reamer Club started on one of its most outstanding pieces of work for the promulgation of Purdue traditions. In November of 1937, a sophomore pharmacy student, Israel "Izzy" Selkowitz, had an idea. He suggested that Purdue have an official mascot, something symbolic of a school rich in engineering heritage. This idea was developed and carried on until the culmination of efforts took place on September 11, 1940, when the first Boilermaker Special was presented to the University. The Purdue Reamer Club was appointed custodian of the mascot at that time and is still carrying out these duties today.

- During the 1950s, the club undertook many money-making tasks, both for the club and the athletic department. The Salty Dogs, a group of campus ragtime musicians, cut two albums for the club to sell to students and alumni. The club also began the freshman-varsity basketball game, a preseason contest to get Boilermaker basketball fans ready for the season. This contest was run completely by the club, and the cost benefited the athletes since 75 percent of the proceeds went to the Reamer Tutoring Fund, which was then used by the athletic department to tutor athletes. Also at this time, the club began to work parking lots for the athletic department, parking cars for athletic contests on the freshman football field, where Mackey Arena now stands. Because of these activities, President Frederick L. Hovde gave the club its motto, "The Spirit of Purdue," in 1951.

- The 1960s brought a time of gradual change to the club as campus unrest hit Purdue. Club membership dropped, as did the membership of many other clubs. Club members tried, unsuccessfully, to raise enough money to send the

Presentation of the key to Boilermaker Special V at its dedication ceremony, September 25, 1993.

Group sing at the Lions Fountain, 1987.

BOILER BYTE

PURDUE CIRCUS

The first Purdue Circus was held on Stuart Field on May 1, 1913. Forty organizations made floats and marched through the main street of Lafayette before the evening performance.

About 300 students performed in the circus in twenty-one acts. Because the circus was a big success, it was continued on a larger scale in 1914—with fifty floats, headed by a grand champion six-horse team. In 1915, more prizes were offered than ever before. In 1916, another gigantic parade was held, but in 1917, when the United States entered World War I, the circus plans were dropped. The circus was revived in 1921, when the Purdue Student Union sponsored it. The last year the circus was held was 1922.

Boilermaker Special to the Rose Bowl in 1967 when funds promised by local agencies fell through.

- In the fall of 1972, the Reamer Club Auxiliary was founded. Although the unofficial organization had been around for years, the Auxiliary was officially given one vote in business meetings of the club. Members of the Auxiliary were easily distinguishable by their gold pots with black felt "R" and pledge boards in the shape of the BMS III. The Auxiliary soon proved its worth to the club and the University and, after much debate, was absorbed into the club in the spring of 1973. At that point, all members of the Auxiliary became full members of the Reamer Club.

- The club took in its first pledge class with both male and female students in the fall of 1974. Since then, women have made significant contributions to the club. In the fall of 1975, the Reamer Club elected its first female president, Kathy Moriarty, one of the pledges taken in the fall of 1974.

- The club continued to raise money and school spirit by parking cars for the athletic department for both home football and basketball games and by selling pep buttons and T-shirts with assorted battle cries and slogans emblazoned upon them. Another activity during football seasons was driving around campus on Friday evenings with the BMS III, the trailer, Reamer Club members, and a pep band from Kappa Kappa Psi and Tau Beta Sigma. The Reamers passed out pep tags to people around campus.

- Raymond S. Jevitt, president of Perkinson Manufacturing in Chicago, brought the BMS IV, the X-tra Special, to life in

1979. His company donated the materials and labor needed to complete the project. The X-tra Special was delivered to the Reamer Club on October 25, 1979.

- In the spring of 1982, the club became caretaker of the world's largest state flag. The flag, measuring seventy-five feet by forty-five feet, was first unfurled at the Purdue-IU basketball game on February 20, 1982. This flag, in addition to the U.S. flag, is an integral part of the pregame show at all home football games.

- The 1980s brought forth a new moneymaking effort. *Purdue University: A Growing Tradition*, a book about Purdue history and traditions, was published in 1988. Two Reamers, Jerry Imel and Carolee Hartman, initiated the idea. The following year, Ann Peat, Joe Wehrheim, and Lisa Hill continued the effort by updating the previous work done. The resulting book, *Purdue Traditions . . . Past, Present, and Future*, was published in December 1989. Profits from these books were used to support BMS III and to help cover repair costs.

- In the fall of 1991, the major project to replace the BMS III was initiated. Purdue alumni and the University Development Office helped the Reamer Club with the immense project, which came to fruition September 25, 1993, when the BMS V was presented to the University.

- In 1995, the club undertook yet another project, the Boilermaker Special VI to replace the existing X-tra Special.

The Boilermaker X-tra Special traditionally leads the football team into Ross-Ade Stadium.

Boilermaker Special I pilot standing in front of Boilermaker Special V, date unknown.

The X-tra Special VI was dedicated October 19, 1996, during Homecoming festivities against Ohio State.

- Beginning with the 1997 Alamo Bowl, the Reamer Club has successfully traveled to five consecutive bowl games to cheer on the Boilermaker football team. These bowls have included the Alamo Bowl in San Antonio, Texas (December 1997 and December 1998), the Outback Bowl in Tampa, Florida (January 2000), the Rose Bowl in Pasadena, California (January 2001), and the Sun Bowl in El Paso, Texas (December 2001). The Boilermaker Special V was driven to each of these bowl games, with the exception of the Rose Bowl in Pasadena, to which the Special was transported in a moving trailer.

- On October 23, 1998, Reamers gathered to celebrate the club's seventy-fifth anniversary with a special banquet held in the north ballroom of the Purdue Memorial Union. At this celebration, the club announced its intentions of a seventy-fifth anniversary project—the restoration of the Lions Fountain to its original working condition as a drinking fountain. The club was able to finish this project and rededicate the fountain on April 22, 2001.

- In March of 2001, Reamer Club members and the Boilermaker Special V traveled to St. Louis, Missouri, to cheer on Purdue Women's Basketball team at the NCAA Final Four.

- In fall 2002, the Reamer Club published a new book, *A University of Tradition: The Spirit of Purdue,* which has become a favorite go-to book for information on Purdue history and traditions. A second edition of the book, expanded and with color photographs, was published ten years later.

- Boilermaker Special VII was put into service on July 30, 2011, and officially dedicated on September 3, 2011, during halftime of the Middle Tennessee football game. A dedication luncheon was held October 1, 2011 to celebrate the new Boilermaker Special VII. It replaced the Boilermaker Special V after nearly eighteen years of service.

The Purdue Reamer Club continues to be a presence of school spirit throughout the University and an ambassador for Purdue across the nation.

Reamers posing with the
Boilermaker Special V outside of
the Rose Bowl, January 2001.

INNIS QUOTE

The Innis Quote originated from Reamer John W. (Jack) Innis, who pledged in the fall of 1966. While Jack was pledging, he experienced what many pledges do, a drop in his grades. The club took any academic trouble very seriously. The Innis Quote was what Jack came up with to demonstrate to the active members his resolve to improve his academic standing, so they would allow him to continue pledging. It was soon adopted by his pledge class (and all that followed) as the only acceptable answer when asked a question by an active of which you did not know the answer.

"Without grades I am nothing to myself, the University, or the Purdue Reamer Club."

REAMER PIN

On October 24, 1984, astronaut Donald Williams, BS ME '64, presented the Reamer Club with his Reamer Pin, which had accompanied him on his first Space Shuttle mission. Williams, past president of the Reamer Club, was on campus for the special Homecoming ceremony honoring the fourteen astronauts who had graduated from Purdue by that time.

A second Reamer Pin traveled into space in 1998—an event that was planned by the spring 1996 pledge class. The following is what it says on the certificate accompanying the pin:

"STS-88\2A, First Assembly Flight of the International Space Station"

"This Purdue Reamer Club Gold Pin was flown aboard the United States Space Shuttle, *Endeavour*, December 4, 1998 to

Purdue Reamer Club Gold Pin
taken into space with Jerry Ross
aboard the United States Space
Shuttle, *Endeavour*.

One of the first things for the crew of the Boilermaker Special to do on road trips is to wash the BMS upon arrival to their destination. Using whatever resources are available, either a garden hose or a drive-in car wash, the Reamers take great pride in the appearance of the University's mascot.

December 15, 1998. Launching from the Kennedy Space Center, Florida, *Endeavour* and its crew of six astronauts joined *Unity* and *Zarya* together, the first elements of the International Space Station. They completed 185 orbits of the Earth, traveling 4.6 million miles before landing on Runway 15 at the Kennedy Space Center, Florida. Signed: Jerry L. Ross, Mission Specialist."

REAMER PREAMBLE

"We, the members of the Purdue Reamer Club, do hereby dedicate ourselves to foster the observance of school traditions, to support major and Olympic sports, to aid in the development of proper school spirit, and to otherwise conduct the activities of the Club in the best interest of Purdue University."

REAMER TIME CAPSULE

Shortly after the seventy-fifth anniversary of the Purdue Reamer Club, a time capsule was sealed. The spring pledge class of 1999 created it as its pledge class project. The time capsule contains memorabilia from years past, pertaining to the Reamer Club as well as the University. The time capsule is not to be opened until the Homecoming football game in the year 2023, the club's 100th anniversary.

THE STATE FLAG

During the spring semester of 1982, Bill Moffit, director of Purdue's "All-American" Marching Band, asked the Reamer Club if it would consider becoming the caretaker of the world's largest Indiana state flag. The club enthusiastically responded that the members would be proud to be involved in this endeavor.

The Reamer road trip crew poses for a picture after the Boilermaker football team defeated the University of Central Florida at the Citrus Bowl for the 1999 regular season opener.

Made of nylon material, the flag expands to be seventy-five by forty-five feet. A symbol of Purdue's state pride, the flag was first unfurled at the Purdue-IU basketball game played at Mackey Arena on February 20,1982. At the first football game that same year, the flag was part of the halftime show. After that, it became part of the "I Am an American" pregame ceremony.

The Indiana state flag and United States flag used during the pregame ceremonies at Ross-Ade Stadium, 2011.

The flag has also done some traveling. It went on the road to be part of the halftime show for the Purdue-Notre Dame game in 1982. In 1984, it traveled to the Hoosier Dome in Indianapolis for the dedication game of the dome, which was played between Notre Dame and Purdue.

TREASURED JAR

According to Reamer Club legend, before the founding of the University, a pickle jar stood in John Purdue's general store. The jar was reputed to contain some of the finest pickles in the land. When he retired and sold his half of the store to his partner, Moses Fowler, Purdue took the jar with him to his new residence, the Lahr House in downtown Lafayette, so that he could remember all the good times it had represented. Upon Purdue's death, his friends saved the jar, knowing how he had felt about it; they kept it as a symbol of fellowship to all.

In 1900, the jar was presented to President Winthrop E. Stone by an incoming freshman named Melvin Glick, whose grandfather has been a close friend of John Purdue. The jar remained in the president's office until the winter of 1920, when President Stone placed it in University Hall. It was the first

Reamers volunteering at a local elementary school fundraiser, 2012.

relic in a John Purdue Memorial Museum, planned secretly by President Stone to be built near the grave. At that time the jar became widely known around campus as a symbol of fellowship.

Although the idea of the museum died after the death of President Stone the following summer, the jar was preserved by each succeeding president. Each class knew quite well its origins and the symbolism of the jar.

In 1960, when University Hall was remodeled, the jar was relocated to the old infirmary. A short time after the jar had been placed in its temporary home, a group of rowdy University of Illinois students stole it. Within a few hours, they were apprehended, but the jar was no longer in their possession.

The whereabouts of the jar remained a mystery until the spring of 1964, when Reamer Club pledge Sheridan L. Miszelevitz discovered Purdue's symbol of friendship partially uncovered from renovations of Ross-Ade Stadium while he was planting clues for a forthcoming walkout. Realizing how much this treasured jar was a part of the traditions of the University, the pledge class believed it only proper to present the rediscovered treasure to President Frederick L. Hovde. In recognition of the jar's recovery, Hovde entrusted the jar to the spring 1964 pledge class of the Purdue Reamer Club so that the fine traditions surrounding the jar could be carried on to future generations at Purdue.

The pledge class decided that a permanent showcase should be set aside in what is now Stewart Center, and that the treasured jar should be displayed for all students to see and appreciate. It was removed only once, on April 3, 1964, when an active was chosen by the pledges to carry the jar after Reverse Lions—an initiation ceremony in which active members switch place with the pledges—had been held. Unfortunately, at 11:24 a.m. on that fateful day, a clumsy guy named Roultney Blake accidentally kicked over the treasured jar as it sat in front of the Lions. It is said that the resounding and mournful crash will long remain in the minds of many students at Purdue, especially those members of the spring 1964 pledge class who cherished the jar so dearly.

Reamer Boilermaker Special crew and Big Bass Drum crew watch from the sidelines as Purdue scores a touchdown, Homecoming 2011.

Some say the pieces were merely thrown away; some say that all the pieces were carefully gathered and kept so that they could be put in the Varsity Walk Award for that year; others contend that the remains were buried near the grave of the founder of the University. The facts behind this are somewhat clouded, but wherever the remains may be, the tradition behind the treasured jar will live forever as one of the great parts of Reamer history.

WHAT THE CLUB DOES TODAY

The Purdue Reamer Club of the present day strives to continue to uphold the values set out by its founders in 1923. While times have changed and the club has evolved through the generations of pledge classes, its core values of supporting Purdue athletics and keeping alive the Spirit of Purdue resonate soundly.

The Boilermaker Specials continue to draw the most publicity for the club as it continues in its duty as caretaker and operator of the official school mascots. The Boilermaker Special VII can often be heard sounding its authentic Norfolk Southern train horn as it passes by Harry's Chocolate Shop or gives rides to enthusiastic Boilermaker fans on Free Ride Fridays the afternoon before home football games. The Boilermaker Special VI, or X-tra Special, can often be found cruising through campus, as club members often enjoy taking it out for the pure joy of boilering up fellow students between classes. The X-tra Special can also be spotted at football, volleyball, and baseball games on a regular basis.

Reamers can most easily be identified from afar by their black pots decked out with as many buttons as can be pinned

BOILER BYTE

SENIOR BEARDS OR MUSTACHES

In the fall of a male student's senior year, it was traditional to grow a beard or mustache. It would be worn until Christmas and, if parents did not object too much, would be kept until graduation day, when the seniors would remove the facial hair. This showed that the labor the senior had put in his final year was finally over and he was ready to go on to better things.

Later it became tradition to shave senior beards on "Senior Cord Day," the Saturday of the first home football game. The tradition faded out in the early 1970s.

onto them. A buttons chairperson in the club designs and creates new buttons almost weekly. Most of the buttons are themed for an upcoming Purdue game, and the bigger the rivalry, the more creative the button's design. Since they stand out in the crowd, pot-wearing Reamers often see face time on video boards and television stations during sporting events.

The club continues to recruit strong pledge classes to build a solid membership. Pledges, along with members, can be found singing around the Stone Lions Fountain twice a week during their eight-week pledgeship, bearing their pots, reamers, and R-shaped pledge boards.

Pledges and members alike sacrifice their time unselfishly to support Purdue athletics in person, and often wait in lines either to camp out for games with the Paint Crew or else to reserve front-row seats for a Reamer section inside of Mackey Arena. In both the spring and fall semesters, the club enjoys "adopting" a non-Olympic sport to demonstrate its support for all Purdue athletes. It also supports the volleyball team by working rotations at every home match, shagging balls, and sweeping the court.

Philanthropy is a major part of the Reamer Club, and each semester actives participate in several philanthropic events. Highway cleanup has been a longstanding tradition for the club, and other activities have included working a soup kitchen,

Current Reamers, Reamer alumni, and friends singing "Hail Purdue" at the end of the Boilermaker Special VII dedication luncheon, October 1, 2011. *Photo courtesy of Janet Stephens, THGphotography.*

penny wars, Habitat for Humanity, and many other small events around campus.

The club also handles the selection of recipients for an athletic award. The Varsity Walk Award is presented to a varsity sport athlete who has "brought the greatest national recognition to the University."

As the Reamer Club continues to move forward—anticipating its 100th birthday in 2023—it will continue to pay homage to its roots and the men who gave independent students at Purdue a voice.

Past and present Reamers singing at the Lions Fountain after the Boilermaker Special VII dedication luncheon, October 1, 2011. *Photo courtesy of Janet Stephens, THGphotography.*

PURDUE PRESIDENTS

Richard C. Owen (1872–74)

Abraham C. Shortridge (1874–75)

John S. Houghman (Acting) (1876)

Emerson E. White (1876–83)

James H. Smart (1883–1900)

Winthrop E. Stone (1900–21)

Henry W. Marshall (Acting) (1921–22)

Edward C. Elliott (1922–45)

Andrey A. Potter (Acting) (1945–46)

Frederick L. Hovde (1946–71)

Arthur G. Hansen (1971–82)

John W. Hicks (Acting) (1982–83)

Steven C. Beering (1983–2000)

Martin C. Jischke (2000–07)

France A. Córdova (2007–12)

Timothy D. Sands (Acting) (2012–13)

Mitchell E. Daniels, Jr. (2013–   )

BUILDINGS

ALTHOUGH NONE OF THE ORIGINAL BUILDINGS that greeted Purdue's first class of students in 1874 are still standing, one nineteenth-century building remains; University Hall, built in 1877. Below is a listing of major buildings significant to the past and present of the University. The first date indicates the building's completion date; following dates are for additions and major renovations.

1874	**BOILER AND GAS HOUSE** (also called Power Plant; now demolished)
1874	**MILITARY HALL AND GYMNASIUM** (now demolished; site of Felix Haas Hall)
1874	**LADIES HALL** (formerly Art Hall, Boarding Hall; demolished in 1927; site of Stone Hall)
1874, 1902	**PURDUE HALL** (formerly Men's Dormitory; demolished in 1961; site of Mathematical Sciences Building)
1874	**PHARMACY BUILDING** (formerly Building No. 2, Science Building; demolished in 1959; site of Steven C. Beering Hall of Liberal Arts and Education)
1877, 1923, 1960, 2007	
	UNIVERSITY HALL (formerly Main Building)
1881, 1888	**AGRICULTURE BUILDING** (now demolished; site of Agricultural Administration Building)

1885   **SCIENCE HALL** (formerly Mechanics Laboratory, Mechanics Hall; demolished in 1916; site of Stanley Coulter Hall)

1889   **ELECTRICAL ENGINEERING BUILDING** (now demolished; site of Wetherill Laboratory of Chemistry)

1902, 2001   **PFENDLER HALL** (formerly Agricultural Hall, Entomology Hall) Named for David C. Pfendler, 38-year faculty member who retired as associate dean in 1974.

1903   **ELIZA FOWLER HALL** (demolished in 1954; site of Stewart Center) Named for benefactor Eliza Fowler.

1904   **POWER PLANT** (demolished in 1925; site of Heating and Power Plant – North)

1904, 1934, 1937, 1949, 1954

    PEIRCE HALL (formerly Stanley Coulter Annex, Biology Annex, Physics Building; partially demolished in 1989-90 to make way for Class of 1950 Lecture Hall) Named for Martin L. Peirce, Board of Trustees member from 1870 to 1875, who gave the University its first tree nursery.

1906, 1927, 1948, 1962, 2006

    GRISSOM HALL (formerly Civil Engineering Building) Named for Virgil "Gus" Grissom, BSNE '50, one of the original seven Mercury astronauts.

1907, 1950   **EDUCATION BUILDING** (formerly Chemistry Building; demolished in 1990; site of Steven C. Beering Hall of Liberal Arts and Education)

1908, 1984   **FELIX HAAS HALL** (formerly Memorial Gymnasium, Computer Science Building)

1908, 2004   **AGRICULTURAL ADMINISTRATION BUILDING** (formerly Agricultural Experiment Station)

1910, 1951   **MICHAEL GOLDEN ENGINEERING LABORATORIES AND SHOPS** (formerly Practical Mechanics Building; partially razed in 1982 to make way for Knoy Hall of Technology) Named for Michael J. Golden, faculty member and director of the practical mechanics program from 1890 until his retirement in 1916.

1910, 1925   **FOREST PRODUCTS BUILDING** (formerly Agricultural Engineering Building, Agricultural Hall Annex, Ag Annex II)

1910   **GROUNDS SERVICE BUILDING** (formerly Judging Pavilion)

1912, 1926   **FORESTRY BUILDING** (formerly horse barn, Agricultural Experiment Station Seed House)

1913, 1947, 1976

SMITH HALL Named for benefactor William C. Smith of Williamsport, Indiana.

1913, 1933, 1947, 1982

UNIVERSITY LIBRARY (incorporated into Stewart Center in 1958)

1915, 1927, 1940, 1998

HORTICULTURE GREENHOUSES

1916 **VETERINARY PATHOLOGY BUILDING** (formerly Veterinary Building, Veterinary Science and Medicine Annex)

1917, 1960 **STANLEY COULTER HALL** (formerly Biology Building) Named for Stanley Coulter, dean of men and the first dean of the School of Science.

1918 **ARMORY HEADQUARTERS FOR RESERVE OFFICERS' TRAINING CORPS**

1919, 1958, 2012

HERRICK LABORATORIES (formerly horse barn) Named for benefactor Ray W. Herrick, founder of Tecumseh Engine Products Company.

1923, 1968 **RECITATION BUILDING CLASSROOMS.**

1923, 1958 **MATTHEWS HALL** (formerly Home Economics Building, Home Economics II) Named for Mary L. Matthews, first dean of the School of Home Economics.

1923, 1925, 1930, 1940

ELECTRICAL ENGINEERING BUILDING

1924, 1930, 1949, 1969, 2003, 2007

ROSS-ADE STADIUM. Named for benefactors David E. Ross, inventor and manufacturer and an 1893 graduate in mechanical engineering, and George Ade, author and humorist and an 1887 science graduate.

1924, 1955, 1994

FOWLER HOUSE (formerly Poultry Science Building) Named for James M. and Harriet O. Fowler. He served as treasurer of the Board of Trustees from 1890 to 1929.

1924, 1929, 1936, 1939, 1956, 1987, 2001, 2007

PURDUE MEMORIAL UNION

1926 **AMERICAN RAILWAY BUILDING** (formerly American Railway Association Building, Mechanical Engineering Annex) Incorporated into Mechanical Engineering Building in 2011.

1926, 1939 **HORTICULTURE BUILDING**

1928, 1932, 1938, 1941, 1969, 2006

CARY QUADRANGLE University residence hall named to honor Franklin Levering Cary, who died at age 18 in 1912.

1928, 1951 **PIERCE CONSERVATORY** (demolished in 1979; site of Psychological Sciences Building)

1928, 1932, 1937, 1951

ENGINEERING ADMINISTRATION BUILDING (formerly Service and Stores Building)

1929, 1940 **AGRICULTURAL AND BIOLOGICAL ENGINEERING** (formerly Agricultural Engineering Building)

1929, 1955, 1987

WETHERILL LABORATORY OF CHEMISTRY (formerly Chemistry Building) Named for Richard B. Wetherill, Lafayette physician and University benefactor.

1929, 1932, 1941, 1948, 1981, 2011

MECHANICAL ENGINEERING BUILDING

1930, 1989 **SCHLEMAN HALL OF STUDENT SERVICES** (formerly Pharmacy Building, Geoscience Building, Geoscience Annex) Named for Helen B. Schleman, dean of women from 1947 to 1968.

1934, 1937, 1939, 2012

WINDSOR HALLS (formerly Women's Residence Halls) University residence halls, five in total being named for Ophelia Duhme, daughter of Moses and Eliza Fowler; Frances M. Shealy, one of three Shealy sisters who provided funding for the hall; Everett B. Vawter, a West Lafayette public servant; Martha E. and Eugene K. Warren, University benefactors; and Elizabeth G. and William R. Wood, University benefactors.

1934, 1940, 1942, 2009

NISWONGER AVIATION TECHNOLOGY BUILDING (formerly Aviation Technology Building, Hangar #1) Named for Scott Niswonger, a 1968 graduate of Purdue's aviation technology program.

1937   **HOVDE HALL OF ADMINISTRATION** (formerly Executive Building) Named for Frederick L. Hovde, University president from 1946 to 1971.

1938, 1999   **LAMBERT FIELDHOUSE AND GYMNASIUM** (formerly Men's Gymnasium and Fieldhouse) Named for Ward "Piggy" Lambert, basketball coach from 1917 to 1945.

1939, 1951, 1976

     BIOCHEMISTRY BUILDING (formerly Agriculture Chemistry Building)

1940   **ELLIOTT HALL OF MUSIC** (formerly Hall of Music) Named for Edward C. Elliott, president of Purdue from 1922 to 1945.

1940, 2002   **FORNEY HALL OF CHEMICAL ENGINEERING** (formerly Chemical Engineering Building, Chemical and Metallurgical Engineering Building)

1940, 1948, 1951, 1961, 1986

     PHYSICS BUILDING

1943   **TERMINAL BUILDING** (formerly Airport Hangar #2) Airport terminal.

1947   **CREATIVE ARTS BUILDINGS 1-2** (formerly FWA 1-5, Naval Science; demolished in 2004; site of Armstrong Hall of Engineering)

1948, 1958, 1969

     HILLTOP APARTMENTS (formerly Married Student Housing – Ross-Ade Apartments)

1950, 1953   **SERVICE BUILDING**

1951, 1962, 1988

     DELON AND ELIZABETH HAMPTON HALL OF CIVIL ENGINEERING (formerly Civil Engineering Building) Named for alumnus and donor Delon Hampton and his mother Elizabeth Hampton. Delon earned a master's degree in 1958 and a doctorate in 1961; both degrees are in civil engineering.

1951, 1958, 1969, 2012

     LILLY HALL OF LIFE SCIENCES Named for the Eli Lilly family, Purdue benefactors.

1953   **MEREDITH HALL** (formerly X Hall) University residence hall named for Virginia C. Meredith, who served on the Board of Trustees from 1921 until her death in 1936.

1954   **HARRISON COURTS #2 AND #3** (now demolished)

1955   **FOWLER COURTS** (formerly State Street Courts; demolished in 1993) Named for James M. Fowler, treasurer of the Board of Trustees from 1890 to 1929.

1955   **POULTRY SCIENCE BUILDING AND POULTRY SCIENCE ANNEX**

1956   **STONE HALL** (formerly Home Economics Administration Building) Named for Winthrop E. Stone, Purdue president from 1900 until 1921.

1956   **TERRY COURTS** (formerly Gable Courts; now demolished; site of Discovery Park)

1956   **TERRY HOUSE UNIVERSITY POLICE HEADQUARTERS** named for Oliver P. Terry, alumnus and benefactor who started the student health service.

1957, 1962, 1967

    PURDUE VILLAGE (formerly Married Student Courts I, II, III and Married Student Housing)

1957, 1962, 2001, 2012

    FRANCE A. CÓRDOVA RECREATIONAL SPORTS CENTER (formerly Recreational Gymnasium) Named for former President France A. Córdova, who served from 2007 to 2012.

1957   **OWEN HALL** (formerly H-1) University residence hall named for Richard Owen, first president of the University.

1957   **NUCLEAR ENGINEERING BUILDING** (formerly Aeronautical, Astronautical and Engineering Sciences Building; Engineering Science Shop Building #1)

1958   **TARKINGTON HALL** (formerly H-2) University residence hall named for author and playwright N. Booth Tarkington, who attended Purdue.

1958   **STEWART CENTER** (formerly Memorial Center) Named for benefactors, R. B. and Lillian Stewart. He retired as vice president and treasurer in 1961.

1958   **OUTDOOR SKATING RINK** (removed in 1983)

1958, 1995   **LYNN HALL OF VETERINARY MEDICINE** (formerly Veterinary School and Medical Building) Named for Charles J. Lynn, benefactor and longtime trustee.

1959   **CHILD DEVELOPMENT AND FAMILY SCIENCES BUILDING** (formerly Child Development and Family Life Building, demolished in 2011)

1959 **HEAVILON HALL** Named for Amos Heavilon, University benefactor whose gifts allowed construction of the original Heavilon Hall engineering building.

1961 **PURDUE STUDENT HEALTH CENTER**

1961 **WADE UTILITY PLANT** (formerly South Power Plant) Named for Walter W. Wade, vice president emeritus for physical facilities.

1961 **GOLF STARTER HOUSE** (now demolished)

1962, 2009 **YOUNG HALL** (formerly Graduate House East, Young Graduate Hall) Named for Ernest C. Young, second dean of The Graduate School, who retired in 1963.

1963 **MCCUTCHEON HALL** (formerly H-4) University residence hall named for John T. McCutcheon, 1889 science graduate and Pulitzer Prize-winning editorial cartoonist.

1963 **SLAYTER CENTER OF PERFORMING ARTS** Named for Marie and R. James Slayter. A 1921 chemical engineering graduate, he was the inventor of numerous fiberglass materials and products.

1964, 2003 **EARHART HALL** (formerly H-8) University residence hall named for aviator Amelia Earhart, career consultant at Purdue from 1935 to 1937.

1964, 2009 **KRANNERT BUILDING** School of Management Named for benefactors Herman C. and Ellnora D. Krannert.

1964 **GRANT STREET PARKING GARAGE** (original demolished and rebuilt in 1995)

1964 **CHAFFEE HALL** (formerly Jet Propulsion Center Library Office Building) Named for Roger B. Chaffee, a 1957 graduate and astronaut who died in an Apollo training accident in 1967.

1965 **DEMENT FIRE STATION** Named for Clayton W. DeMent, retired director of safety and security.

1966 **HARRISON HALL** (formerly H-5) University residence hall named for Benjamin Harrison, twenty-third president of the United States and Purdue trustee from 1895 until his death in 1901.

1967, 2011 **MACKEY ARENA** (formerly Purdue Arena) Named for Guy J. "Red" Mackey, athletic director from 1942 to 1971.

1967, 1982 **MATHEMATICAL SCIENCES BUILDING**

1968 **HAWKINS HALL** (formerly Hawkins Graduate House, Graduate House West) University residence hall named for George A. Hawkins, retired dean of engineering and vice president of academic affairs.

1970, 1987 **FREEHAFER HALL** Named for Lytle J. Freehafer, vice president and treasurer emeritus.

1970 **HEINE PHARMACY BUILDING** Named for Robert E. Heine, Purdue trustee from 1968 to 1981.

1970 **SHREVE HALL** University residence hall named for Eleanor B. Shreve, author, educator, and wife of R. Norris Shreve, former head of chemical and metallurgical engineering.

1972 **BROWN LABORATORY OF CHEMISTRY** (formerly Chemistry Building East) Named for Nobel Laureate Herbert C. Brown the R.B. Wetherill Research Professor Emeritus of Chemistry.

1977 **JOHNSON HALL OF NURSING** (formerly Nursing and Allied Health Sciences Building) Named for Helen R. Johnson, head and professor emeriti of nursing.

1977 **POTTER ENGINEERING CENTER** Named for A.A. Potter, dean of engineering from 1920 to 1953.

1980 **PSYCHOLOGICAL SCIENCES BUILDING**

1981 **WHISTLER HALL OF AGRICULTURAL RESEARCH** (formerly Agricultural Research Building) Named for Roy L. Whistler, professor emeritus of food science.

1982, 2011 **INTERCOLLEGIATE ATHLETIC FACILITY**

1982 **HICKS UNDERGRADUATE LIBRARY** Named for John W. Hicks, professor emeritus of agricultural economics, senior vice president emeritus, and acting president of the University from 1982 to 1983.

1983 **KRANNERT CENTER FOR EXECUTIVE EDUCATION AND RESEARCH**

1984 **HANSEN LIFE SCIENCES RESEARCH BUILDING** (formerly Life Sciences Research Building) Named for Arthur G. Hansen, president of Purdue from 1971 to 1982.

1984 **KNOY HALL OF TECHNOLOGY** Named for Maurice G. Knoy, president of the Board of Trustees from 1968 to 1979.

1986 **VISITOR INFORMATION CENTER** (in Northwestern Avenue Parking Garage)

1988 **MATERIALS AND ELECTRICAL ENGINEERING BUILDING**

1989	**THE PURDUE EXPONENT BUILDING**
1990	**CLASS OF 1950 LECTURE HALL** Named for the Purdue Class of 1950, whose members contributed more than $1 million toward its construction.
1990	**MOLLENKOMPF ATHLETIC CENTER** Named for Jack Mollenkopf, football coach from 1956 to 1969.
1991	**ANIMAL DISEASE DIAGNOSTIC LABORATORY**
1992	**STEVEN C. BEERING HALL OF LIBERAL ARTS AND EDUCATION** (formerly Liberal Arts and Education Building) Named for Steven C. Beering, who served as President from 1983 to 2000.
1993	**HILLENBRAND HALL** University residence hall named for John and William Hillenbrand, University trustees. John, William's father, served from 1913 to 1947; William from 1967 to 1975.
1998	**NELSON HALL OF FOOD SCIENCE** (formerly Food Science Building) Named for Philip E. Nelson, founding head of the Department of Food Science.
1999	**BLACK CULTURAL CENTER**
2001	**BOILERMAKER AQUATIC CENTER**
2003	**FORD DINING COURT** Named for Purdue graduates Fred and Mary Ford. He served as executive vice president and treasurer for nearly 25 years.
2004	**LAWSON HALL OF COMPUTER SCIENCE** Named for alumnus H. Richard Lawson and his wife, Patricia A. Lawson.
2004	**MORGAN CENTER FOR ENTREPRENEURSHIP** Funded by the Burton D. Morgan Foundation; Morgan was a 1938 Purdue alumnus.
2004	**DAUCH ALUMNI CENTER** Named for Dick and Sandy Dauch. Mr. Dauch is a 1964 alumnus.
2005	**BIRCK NANOTECHNOLOGY CENTER** Named for alumnus and Purdue Board of Trustee member Michael Birck and his wife Kay Birck.
2005	**BINDLEY BIOSCIENCE CENTER** Named for 1962 graduate William E. Bindley.
2005	**ARMSTRONG HALL OF ENGINEERING** Named for alumnus astronaut Neil Armstrong.
2005	**PAO HALL OF VISUAL AND PERFORMING ARTS** Named for Yue-Kong Pao, international business leader and visionary.

2006	**JISCHKE HALL OF BIOMEDICAL ENGINEERING** Named for former President Martin C. Jischke, who served from 2000 to 2007.
2007	**MANN HALL** Named for Gerald and Edna Mann, University benefactors.
2009	**HOCKMEYER HALL OF STRUCTURAL BIOLOGY** Named for Wayne T. and Mary T. Hockmeyer. Mr. Hockmeyer is a 1966 alumnus.
2009, 2012	**FIRST STREET TOWERS** University residences located on former site of Fowler Courts.
2010	**HALL FOR DISCOVERY AND LEARNING RESEARCH**
2011	**HANLEY HALL** Named for Purdue alumni Bill and Sally Hanley.
2012	**MARRIOTT HALL** Named for the J. Willard and Alice S. Marriott Foundation, lead donor.
2012	**PARRISH LIBRARY OF MANAGEMENT AND ECONOMICS** Named for Purdue graduate Roland G. Parrish.